MODERN JUDAISM

Modern Judaism

Dan Cohn-Sherbok
Lecturer in Jewish Theology
University of Kent
and
Visiting Professor
Middlesex University
University of Wales, Lampeter
University of St Andrews

First published in Great Britain 1996 by
MACMILLAN PRESS LTD
Houndmills, Basingstoke, Hampshire RG21 6XS
and London
Companies and representatives
throughout the world

A catalogue record for this book is available
from the British Library.

ISBN 0–333–62101–8 hardcover
ISBN 0–333–62102–6 paperback

First published in the United States of America 1996 by
ST. MARTIN'S PRESS, INC.,
Scholarly and Reference Division,
175 Fifth Avenue,
New York, N.Y. 10010

ISBN 0–312–16188–3

Library of Congress Cataloging-in-Publication Data
Cohn-Sherbok, Dan
Modern Judaism / Dan Cohn-Sherbok.
p.   cm.
Includes bibliographical references and index.
ISBN 0–312–16188–3
1. Judaism—History—Modern period, 1750–   2. Jewish sects–
–History—19th century.   3. Jewish sects—History—20th century.
I. Title.
BM195.C64   1996
296'.09'03—dc20   96–12368
                                                        CIP

10   9   8   7   6   5   4   3   2   1
05   04   03   02   01   00   99   98   97   96

Printed in Great Britain by
Ipswich Book Co. Ltd, Ipswich, Suffolk

For Lavinia

Contents

Introduction

In our recent book, *The American Jew* – an examination of current attitudes within the American Jewish Community today – the manager of a kosher-style restaurant in a typical American City recounts his experiences as a young boy growing up in an Orthodox synagogue:

> I could not reconcile anything these people were talking about with anything that made sense: miracles, prohibitions – keep the whole thing! There was one thing that set the seeds in motion very early on. I used to go to the Science Museum. The folks took me; I went there all the time. I loved it. You see these prehistoric things, and all that stuff. When I learnt how to read, I see these things are sixty million years old. They got dates on 'em. How come then, in religion school, the calendar is 5,000 and some years old? So I start thinking about it. This was when I was probably seven or eight. And I say, 'There's something wrong here. These people are telling me the world started 5,000 years ago and these things are sixty million years old! So I go in to the rabbi and say, 'How come?' He says, 'That's the way it is.' And I say, 'How can you say that's the way it is. I'm reading the Bible already, and I don't see anything about dinosaurs in there. Somewhere, somebody's got something wrong. I don't know who, but somebody's got something wrong.' (D. and L. Cohn-Sherbok, 1994, 246)

Such sentiments reflect the attitude of many Jews to organized religion. No longer is Jewry united by an overarching religious structure as an integrated community. Rather the Jewish people has fragmented into a variety of sub-groups with conflicting ideologies. In addition, there are many Jews today who have dissociated themselves completely from any form of religious belief or practice.

Given such diversity, is it possible to formulate a philosophy of Judaism which will be able to provide a framework for Jewish existence in the twenty-first century? Recently a number of Jewish thinkers have grappled with this issue. Pre-eminent among such writers Jonathan Sacks, the Chief Rabbi of the United Hebrew Congregations of the British Commonwealth, proposes in *One*

People? a new conception of Jewish existence in a future age. According to Sacks, contemporary Jewish life is beset with conflict. No longer is the Jewish people united by a common basis of belief and observance. Instead Jews are divided by conflicting religious convictions as the Jewish nation has fractured and fragmented as never before. To overcome such confusion, Sacks advocates an inclusive ideology which would embrace all segments of the Jewish community regardless of their religious orientations. Sacks is critical of those who disparage the various branches of non-Orthodox Judaism. Such animosity, he believes, undermines the traditional understanding of *Klal Yisrael* (Jewish peoplehood). In its place he endorses an inclusivist stance which recognizes the positive value of all forms of Judaism while refusing to grant these various branches religious legitimacy.

In Sacks's view, the future of the Jewish people can be assured only if they return to the faith of their ancestors. Despite the disintegration of modern Jewish life, it is possible for Jews to regain a love for tradition. Drawing on the biblical narrative, he formulates a vision of the Jewish future in which traditional Jewish life will be renewed:

> The primal scene of Jewish history, is of the Israelites in the wilderness, fractious, rebellious, engaged in endless diversion, yet none the less slowly journeying towards the fulfilment of the covenantal promise. No image seems to be more descriptive of contemporary Jewry ... The inclusivist faith is that Jews, divided by where they stand, are united by what they are travelling towards, the destination which alone gives meaning to Jewish history: the promised union of *Torah*, the Jewish people, the land of Israel, and God. (Sacks, 1993, 228)

This vision of a return to tradition has also animated Sacks's quest to educate Jewry. In his book *Will We Have Jewish Grandchildren?*, Sacks maintains that it is only through revitalization of Jewish education that we can assure the survival of the Jewish nation.

At the core of Jewish Continuity is the realization that Jewish identity in the diaspora is not something that happens of its own accord. It must be learned and lived, acted out and constantly reinforced. In this process, much depends on our choices as individuals. Much, too, depends on our decisions as a community ... we must aim at a community in which: 'Jewish youth are exposed to and involved in a confluence of cognitive-affective Jewish experiences in a Jewish school (preferably elementary and secondary day school), synagogue, youth group, summer camp and home (via Jewish family education, where appropriate). And all this must be capped by a Israel experience during the teen years especially a post-high school year of study in Israel. We must take collective delight learning and growing as Jews.' (Ibid. 122–3).

Here then is a traditional response to the perplexities of contemporary Jewish life. According to Sacks, Orthodox Judaism provides an overarching ideology for the modern age. Yet is such an approach viable? There is little doubt that Reform, Conservative, Reconstructionist and Humanistic Jews, as well as non-believers would find Sacks's proposals unacceptable. Given the drift away from traditional patterns of Jewish life, there is simply no way that world Jewry will be able to come to a common view concerning the fundamentals of Jewish belief and practice as he recommends – today no uniform pattern of Jewish existence can be imposed from above, nor is it likely to emerge from within the Jewish community. Arguably what is needed instead is a more realistic conception of Jewish life if Jews and Judaism are to continue into the next century and beyond. The purpose of this book is to offer a panoramic overview and critical evaluation of the different sub-groups in contemporary Jewish life in the quest to provide an alternative vision of Judaism for the modern age.

The book begins with a description in Chapter 1 of the various divisions within modern Judaism based on *The American Jew*. Although this book was based on a cross-section of Jews in a typical American city, it provides an impressionistic picture of contemporary attitudes. On the far right, strictly Orthodox Jews have embraced a way of life as enshrined in sacred sources. Determined to preserve the Jewish heritage, these Jews have isolated themselves from the main currents of modern life. Moving across the religious spectrum, Traditionalists similarly desire to uphold the central tenets of the faith though they seek to combine such an aspiration with an acceptance of secular society: such neo-Orthodox attitudes offer a means for adapting to contemporary circumstances. A more liberal approach to the Jewish tradition has been advanced by Conservative, Reconstructionist and Reform Jews who acknowledge the need for adaptation and change. In their view, what is required today is a reformulation of the essential features of Judaism.

On the far left, however, Jewish radicals have pressed for both political and religious modification as well as alternative lifestyles. Finally, within the community there is also a growing number of individuals who have severed their links with organized religion. Modern Judaism, therefore, has ceased to be a monolithic structure; instead the Jewish community is deeply divided over the most fundamental features of the faith.

Surveying the various divisions within Jewish community, Chapter 2 traces the origin and development of Orthodox Judaism through the centuries. In ancient Israel the community was united by a common inheritance based on God's revelation to his chosen people. According to tradition, God revealed the Written *Torah* to Moses on Mount Sinai; determined to ensure the strict observance of Jewish law, the rabbis elaborated the biblical precepts so as to make them relevant to changing circumstances. As time passed, this system of *halakhah* (Jewish law) served as the basis for Jewish life. However, in the post-Enlightenment period reformers sought to modify the Jewish heritage. Yet arguably such a deeply held commitment to the past no longer provides a viable form of Jewish living in the modern age.

Like Orthodox Jews, the Hasidim are staunch supporters of the traditional Jewish way of life. As Chapter 3 explains, in the nineteenth century the Hasidic movement emerged as a reaction to the strict formalism of Orthodoxy. The founder of this movement, the Baal Shem Tov, attracted a wide circle of followers who passed on his teaching; after his death his disciple Dov Baer of Mezhirech became the leader of this sect. Due to his influence Hasidism spread throughout Eastern Europe. However because of its adoption of new patterns of belief and practice, Hasidism was fiercely opposed by the rabbinic establishment, particularly the authorities in Vilna. Despite such denunciations, Hasidism was officially recognized by the Russian and Austrian governments and succeeded in gaining a wide circle of followers. In the modern world, this revitalized form of Judaism has emerged as a major force on the Jewish scene. But because of its adherence to archaic forms of Jewish existence, it is inconceivable that the Hasidic movement could serve as an overarching framework for world Jewry in the twenty-first century.

From the time of the Enlightenment, Jews were not obliged to live in isolated communities; in this new environment a number of Jews sought to modify the tradition. Chapter 4 outlines the evolution of the Reform movement from its origin at the beginning of the nineteenth century. These advocates of Jewish reform initially sought to modify public worship and modernize education. Not surprisingly, their programmes were rejected by the Orthodox who regarded any alteration to tradition as heretical. In the face of such hostility, European Reform leaders organized a series of synods to formulate a coherent policy; in the United States Jewish reformers similarly pressed for religious modification. In 1885 a synod of American Reform rabbis produced a list of formal principles, the Pittsburgh Platform; subsequently a new declaration of precepts, the Columbus Platform, was issued in 1937. This statement advocated a return to beliefs and practices that had previously been discarded by the movement. After the Second World War, Reform Judaism continued to develop, and in 1971 the Central Conference of American Rabbis formulated a new set of principles, the San Francisco Platform. However despite the growth of Reform Judaism world-wide, it is difficult to see how the ideology of reform could serve as a basis for reconstructing Jewish life in the next century.

Chapter 5 continues this exploration of the various forms of non-Orthodox Judaism. Emerging from the ranks of Reform, the leaders of Conservative Judaism propounded a new approach to the tradition. Critical of the radical stance espoused by leading reformers, such figures as Zacharias Frankel argued that a more moderate alteration of Jewish practice was needed to meet contemporary circumstances. In the United States adherents of positive-historical Judaism sought to establish a seminary to train rabbis at the beginning of this century. In the 1920s and 1930s the Conservative movement underwent considerable growth and embraced a degree of uniformity. None the less there was a general reluctance to enunciate a comprehensive philosophical position. As a result, there is widespread uncertainty within the movement about its underlying principles. Like Reform Jews, adherents of Conservative Judaism have advanced a wide range of interpretations of Judaism, and this lack of ideological coherence constitutes Conservative Judaism's fundamental deficiency for modern Jewry: despite its defence of a traditional Jewish way of life, the movement is deeply divided over the major elements of the faith.

As Chapter 6 demonstrates, Reconstructionist Judaism is an offshoot of the Conservative movement, offering a non-supernatural understanding of the tradition. Under the influence of Mordecai

Kaplan, Professor of Homiletics at the Jewish Theological Seminary, Reconstructionism attempted to reformulate the Jewish heritage to meet the demands of contemporary life. Judaism, Kaplan believed, is essentially the concretization of the collective self-consciousness of the community. The Jewish faith is a civilization which is manifest in *sancta*. Such *sancta* commemorate what the Jewish people hold most sacred and provide continuity through history as well as fortify the collective conscience. Conceived in this way, the Jewish faith includes history, literature, language, social organization, sanctions, standards of conduct, social and spiritual ideas and aesthetic values. By concentrating on Judaism as a civilization, Kaplan was able to activate Jewish concern and commitment to peoplehood and tradition in his presentation of the nature of the Jewish faith. Over the years the Reconstructionist movement has undergone considerable development; it now has its own rabbinical seminary, federation of synagogues and *havurot* (prayer groups) as well as an association of Reconstructionist rabbis. None the less, due to its rejection of any form of supernaturalism, it is difficult to see how this new interpretation of the tradition could serve as a framework for Jewish living in the future – despite the impact of secular values on the Jewish community, many Jews are today searching for a contemporary form of spirituality based on the religious traditions of the past.

Less traditional in orientation, Humanistic Judaism – as described in Chapter 7 – similarly espouses a non-theistic interpretation of the Jewish heritage. Under the leadership of Rabbi Sherwin Wine, this movement originated in the 1960s in Detroit, Michigan: unlike the other branches of mainstream Judaism, it acclaims the Humanistic dimensions of the tradition. On this basis, holidays and life-cycle events have been reformulated so as to highlight their humane characteristics. According to the advocates of this new movement, the central doctrines of the Jewish faith need to be reassessed in the light of contemporary knowledge and scientific discovery. Promoting a secular form of Jewish existence, Humanistic Jews argue for a de-mythologized form of Judaism. However although the movement currently has a following of about 40 000 members, it is unlikely that this radical translation of Judaism could serve as a viable ideology for the Jewish community. The Holocaust has eclipsed the optimistic attitudes generated by the Enlightenment, and, like Reconstructionist Judaism, Humanistic Judaism offers no foundation for a Jewish form of spirituality in the modern age.

A final ideology adopted by many twentieth-century Jews is Zionism. As Chapter 8 indicates, originally a small number of religious Jews in the nineteenth century, (including Yehuda hai Alkalai and Zwi Hirsch Kalisher) argued that the land of Israel should be settled in order to hasten the coming of the Messiah. In their view, colonies of devout Zionists should rebuild Palestine in anticipation of Messianic redemption. Paralleling this religious development, other secular Jews such as Moses Hess, Leon Pinsker and Theodor Herzl stressed that the creation of a Jewish state could only come about through human effort rather than divine intervention. As a result, they argued for the creation of Jewish settlements in order that the Jewish nation would cease to be a minority group within a gentile culture – this, they believed, was in the past the central cause of anti-Semitism. Through the efforts of these brave individuals a Jewish State was eventually created, and today the state of Israel is accepted by Jews world-wide regardless of their religious affiliation. Yet the recognition of Israel does not provide a framework for Jewish living, nor does it ensure the continuation of Judaism in the future.

Given the deficiencies of these various religious movements and ideologies within the Jewish community, there is a pressing need for new philosophy of Judaism which could provide a unifying basis for Jewish life in the next century. Arguably such a new interpretation of the tradition – referred to in Chapter 9 as Open Judaism – should be grounded in a recognition of the realities of modern Jewish existence. This new formulation of Judaism is based on the recognition that there is a fundamental distinction between the Divine as-it-is-in-itself and the Divine-as-perceived. Aware of the inevitable subjectivity of all religious belief, Jews should feel free to select those features of the Jewish heritage which they find spiritually meaningful. Unlike the major branches of Jewry, this new interpretation of Judaism would allow each individual independence of thought and action. Such a liberal approach would acknowledge the true nature of contemporary Jewish life, extolling the virtue of personal freedom of decision-making which has become the hallmark of the modern age.

1

Modern Jewish Diversity

Through the centuries the Jewish community was united by a common religious tradition. However from the time of the Enlightenment the monolithic system of Judaism underwent a process of fragmentation. As a consequence, Jewry today is divided into a variety of subgroups with their own religious identities. On the far right, ultra-Orthodox Jews adhere to the traditional way of life as outlined in Jewish legal sources. Determined to preserve their identity, these individuals isolate themselves from the main currents of modern life. Like these Orthodox Jews, Traditionalists also follow Jewish law, yet they seek to combine their loyalty to the tradition with an acceptance of contemporary society. Such neo-Orthodoxy strives to achieve a positive accommodation with the modern world. Moving across the religious spectrum, Conservative, Reconstructionist and Reform Jews have in their different ways attempted to reform the tradition in the light of current knowledge: this growing segment of the community advocates positive integration and assimilation. On the far left, Jewish radicals have espoused political and religious strategies for change as well as alternative Jewish lifestyles. Finally, the community also contains many individuals who seek to distance themselves from the faith. Arguably such acute diversity requires the formulation of a new philosophy of Judaism which could embrace these varied and opposing approaches to the Jewish heritage.

THE DISSOLUTION OF TRADITIONAL JUDAISM

Under the impact of modern science and contemporary secular trends, the monolithic system of Jewish belief and practice has undergone a process of dissolution. Regarding the concept of God, a number of Jewish thinkers have found it increasingly difficult to accept the fundamental tenets of the Jewish faith: some wish to modify various elements of Jewish theism, imposing limits to God's

1

omnipotence or omniscience; others have sought a more radical solution, wishing to substitute the concept of a supernatural deity in naturalistic terms. The Reconstructionist thinker Mordecai Kaplan, for example, asserted that the idea of God must be redefined – the belief in a supernatural deity must be superseded by a concept of God as 'man's will to live'. At the far end of the religious spectrum an even more radical approach has been advanced by Humanistic Jews who wish to dispense with God altogether. For these Jews, it is possible to live a Jewishly religious life without any acknowledgement of a divine reality. Thus, across the various groupings in contemporary Judaism there exists a wide range of different and conflicting beliefs about the nature of the Divine – no longer is the Jewish community committed to the view that God created and sustains the universe, guiding it to its ultimate fulfilment.

Similarly, for many Jews, the traditional belief in *Torah MiSinai* (God gave the *Torah* to Moses on Mount Sinai) no longer seems plausible. The rabbinic understanding of *Torah* as revealed to Moses and infallibly transmitted through the sages has been undermined by the findings of modern scholarship. Thus from the earliest period, reformers continued to believe in divine revelation, but they were anxious to point out that God's disclosure is mediated by human understanding. According to Reform Judaism, the Bible is a spiritual record of the history of ancient Israel, reflecting the primitive ideas of its own age. Similarly, the Conservative movement views Scripture as historically conditioned and mediated through human apprehension. As the Conservative scholar Solomon Schechter explained, the *Torah* is not in heaven – it is on earth and must be interpreted to be understood. For Reconstructionist Jews, the *Torah* is a human document, shaped by those who composed this epic account of Israel's origins and development. In this light, the Reconstructionist movement seeks to incorporate the Bible into the life of its members without ascribing to it a supernatural origin. Humanistic Jews share a similar veneration of the *Torah* even though they do not believe it was divinely revealed. Hence, as in the case of beliefs about God, there are fundamental differences of opinion regarding the status of Scripture among the various branches of contemporary Judaism.

The doctrine of messianic redemption has likewise been radically modified within the various branches of non-Orthodox Judaism. In the earliest stage of development, reformers rejected the notion of a personal Messiah; instead they believed that the Messianic Age was beginning to dawn in their own time. In their view, history was evolving progressively towards an era of liberty, equality and justice for all people. Even though the events of the twentieth century have eclipsed these earlier messianic expectations, Reform Judaism still embraces the conviction that human progress is possible in the modern world. Similarly, many Zionists saw the founding of a Jewish homeland as the fulfilment of messianic hope. Rejecting the belief in a personal Messiah, they advocated a naturalistic interpretation of historical progress in which the Jewish people would be restored to the land of their ancestors. Such reinterpretations of traditional belief are indicative of the general shift away from supernaturalism in the modern world.

The doctrine of the resurrection of the dead has likewise been largely rejected in both the Orthodox and non-Orthodox camps. The original belief in resurrection was an eschatological hope bound up with the rebirth of the nation in the Days of the Messiah, but as this messianic concept faded into the background so did this doctrine. For most Jews, physical resurrection is simply inconceivable in the light of the scientific understanding of the world. Thus, the Orthodox writer Joseph Seliger criticized the doctrine of resurrection as unduly materialistic. According to Seliger, in the ancient world the Afterlife was depicted in terms of earthly existence. The Egyptians, for example, believed so strongly in the bodily aspect of the Afterlife that they mummified the body and erected pyramids to protect it. In Seliger's view, such a notion is a mistaken folk-belief and has little in common with the Law of Moses. Judaism, he maintained, does not in fact adhere to the belief in physical resurrection but to belief in the immortality of souls.

In the Reform community a similar attitude prevails. Thus the Pittsburgh Platform categorically rejects the doctrine of the soul and such a conviction has been a dominant feature of the movement in subsequent years. Reform Jews, the Platform states:

> reassert the doctrine of Judaism that the soul is immortal, grounding this belief on the divine nature of the human spirit, which forever finds bliss in righteousness and misery in wickedness. We reject as ideas not rooted in Judaism the belief in bodily resurrection and in Gehenna and Eden (Hell and Paradise) as abodes for eternal punishment or reward.

The belief in eternal punishment has also been discarded by a large number of Jews partly because of the interest in penal reform during the past century. Punishment as retaliation in a vindictive sense has been generally rejected. As Louis Jacobs has remarked: 'the value of punishment as a deterrent and for the protection of society is widely recognized. But all the stress today is on the reformatory aspects of punishment. Against such a background the whole question of reward and punishment in the theological sphere is approached in a more questioning spirit' (Jacobs, 1964, 364). Further, the rabbinic view of Hell is seen by many as morally repugnant. Jewish theologians have stressed that it is a delusion to believe that a God of love could have created a place of eternal punishment.

Traditional theological belief has thus lost its force for a large number of Jews in the modern period – no longer is it possible to discover a common core of religious belief underpinning Jewish life. The community instead is deeply divided on the most fundamental features of the Jewish tradition. Likewise, there is a parallel disunity within Jewry concerning Jewish observance. As far as Orthodoxy is concerned, it is in theory a system of law, going back consistently and without interruption for thousands of years to the beginning of Jewish history; all the elaborations of *halakhah* in the later Orthodox Codes are held to be rediscoveries rather than novelties. Yet, this picture of an eternal developing legal system breaks down when we face its astonishing shrinkages in contemporary society – great areas of Jewish law have disappeared for a wide variety of reasons. Frequently, individuals who consider themselves Orthodox have simply ceased to resort to rabbinical courts in a number of areas of life. There is thus a large gap between the Orthodox system of practice and the limited observance of Jewish life within a large segment of the Orthodox Jewish community.

The rapidly contracting area of observance within Orthodoxy is in part the reason for the existence of Conservative Judaism. Since its inception, Conservative rabbis have been anxious to make Jewish law more flexible so as to provide for change legally. This approach to the tradition has provided a framework for the reinterpretation of Jewish law in the light of changed circumstances and modern needs. While acknowledging the historical importance of the Jewish heritage, the movement has sought to discover new ways to adjust the legal system where necessary. As a result, many traditional observances have been abandoned and other features altered to suit contemporary circumstances. In this way Conservative Judaism has provided a means of legitimizing deviations from tradition, thereby contributing to the further shrinkage of the Jewish legal code.

Similarly, within Reform Judaism, there has been an attempt to reinterpret Jewish law in the light of contemporary conditions. As the Reform Jewish scholar Solomon Freehof explained:

> Some of its provisions have passed from our lives. We do not regret that fact. But as to those laws that we do follow, we wish them to be in harmony with tradition ... Our concern is more with people than with the legal system. Wherever possible, such interpretations are developed which are feasible and conforming to the needs of life. Sometimes, indeed, a request must be answered in the negative when there is no way in the law for a permissive answer to be given. Generally the law is searched for such opinion as can conform with the realities of life. (Freehof, 1960, 22–3)

Due to such a liberal approach to the tradition, even greater areas of the legal system have been rejected within the ranks of Reform Judaism. For many Reform Jews, traditional Jewish Law has no bearing on their everyday lives.

In contemporary society, then, there is a wide divergency concerning Jewish observances and ceremonies. At the far right, ultra-Orthodox Jews scrupulously adhere to the tradition, yet within the Orthodox camp there are many who have ignored the dictates of Jewish law. Within Conservative Judaism deviation from the *halakhah* is legitimized, resulting in the abandonment of large areas of the tradition. And on the left, within Reform and Humanistic Judaism, there is a virtual abandonment of the traditional Code of Jewish Law. Hence, within modern Judaism there is no agreement about either practice or religious belief: the monolithic character of traditional Judaism as it existed from ancient times to the Enlightenment has been replaced by chaos and confusion across the religious spectrum. Jews disagree as to the fundamentals of the faith and the place of Judaism in their lives.

THE ULTRA-ORTHODOX

Throughout history Jews have affirmed their faith in one God who created the universe; as a transcendent Deity he brought all things into being, continues to sustain the cosmos, and guides humanity to its ultimate destiny. In addition, Orthodox Judaism affirms that God revealed the *Torah* (the Five Books of Moses) as well as the Oral Law to Moses on Mount Sinai. This belief guarantees the validity of the legal system, as well as Israel's pre-eminence among the nations.

Today Orthodox Jews continue to subscribe to these fundamental doctrines, secure in the knowledge that they are fulfilling God's will: such a commitment serves as the framework for the modern Orthodox way of life. In *The American Jew*, we describe a Sabbath meal as observed in a typical strictly Orthodox Jewish household – this celebration illustrates how ancient patterns of observance have been integrated into contemporary Jewish existence:

> When we arrived on Friday evening the house was abuzz with activity. Hairdryers hummed; children shouted and stamped; there was the constant sound of running feet. An urgent message was conveyed down the intercom. A telephone call must be returned immediately because the telephone, according to Jewish law, could not be used on the Sabbath. Our hostess emerged from her bedroom in her bathrobe; she was in the process of putting on her make-up and her head was completely covered by a scarf. Then the door opened and the men returned from synagogue. 'Good *Shabbos*, good *Shabbos*!' they said to the women. Besides all the husbands there were various nephews and rabbinic students. They were all dressed in dark suits and big hats. An elegant young Hasid with a long red beard wore a magnificent *streimel* (fur hat) above his kaftan. The head of the house took his seat at one end of the table and the Rabbi sat at the other. Blessings over the wine were said by every man present, one after the other. Then Sabbath songs were led by the younger son-in-law. The women did not sing – they listened. And then the food was served.   (D. and L. Cohn-Sherbok, 1994, 180–1)

Wary of modern life, such ultra-Orthodox Jews are anxious to preserve the Jewish way of life through a process of intensive education – for these Jews there can be no compromise with secularism. As the patriarch of the ultra-Orthodox community explained to us:

> I am aware that the environment of the United States is so powerful that unless the Jewish people created an intense atmosphere for themselves, it would be difficult to sustain themselves. A reli-

gious person can be involved in the secular world, but in order to
sustain himself, he must have a strong anchor or background.
I've always thought that. I can never remember thinking any differently. I know you have to make a choice; you have either to be
intensely Jewish and be taught about it, or you disappear as a
Jew. You weren't going to be able to ride the fence for too long.
(Ibid., 183)

Such attitudes permeate all aspects of Jewish life from the earliest
age. Among the ultra-Orthodox education for boys is rigorous, following the curriculum established in ancient times. Describing his
experiences living in a *yeshiva* (rabbinical seminary) one Orthodox
boy explained the strict discipline imposed on all students:

My whole life changed when I came here. At home I had my own
room; I was able to come whenever I wanted; in the fridge there
was always something to eat. Here in the dorm, its not your
room; it's not your space. The dorm consists of apartments.
There's just room space and a bathroom. Each apartment has
space for five. You have your own bed, closet and dresser. No
desk. You study in the *yeshiva*. You are allowed to put things on
the wall. Obviously sports figures get up there, but they really
discourage that. Lots of people stick up famous rabbis or scenery
from Israel. They really don't have pictures of family – they may
have them in their wallet. You have to have a dark *Shabbos* suit
and a white *Shabbos* shirt. It's the dress code that every child
wears a tie, and not casual stuff. Nothing overly loud, and a
black velvet *yarmulke* ... Having a relationship with a girl – that's
taboo. There are no proms, no discotheques ... They just don't
want you to be out of the *yeshiva* ... The boys do read newspapers, that's not forbidden. (Ibid., 173–4)

Within ultra-Orthodox circles, expectations for girls are of a different nature: Jewish young women are reared to become loyal and
dedicated mothers and homemakers. Explaining the nature of their
upbringing, the Governor of an Orthodox Girl's High School
stressed the importance of parental supervision in choosing a
husband:

With my eldest daughter, she was in seminary. A friend of a
friend said, 'I know a real nice boy for you.' This girl had lived in

the boy's parents' house, and she thought they would be a real good match. As it turned out, it was! She's now married has had two babies of her own. We try to check out the boy to see if things match each other. You always know somebody who knows somebody. So basically we called up and checked up on the school and the synagogue and the rabbi and so on. Sometimes you check up and it's a wonderful person, but it's not for your child. You want somebody suitable for them. There was times that I called, and I didn't like what I heard. There's no point for her to go out with somebody if you know it's not going to work out ... I've never had a problem with this. If I say, 'I do not care for this person', I do not think she would go against me. (Ibid., 107–8)

Strict adherence to Jewish law is demanded within the context of ultra-Orthodox Judaism: committed to the doctrine of *Torah Mi Sinai* (the belief that God revealed the *Torah* to Moses on Mount Sinai), Orthodox Jews are obliged to keep all biblical and rabbinic ordinances. To accomplish this in a modern setting requires determination and scrupulous care. With regard to the regulations concerning *kashrut* [food laws], for example, contemporary life has created numerous complexities requiring expert advice. In the words of the *kashrut* supervisor:

It doesn't sound like much, but I help *kosher* between three and four homes a month. I speak to people; I go through their kitchen; I tell them what to expect; and also I try not to force my standards upon people. I try to make it as easy for them as I can ... when we *kosher* a pot, there's no hocus-pocus; we put it into a big pot of boiling water and then cold water. Everything has to be done: pots, stoves, sinks, silverware. Before you use your pot, you should take it and keep it in the ritual bath – you make a blessing there.   (Ibid., 135)

Although the Orthodox constitute only a small segment of the Jewish community, they are a growing segment anxious to draw other Jews to traditional Judaism. Recently, there has been a burgeoning of Orthodox programme schemes designed to make *Torah* Judaism attractive to the less observant and unaffiliated. One of those who spoke to us was an *yeshiva* official whose job was to create such programmes for the general Jewish population.

Describing the *yeshiva* adult educational programme, he stated that:

> It is directed towards any Jewish person or their spouse who really has very limited or no Jewish background. As people get older, they start to ask themselves, 'What's life all about?' My objective is to educate people and let people make their own decisions. Judaism smacks in the face of a lot of the philosophies and ways and beliefs of American society. To that I say: 'if Abraham had caved in to the beliefs of his time, we would all now be pagans. Judaism did not give in to the times ... that's how it remained Judaism!' ... I think the return to *Torah* Judaism is part of God's plan. There's a very beautiful song and when I got married I marched down to the marriage canopy to its tune: 'Behold the days are coming, promises God, and I will send a hunger in the land, not a hunger for bread, not a thirst for water, but to hear the word of God.' (Ibid., 104–5)

TRADITIONALISTS

Within the Jewish community there are a considerable number of Jews who – while considering themselves Orthodox in orientation – are less strict about Jewish observance than the ultra-Orthodox. These Traditionalists attempt to steer a middle course, combining the Jewish heritage with a contemporary life-style. Such a Traditionalist approach is a modified form of Orthodoxy (similar to right-wing Conservative Judaism). Explaining the difficulties inherent in such a position, one of the Traditional rabbis remarked:

> I'm called the 'middler' ... cars going down the middle of the street get hit by other cars going in both directions! I'm a moderate politically and religiously ... we Jews fought for Americanization, and we got it up to a great point, and now we're realizing the consequences ... mixed marriages and a lack of observance. We live in a society that emphasizes autonomy and individual choice. It's not too hot on nationalism or ethnic identity or religious beliefs. People start to marry late, to have alternative lifestyles, to live together before marriage, to be homosexual, bisexual, to adopt and have children as single people. Anything goes in America. The whole smorgasbord is bound to

affect the Jewish people. Those of us in the middle are caught in a bind. We have sympathies for choice and for rights, but religiously, it's very difficult. So we're hit by both sides (Ibid., 20)

Yet despite such difficulties, the advocates of Traditionalism maintain that such an approach provides the framework for authentic Jewish living in the modern age. Another of the Traditional rabbis emphasized that an accommodation with the realities of contemporary society can draw Jews back to the Jewish heritage:

I discovered a long time ago that there are many Jews who are not prepared to be connected to the Jewish community through religion. So I became active in the wider community in the hope that if I build a relationship with people on some other basis, they could feel more connected to what I really represented to them – which is traditional Judaism. It was that that led me to create entities in this community, with which people could identify, even if they aren't religious institutions.   (Ibid., 98–9)

Responding to the Orthodox criticism that such activity is simply a temporary remedy to an intractable problem, he replied:

People … say to me that if only I could have taken my talents and focused them on Orthodox institutions, I could have built something that would last. All of these things will disappear when I'm gone … I sort of agree, and I am concerned with the future of Judaism … Nevertheless, I feel a compulsion to minister to the wider community because they're here now and they need my gifts. Even terminal cancer patients need help.   (Ibid., 100)

Although worship in Traditional synagogues is usually the same as found in strictly Orthodox communities, men and women are allowed to sit together. This is an important infringement of Jewish law as the traditional cantor explained; however he stressed that he still considered himself Orthodox:

Beit Torah was always a traditional synagogue. It couldn't be Orthodox because they had men and women sitting together. I accepted this, but my parents didn't like it, coming from an Orthodox background. At home I still keep *kosher*, I still have a completely Orthodox life. You bet! I will not eat in restaurants; I

never ride on the Sabbath; I am still Sabbath observant. You bet!
The congregation wanted that, I was at *Beit Torah* for twenty-two
years, I always lived near the synagogue so as I could walk.
(Ibid., 42)

Reflecting on the changes he observed during his life as a cantor, he
sadly observed the current lack of interest in the liturgy:

People do not appreciate the cantor as they did years ago. No.
Because today it's 'one two, three,' time schedule in the synagogue. The service must be done in a certain amount of time, and
the attendance has fallen down. People don't understand the way
it used to be. The old-timers used to come and appreciate the
cantor. They loved the music. Today they don't know what
prayer means. They say it takes up too much time. They want to
be out by 12 o'clock. They don't appreciate it.   (Ibid., 43)

Within Traditional Judaism major changes have been made in the
status of women. In the past Judaism was essentially a patriarchal
religion with clearly defined roles for men and women. According
to Jewish law, women are exempt from time-bound positive commands – as a result they are not expected to take an active part in
prayer and worship. Today however Traditional synagogues actively encourage women to take a more central role in religious observance. In some congregations women have even assumed
positions of leadership. Commenting on her role, the woman
President of a Traditional synagogue stated:

My initial feeling was – oh, the token woman! You make her
Secretary, and that's as far as it would get! Then after a short
period of time, I got to be Vice-President and then was First Vice-
President and next in line ... Was there any difference in being a
woman President? I did not sit up on the *bimah* [dais] during services which the President normally does ... I didn't arrive early
because after all I didn't count in the *minyan* [quorum] ... The
woman is supposed to defer to the man! As the President of
course, I was certainly not deferring! But it didn't bother me if I
were up there or not. It didn't make any difference.   (Ibid., 45–6)

Although Traditional congregations do not allow women to be
rabbis or cantors, there has been a growing recognition of women's

talents. Thus, even though a woman would not be allowed to function as a cantor, the Traditional cantor being interviewed was prepared to train a woman to serve as a cantor in a Reform synagogue. Commenting on her abilities, he said proudly: 'She's my student. She's a lovely, lovely, very talented, very pretty young lady with a beautiful voice. She's not Orthodox, but she wanted to know the traditional liturgy, how it sounds. She was anxious to learn and why not?' (Ibid., 43)

As far as girls are concerned, Traditional synagogues have *Bat Mitzvah* as well as *Bar Mitzvah* ceremonies. In many respects such services are the same, yet as one *Bat Mitzvah* student pointed out there are differences:

> I had to learn my *Haftarah* [prophetic reading] and my speech. I wasn't reading from the *Torah* scroll, no ... The service was on Saturday night. It wasn't in the synagogue; it was in the chapel. My grandparents' friends all came, and I was allowed to invite some friends. It was around 200 – maybe not even that many. There was a big *Bar Mitzvah* in the synagogue on Saturday morning. I didn't know the boy ... I wore a new dress ... It was all over blue sequins with a white satin shirt and jacket. It sparkled ... we were at the synagogue very early ... I did my *Haftarah* – and I said my speech ... Then I said my *Bat Mitzvah* prayer in front of the Ark. Then we had the *Havdalah* [the conclusion of the Sabbath ceremony] ... Doing a *Torah* portion takes the boys much longer. I didn't think I'd have been allowed to do that. It didn't bother me. I enjoyed it. I'm glad I did it.   (Ibid., 161–2)

At an even younger age, girls and boys attend traditional day schools where students learn the same subjects. The curriculum consists of both Jewish and secular studies. Describing a typical day, one girl student said:

> At school we have Hebrew and Judaic. In Hebrew we read stories and translate them. Hebrew is forty-five minutes and Judaic is fifty-five minutes each day ... we have *shaharit* [morning prayer] every morning for half an hour, and once a week we have a *Torah* service on Thursday.   (Ibid., 158)

Traditional Judaism thus differs from strict Orthodoxy in its attempt to harmonize Jewish values with modern life. Although less rigorous in its approach to the Jewish heritage, it none the less fosters a positive attitude toward the tradition.

REFORMERS

From the time of the Enlightenment, Jewish reformers sought to revaluate the Jewish faith, modifying the tradition to meet modern needs. The aim of these progressive Jews was to make Judaism relevant to contemporary society. Initially Reform Judaism paved the way for such a process of modernization. Subsequently more traditionally-minded reformers established the Conservative movement and as an alternative approach to the heritage. More recently, the Reconstructionist movement emerged out of Conservative Judaism as a non-supernaturalistic interpretation of the tradition.

Although the adherents of Conservative Judaism stress the importance of Jewish observance, they do not integrate the corpus of Jewish law into their everyday lives. In this respect they resemble Traditionalists. As the Conservative rabbi explained, the members of his synagogue like to think of themselves as Orthodox, even though they are lapsed in practice: 'They like to think of themselves as Orthodox. They like an Orthodox style, but that's not how they live their lives ...' (Ibid., 22).

In recent years the Conservative movement fostered the creation of small, home-based groups (*havurot*) that hold their own religious services without rabbinic leadership. These groups encourage active participation and a return to traditional observance. As the lay leaders of one group explained:

Sarah: A co-ed *Talmud* group meets every Thursday noon. And on Friday morning a smaller group meets to talk about the *Torah* portion and holds a short service. Only men are involved in that.

Don: That service is really wonderful because it's done with all the set Psalms in the liturgy. We go through the entire service with traditional melodies as well. We even dance a lot.

Sarah: And then on Friday, we've decided to observe Friday night as a huge celebration. Initially we held Friday night services, but we discovered that they disrupted the Sabbath atmosphere. It's paradoxical that there's nothing

more disruptive to a real *Shabbat* than having to attend
formal worship; we had to get our children ready and
drive them from all over the city.

Don: But on Saturday mornings we have regular services.

Sarah: We've only just started that. Previously we only held services twice a month since people were used to spending
Saturdays on sport or doing errands or whatever. The
idea of committing two *Shabbats* a month sounded enor-
mous at first. Then eventually we took a big step and
made it three. Shortly afterwards we said, 'Hey we want
to do it all the time.'

Don: One principle of our group is that you can't transmit
Jewishness to your children just by telling them to do
something. The parents have to lead by example. The
kids learn that this is what's actually done. The hope
with all our children is that as they get older, they'll form
their own Jewish homes.   (Ibid., 49)

As an off-shoot of Conservative Judaism, Reconstructionist
Judaism is a relatively new movement – it is traditional in observance, but non-theistic in orientation. In the community we interviewed, the Reconstructionist congregation was composed of *havurah*
groups united into a Federation. As the lay leader explained:

At this point we have approximately 200 households divided into
about sixteen *havurahs*. We have group events as well as High
Holy Day services. We also have a religious school which has
about sixty-five kids. That happens every Sunday plus there is a
Wednesday programme for Hebrew school. Typically we have
Friday night services once a month and one *havurah* organizes the
programming. Last time we had about 150 people show up.
    These *havurahs* range from four or five families up to, in some
instances, fourteen and fifteen families. They meet in each other's
homes. What do they do? They all do a variety of different things,
from scholarly discussions to life-cycle events to Sabbath dinners,
to picnics. They choose their own programmes.   (Ibid., 51)

Unlike Conservative and Reconstructionist Judaism, the Reform
movement fosters a more liberal approach to the tradition in terms
of both belief and practice. Embracing the principle of contemporary relevance, Reform Jews affirm those features of the Jewish her-

itage that they find spiritually meaningful. Distancing itself from Orthodoxy, Reform Judaism also embraces a number of practices censured by the Orthodox establishment. For example, in 1983 the Reform rabbinical association (the Central Conference of American Rabbis) decreed that the child of either a Jewish mother or Jewish father should be regarded as Jewish. By expanding the determination of Jewishness to include children of matrilineal and patrilineal descent, the American Reform movement defined as Jews individuals whom other branches of Judaism regard as gentiles; this means that neither these persons nor their descendants can be accepted as Jews by the Orthodox religious establishment. In addition, Reform Judaism has also adopted conversion procedures which differ from the Orthodox process – as a result, its converts are not accepted by the Orthodox community.

Such changes to the tradition have been made because of the rise in mixed marriages. The quest to integrate the offspring of such unions into the community has become an important aim of the Reform movement. In the words of one of the Reform rabbis we interviewed:

> The thing that this congregation has become known for is the outreach work we've done. We do a lot of stuff here with outreach. We developed some programmes for people who already had converted to Judaism – how to integrate them into the congregation. We did some groups for parents in a mixed marriage. Then we did a group for non-Jewish parents. Then we decided the one missing piece was for kids whose parents had intermarried, and we created another programme called, 'Every Day, the Jewish Way'. Intermarriage is not on the horizon. It already is ... maybe a third of the congregation is intermarried. I really don't know.   (Ibid., 28)

The Director of 'Every Day, the Jewish Way' amplified the initiatives taken by the Reform Congregation to draw intermarried couples to the Temple. In her view, it is vital that children of intermarriages be brought up as Jews:

> I do communicate to them that I feel unequivocally that it is better for a child and for a whole family if there is a decision to raise a child in one religion. Whether one partner maintains her own religion but is supportive of the decision, or whether there is

a conversion, there should be one religion for the child. Research shows that adults who are brought up between two worlds are caught in the middle and spend much of their adult lives trying to find out who they are.   (Ibid., 296)

One adult who had converted to Judaism spoke to us about her experiences. For this individual, Reform Judaism provided a framework for an authentically Jewish life style:

I went to every synagogue in town before I made the decision. It was a really big deal for me, and I wanted to be sure wherever I converted I felt comfortable. The people at Temple Shalom were the most warm and open and caring – that always makes you feel good. The classes lasted for almost a year ... we learned about the differences between the types of Judaism; we had a lot of books to read; we didn't have to do any Hebrew; we met with people who showed us how to do the blessings; and we learnt about the holidays.   (Ibid., 300)

Another liberal feature of Reform Judaism has been its acceptance of women as both rabbis and cantors. In 1972, the Reform movement ordained the first woman rabbi; in subsequent years an increasing number of women have entered the rabbinate. Yet, as the woman rabbi in the community stressed, the quest for recognition is difficult even though the Reform movement has embraced the principle of equality of the sexes.

As far as jobs go, once you are a rabbi, it's not necessarily that congregations won't hire women, but that the differential in pay between women and men in rabbinical positions is as much as 20 per cent. You see, we keep getting pregnant, and they don't like that too much ... as an educator, I was never seen as a real rabbi. The assistant rabbi was named associate before it was even thought to make me associate ... I always had to be better, to speak better, be more creative. I had to come up with new things all the time whereas the associate male colleague could do the same thing.   (Ibid., 34–5)

Despite such criticism, Reform Judaism has been an influential force in modern Jewish life. With its national and local organizations and vast number of synagogues, it provides a progressive approach to the tradition that appeals to many Jews in search of an authentic expression of Judaism in tune with the realities of contemporary society.

RADICALS

Moving across the religious spectrum, the contemporary Jewish community also includes individuals who, though seeking to identify as Jews, have adopted alternative approaches to the tradition. Recently, for example, Humanistic Judaism has undergone significant growth: today there are approximately 40 000 Jews worldwide who subscribe to the principles of Jewish Humanism.

Like Reconstructionist Judaism, Humanistic Judaism has abandoned the traditional belief in a supernatural Deity. In its place, Humanistic Jews have substituted a commitment to Humanistic principles enshrined in the Jewish heritage. Thus in a statement of the principles of Humanistic Judaism, the Federation of Humanistic Jews proclaims:

> Every person is entitled to life, dignity and freedom. We believe in the value of Jewish identity and in the survival of the Jewish people. Jewish history is a human story.

Dedicated to Humanistic values, members of this new movement are anxious to eliminate those features of the Jewish faith which they regard as undermining their core principles. Yet for these individuals such a quest involves a considerable struggle, as a Humanistic couple explained:

Edie: I called the Humanistic Jews' headquarters, and I got their prayerbook, and I was doing mini-versions of their services. We would have our friends over to Passover and whenever we got to a certain point they would say, 'This isn't right!'

Jay: They would ridicule us and make jokes.

Edie: We had a beautiful liturgy, but they would demand the traditional service about killing first-born babies. Humanists don't kill babies. I would get so mad.

Jay: We're vegetarians and our friends would say they were going to a meatless, godless Passover!

Edie: Yet we knew they didn't themselves believe in an all-powerful, all-loving God. I would feel really confused about it all. We were so on our own. Then in 1991, I got a phone call from someone who was trying to get a Humanistic group formed and it worked out. Right now we are a bona fide affiliated group accepted by the national body. (Ibid., 65–6)

Another group within the Jewish community which has experienced considerable hostility are gay Jews. Traditional Judaism condemns homosexuality, and as a result gay Jews frequently find they are subject to official opposition from the Jewish establishment. As a gay couple explained:

Tim: I deal with a lot of traditional rabbis ... all these traditional congregations look at us as if we have illnesses.

Gerald: The official position is that we're supposed to abstain from sexual activity.

Tim: What do I expect from them? Five years ago I would have said, 'You change your attitude!' Today I understand it's not going to happen.

Gerald: We have had a problem with the *Jewish News*.

Tim: Yeah. We were just like any other new congregation and right at the beginning we did have a few listings [in the newspaper]. Then we were dropped. They argued it was a privately owned newspaper, and they could decide what would be put in it. (Ibid., 55–6)

Despite such an official rejection, gay Jews have been accepted within the more liberal branches of Judaism. As this couple added:

Gerald: The Reform movement was coming to terms with homosexuality, and that made a difference. I'd been a member of the Reconstructionists since 1984, and they also were accepting. Now they even allow gays to be rabbis.

Tim: So does the Reform movement. The rabbi of Temple Shalom has been the most active supporter of the gay congregations. (Ibid., 55)

In addition to those Jews at the fringes of religious life, there are also a significant number of Jews involved in radical politics: these individuals have become deeply concerned about Israeli policies concerning the Palestinian problem. Frequently, they too have been subject to adverse criticism from the Jewish establishment. One such activist recounted his experiences in this regard:

> Basically, we have adopted the two-state position in the Middle East, and we have consistently supported Palestinian rights. As you can imagine, that puts us very much on the fringe of the organized Jewish community. The mainstream Jewish community tries to perpetuate the myth that there really was no Palestinian community, that the Jewish settlers entered an empty land ... How have we been received? With anger, with derision, with hostility. I think there's been a conscious attempt by the mainstream organizations to marginalize us, to present us as fringe elements, wackos.   (Ibid., 262–3)

Another important development within modern Judaism has been the emergence of Jewish feminism. In the past Judaism was essentially a patriarchal religion with clearly defined roles for men and women. Because women were exempt from positive time-bound commands, they did not take an active part in Jewish life. In recent years, however, Jewish women have sought to participate on an equal basis with men. Although very little has changed in the Orthodox community, the non-Orthodox branches of Judaism have actively encouraged women to become full participants in the faith. Yet, as one Jewish feminist commented to us, it is difficult to overcome the inherent sexual bias of the tradition:

> Obviously Judaism is a patriarchal religion; obviously it's institutionalized sexism. It's role-based; it's gender-based. As far as feminists go, I have so much experience of women starting off exploring their Judaism and ending up being goddess worshippers. I've seen this trend a lot. I went to this fascinating lecture by someone called Starhawk, who's written several books. She was born Jewish, and she said in her talk that's she's a little bit of everything. And you can see why. She's having a great time; she's banging a drum; she's the centre of her life.

Yet for this feminist, a new vision of the faith is a possibility:

> I'm not going to waste my time being actively opposed to any Jewish institution. I'm much more interested in the positive side. Reinforcing and listening to Jewish women who have done

something significant, resurrecting Jewish heroines, encouraging
Jewish women's accomplishments.   (Ibid., pp. 258–60)

A very different approach to the heritage was expressed by a
Jewish astrologer we met. As she explained, her early experience
of Judaism was devoid of spirituality. Growing up in a Reform
context, she found little to deepen her faith:

> You really want me to tell you what I learnt at Temple Shalom? I
> learnt that there was something morally wrong with chewing
> gum … and that's about it … What I got from Temple Shalom
> was roughly the equivalent of spiritual bankruptcy. It was
> definitely not a positive experience. It was serving a jail sentence.
> What I learnt at religion school was about Jewish baseball. They
> were trying to secularize the religion.   (Ibid., 242–3)

In place of established religion, this person turned to Jewish astrol-
ogy to discover a source of spirituality:

> What astrology taught me is that we have a universe which is
> orderly and structured. Science is based on predictability as well
> … in the Middle Ages Jews were the best astrologers. I also found
> that a lot of traditional Jewish superstitions are solidly grounded
> in metaphysical and astrological principles … So suddenly, a great
> many of those superstitions made sense – when they made no
> sense at all in terms of enlightened reason … Astrology is very
> much part of the Jewish tradition. Not many people know that, but
> it is an ancient part of the tradition. The more I study, the more I
> realise that it is part of my birthright.   (Ibid., 242–4)

In their different ways these radical Jews have distanced themselves
from the mainstream currents of modern Judaism. Standing outside
the contemporary framework of the tradition, they have found new
ways of making the Jewish heritage meaningful in their lives.

THE UNAFFILIATED

Within the Jewish community, there are also many individuals who
have disassociated themselves from Judaism – some of these
persons have simply assimilated into the secular world. As one of

these assimilated Jews told us, he married a non-Jew and through the years had no particular affinity with the tradition:

> I've never belonged to a synagogue in Metropolis. As a matter of fact, it's fair to say I've never really thought about the question. Beth and I were a unit. We lived in a world which had frequent contact with both the Jewish and non-Jewish world. We didn't have children. How would I have brought them up? You're asking me a hypothetical question that I don't know that I can answer. I think probably as agnostics and with the moral virtues, and that's it! I would say I am not religious. I was not particularly interested in Jewish religion, even in Jewish history. I don't even recall any religious discussions. Did I think of myself as a Jew? No ... that was not my uppermost thought and reaction ... Over the years, I may have become slightly more sensitive to being a Jew, but it is not my first consideration in meeting people or in doing things. In fact it's way down the list. (Ibid., 196–8)

Some of the unaffiliated Jews we met lost interest in Judaism because they were unable to accept the religious principles of the faith; for these Jews, belief in God was simply unimaginable. This was the view of a Holocaust survivor who had been brought up in a secular household – for this person beauty had in later life taken the place of religious commitment:

> I cannot tell you that I particularly believed in a God. I believed so strongly in my parents that they took on the role of authority. In my reliance on them, I did not ever have the desire to believe in something besides us. The authority and the meaningfulness was really taking place within our household. Belief or non-belief in God never came up. We did not take much notice of religious holidays except that we were taken out of school, which was very nice! ... Beauty has been my passion. Music was what connected me with my parents, and my experience is that when it is beautiful, it is uplifting. I travel a lot for opera, and it is uplifting to me as an experience. (Ibid., 239–42)

Because aesthetics play such a fundamental role in this person's life, she and her husband decided that at their deaths sculpture and music would take the place of a formal religious observance:

We know that we wanted to be cremated. We don't want a tomb-
stone, but we commissioned this piece of sculpture carved by a
husband and wife team. It's a large book made of Florentine
marble. It's warped and it represents age. When one of us dies,
the other one will pay for a quartet to play in the house. There
will be good food, good drink and good music. People can talk
about the departed one. The ashes will be put in pots which I've
already commissioned and these will be buried in the cemetery
and the book will go on top.   (Ibid., 239–42)

Other Jews have found it increasingly difficult to identify with
the Jewish community because they have intermarried. In one in-
stance, the person we spoke to had also adopted an Oriental child.
Although this individual regarded herself as Jewish, she and her
husband did not wish to identify with the Jewish community and
sought to raise their child as a secular humanist:

I want her to grow up as a secular American humanist. I want
her to care about other people, to have a sense of responsibility
for her community, and to take pride in herself and her varied
background. I do not particularly want her to have a Jewish education. I don't think I will send her to religion school. We talk a
lot about Vietnam and that background. She's a Vietnamese
American, and we encourage her also to think about being an
American – Thanksgiving and pumpkin pie, and all that. She
may, as an adolescent, join some other religion. I don't know.
(Ibid., 277)

The growth of intermarried couples has had a profound effect on
Jewish identity. As we have seen, a number of Jewish institutions
have attempted to integrate these couples and their children, but
this has proved difficult in many cases. Often the non-Jewish
partner is perplexed how to integrate his family into a Jewish
setting. Thus a non-Jewish spouse told us of his confusion.

A few years ago, when the kids were six or so, we were thinking
about how to give them a proper sense of values. So we sent
them to the Temple Shalom 'Every Day, the Jewish Way' programme. Tom went for one year. He had a scepticism which I
share, so he dropped out. Barbara, my daughter, went for two
years. She enjoyed it, but they both thought it too slow; they were

a bit bored ... We go to the Presbyterian church about once a year to listen to the hymns. I have great affection for the Quakers, but at this point my politics and theirs differ. We made one other stab at religious training besides the Temple Shalom programme. They learnt Hebrew for a year with a tutor. The last two or three years they have not got much religious training. In the home, for a number of years, we lit Friday night candles. We have a Christmas tree and presents – they get both Hanukkah and Christmas presents! In past years, we've been through short forms of the Passover service. Easter eggs? Sometimes, yeah ... Would I want them to marry someone Jewish? The quality of person is more important to me than the religion. (Ibid., 340).

For a number of converts to Judaism, there is similarly a sense of unease about Jewish identity. One of the converts we interviewed spoke at length about her negative feelings toward the community:

When we announced we were going to get married, the balloon went up ... His family insisted, absolutely insisted, on a Jewish wedding, and if we were to have a Jewish wedding, then I had to convert. There was no option ... to begin with, I went along with it. I wanted to please his folks. But it was a bummer from the start. I had an awful interview with the rabbi. Without exactly saying so, he made it quite clear he couldn't understand why a boy like Joe would want to get involved with a little tramp like me ... Anyway, I went along to the weekly conversion class. I had to ... Every week we had to go to the Temple ... It was all so silly ... and so different from what I was used to ... Our kids ... We're not bringing them up in any religion. They can decide for themselves when they're old enough ... It was all a long time ago now. I wish I had something more positive to tell you. (Ibid., 303–5)

Such individuals, though formally part of the community, have fallen away from any form of Jewish practice. Others, too, have dropped out of Jewish life even though they are perceived as Jewish by the community because of their birth. Some of these Jews have sought spiritual enlightenment in other religions. One Jewish girl we talked to had been so disenchanted with the Judaism of her youth, that she became a Hare Krishna devotee. Movingly she explained her spiritual journey away from Judaism:

When did I check out of Judaism? I don't know. I don't think in that way. My mind and body will probably always be Jewish. There will always be a Jewish part of me. But I am a spirit-soul, and the knowledge of Bhakti has been very fulfilling. I feel my identity with this tradition predates my identity with Judaism. I felt it very strongly. It all clicked when I first went to India ... Personally I don't feel that God is going to mind if you worship Him by bowing down, or standing up, or calling Him one name or another. The point is to call God.   (Ibid., 315–17)

Another person we interviewed had broken with Judaism and become a Roman Catholic. Yet, she too was conscious of her Jewish origins and still perceived herself as Jewish:

The second Christmas I was here I went to Mass with some friends, and that night I decided it was time to become a Christian. I was living Christianity anyway. I started going to classes immediately in January, and I continued for over a year ... I'm much happier. I finally feel I belong. I always prayed to be part of a larger family, and I've got very involved with the church in all sorts of projects. Catholics want to get back to their roots. I always thought I had better hide my Judaism, but it's very special to the Church that I was a Jew – very precious. I'm asked to speak; I've conducted Passover seders [home cere-monies]; I've read the Old Testament in Hebrew.   (Ibid., 312–13)

The unaffiliated members of the Jewish community hence range across a broad spectrum of belief and practice. Yet despite the dif-ferences in approach, they have all disassociated themselves from the formal established structures of the faith.

2

Orthodox Judaism

The origins of Orthodox Judaism stretch back across 4000 years to the beginnings of the Jewish nation. From the patriarchal period to the institution of rabbinic Judaism in the Hellenistic period Jews were bound by the covenant contracted with Moses on Mount Sinai. With the emergence of the Pharisees the belief in *Torah MiSinai* (the revelation of the *Torah* on Mount Sinai), became a cardinal principle of the faith. Determined to ensure the strict observance of the law, the rabbis engaged in extensive interpretation of the Written Law – their discussions were later recorded in the *Mishnah*, *Talmud* and *Code of Jewish Law*. Throughout the Middle Ages, the system of *halakhah* (Jewish law) served as the basis for Jewish existence. However under the influence of the Enlightenment, Jewish reformers sought to modernize the tradition. In response, traditionalists insisted on the continuity of the Jewish heritage; these defenders of the faith denounced any alteration to Jewish belief and practice. Yet arguably such a vigorous championship of Orthodoxy suffers from a number of serious defects due to traditional Judaism's unwillingness to confront the challenges of the modern age.

BIBLICAL AND RABBINIC ORIGINS

The history of the Jewish nation began in ancient Mesopotamia where successive empires flourished and decayed before the Jews emerged as a separate people. According to the Bible, Abraham was the father of the Jewish nation; initially known as Abram, he came from Ur of the Chaldeans. Together with his family he went to Haran and later to Canaan, eventually settling in the plain near Hebron. Abraham was followed by Isaac and Jacob whose son Joseph was sold into slavery in Egypt; in time the entire Hebrew clan moved to Egypt where they flourished for centuries until a new Pharaoh decreed that all first-born Hebrews should be put to death.

To persuade Pharaoh to let the Jewish people go, Scripture records that God sent a series of plagues upon the Egyptians. After this devastation, Moses, the leader of the people, led his kinsfolk out of Egypt; after wandering in the desert for forty years, the Israelite clan finally entered into the land that God had promised them. Under Joshua's leadership, the Hebrews conquered the existing inhabitants. After Joshua's death the people began to form separate groups: at first there were twelve tribes named after the sons of Jacob. During this period the country was ruled over by twelve national heroes who served successively as judges.

Frequently the covenant between God and his chosen people – first formulated by Moses – was proclaimed at gatherings at national shrines. Such an emphasis on covenantal obligation reinforced the belief that the Jews were the recipients of God's loving kindness. In a more settled existence, the Covenant expanded to include additional legislation, including the provisions needed for an agricultural community. During this epoch it became increasingly clear to the Jewish population that the God of the covenant directed human history: the Exodus and the entry into the Promised Land were viewed as the unfolding of a divine plan.

Under the judges, God was conceived as the king of kings, however in time the nation yearned for a human monarch; as a result Saul was elected as king, but in later years the Israelite nation divided into two kingdoms. It was against this background that the pre-exilic prophets (Elijah, Elisha, Amos, Hosea, Micah and Isaiah) endeavoured to bring the nation back to the true worship of God. Righteousness, they declared, is the standard by which all people are to be judged, especially kings and rulers.

During the first millennium BCE the Jews watched their country emerge as a powerful state only to see it sink into spiritual and moral decay. Following the Babylonian conquest in 586 BCE the Temple lay in ruins, Jerusalem was destroyed, and the people despaired of their fate. This was God's punishment for their iniquity, which the prophets had predicted. Yet despite defeat and exile, the nation arose from the ashes of the old kingdoms. In the centuries which followed, the Jewish people continued their religious traditions and communal life. Though they had lost their independence, their devotion to God and His law sustained them through suffering and hardship and inspired them to new heights of creativity. In Babylonia, the exiles flourished, keeping their religion alive in the synagogues. When in 538 BCE King Cyrus of Persia permitted the

Jews to return to their former home, the nation underwent a transformation: the Temple was rebuilt, and religious reforms were
enacted. This return to the land of their fathers led to a national
restoration and a renaissance of Jewish life which was to last until
the first century CE.

With the destruction of the Temple in 70 CE, Jewish life underwent a major transformation: no longer were Jews secure in their
own country – instead they were compelled to live in exile. Despite
such devastation, Palestinian rabbinic scholars continued to engage
in the interpretation of Scripture. The most important scholar of the
early rabbinic period was Judah ha-Nasi, the head of the Sanhedrin,
whose main achievement was the redaction of the *Mishnah* (a compendium of the Oral *Torah*) in the second century CE. This volume
consists of the discussions and rulings of sages whose teachings
had been transmitted orally. According to the rabbis, the law
recorded in the *Mishnah* was given orally to Moses along with
the written law: 'Moses received the *Torah* from Sinai, and handed
it down to Joshua, and Joshua to the elders, and elders to the
prophets, to the men of the Great Assembly'. This view implies that
there was an infallible chain of transmission from Moses to the
leaders of the nation and eventually to the rabbis.

The Sanhedrin, which had been so fundamental in the compilation of the *Mishnah*, met in several cities in Galilee, but later settled
in the Roman district of Tiberius. Simultaneously other scholars established their own schools in other parts of the country where they
applied the *Mishnah* to daily life (together with other rabbinic
teachings not contained in the *Mishnah*). By the first half of the
fourth century Jewish scholars in Israel had collected the teachings
of generations of rabbi in the academies of Tiberius, Caesarea and
Sepphoris. These extended discussions of the *Mishnah* became the
Palestinian *Talmud*. The views of these Palestinian sages had an important influence on scholars in Babylonia, though this work never
gained the same prominence as that of the Babylonian *Talmud*.

Paralleling the development of rabbinic Judaism in Palestine,
Babylonian scholars founded centres of learning in Mesopotamia:
the great third century teacher Rav established an academy at Sura;
his contemporary Samuel was head of another academy at
Nehardea; and after Nehardea was destroyed in an invasion in
259 CE, the school at Pumbeditha became a dominant centre of
Jewish learning. The Babylonian sages continued the Galilean tradition of disputation, and the fourth century produced two of the

most distinguished scholars of the *Talmud* period, Abbaye and Rava. With the decline of Jewish institutions in Israel, Babylonia became the most important place of Jewish learning.

By the sixth century Babylonian scholars completed the redaction of the Babylonian *Talmud* – an editorial task begun by Rav Ashi in the fourth to fifth century at Sura. This massive work parallels the Palestinian *Talmud* and is largely a summary of the rabbinic discussions that took place in the academies. Both *Talmuds* are essentially elaborations of the *Mishnah*, though neither commentary contains material on every *Mishnah* passage. The text itself consists largely of summaries of rabbinic discussions: a phrase of the *Mishnah* is interpreted, discrepancies resolved and redundancies explained. In this compilation of law, conflicting opinions of the earlier scholars are contrasted, unusual words are explained and anonymous opinions are identified. Debates between outstanding scholars in one generation are often cited, as are differences of opinion between contemporary members of an academy or a teacher and his students. The range of talmudic exploration is much broader than that of the *Mishnah* itself and includes a wide range of rabbinic teachings about such subjects as theology, philosophy and ethics.

By the eighth century the Muslim empire began to undergo a process of disintegration; this process was accompanied by a decentralization of rabbinic Judaism. The academies of Babylonia began to lose their hold on the Jewish scholarly world, and in many places rabbinic schools were established in which rabbinic sources were studied. The growth of these local centres of scholarship enabled teachers to exert their influence on Jewish learning independent of the academies of Sura and Pumbeditha. In the Holy Land, Tiberius was the location of an important rabbinical academy as well as the centre of the Masoretic scholars who produced the standard text of the Bible. In Egypt, Kairouan and Fez became centres of scholarship. But it was in Spain that the Jewish community attained the greatest level of achievement in literature, philosophy, theology and mysticism.

Despite the development of Jewish learning and culture in medieval Spain, the Jewish community was expelled in 1492. Among those who emigrated from Spain to the Balkans was Joseph Caro who in the 1520s commenced a study of Jewish law, the *House of Joseph*, based on previous codes of Jewish law. In addition he composed a shorter work, the *Shulhan Arukh* (Code of Jewish Law), which has become the authoritative code of law in the Jewish world. While working on the *Shulhan Arukh*, Caro emigrated to Safed in Israel which had become a major centre of Jewish religious life. Here talmudic academies were established and small groups engaged in the study of kabbalistic (mystical) literature as they piously awaited the coming of the messiah.

During this period Poland had also become a great centre of scholarship. In the rabbinical academies the method of *hilluk* (the differentiation and reconciliation of rabbinic opinions) fostered the study of talmudic law. In addition, a number of scholars began to collect together the legal interpretations of previous scholars, and commentaries were written on the *Shulhan Arukh*. In order to regulate Jewish life in the country at large, regional federations were created which administered Jewish affairs. Further, a Council of the Four Lands, composed of eminent rabbinical and lay leaders, met twice a year to allocate taxes to the synods of *kehillot*, select and finance Jewish representatives to the royal court, and issue ordinances concerning interests and activities.

Although eastern European Jewry suffered a series of massacres in the seventeenth century, Lithuanian Jewry underwent considerable renewal. Because of its proximity to Russia as well as its trade connections with Russia and the West, Jews in Vilna and other Lithuanian towns flourished during this period. Vilna in particular became a centre for Jewish scholarship. There traditional rabbinic learning reached great heights. The central figure of the eighteenth century was Elijah ben Solomon Zalman, known as the Vilna Gaon. The appearance of the Vilna Gaon reflects the revitalization of the sixteenth- and seventeenth-century rabbinic tradition. His writings embraced commentaries on the Bible, the *Mishnah*, the Babylonian and Jerusalem *Talmuds*, midrashic literature, the *Shulhan Arukh*, and kabbalistic texts. In this enclosed world of intense Jewish observance, Jews piously upheld the traditions of their forefathers in the face of the countervailing currents of the Enlightenment.

THE EMERGENCE OF ORTHODOX JUDAISM

Throughout the Middle Ages Jewish life centred around the traditional observance of the law. Wherever they lived Jewish communities were self-governing, exercising their own educational, welfare and judicial functions. With the growth of the Enlightenment, however, ancient patterns of self-governance began to disintegrate.

Freed from the restrictions of the past, Jews began to enter into the mainstream of Western European society. Pre-eminent among the early advocates of cultural assimilation was Moses Mendelssohn; born in Dessau, he travelled to Berlin as a young student where he pursued secular as well as religious studies and befriended leading figures of the German Enlightenment. As well as publishing a number of theological studies, Mendelssohn sought to modernize Jewish life by translating the Pentateuch into German so that Jews would be able to learn the language of the country in which they lived. In addition, he spearheaded a commentary on Scripture which combined Jewish scholarship with secular thought.

When challenged by a Christian apologist to explain why he remained loyal to the Jewish faith, he published a defence of the Jewish religion. In this study, he contended that Judaism does not coerce the mind through dogma. 'The Israelites possess a Divine legislation – statutes, commandments, rules of conduct, instruction in God's will and in what they are to do to attain temporal and eternal salvation. Moses, in a miraculous and supernatural way, revealed to them these laws and commandments, but not dogmas.' According to Mendelssohn, Jews should not absolve themselves from following God's law. 'Adopt the mores and constitution of the country in which you find yourself,' he declared, 'but be steadfast in upholding the religion of your fathers, too ... I cannot see how those who were born into the household of Jacob can in good conscience exempt themselves from the observance of the law.' (Seltzer, 1980, 563–4). Thus, despite Mendelssohn's advocacy of Jewish emancipation, he followed the traditions of his ancestors and urged the retention of distinctive features of the Jewish faith.

Following Mendelssohn's example, a number of Prussian followers known as *maskilim* (advocates of the Jewish Enlightenment) fostered a Jewish Enlightenment – the *Haskalah* (Enlightenment) – which encouraged Jews to abandon medieval patterns of life and thought. Influenced by such progressive ideas, a number of reformers sought to revitalize the Jewish heritage through liturgical and theological change. Such a radical approach to the Jewish tradition provoked a hostile response from a number of leading Orthodox rabbis, a reaction which stimulated the creation of the Neo-Orthodox movement. For these traditionalists the written and oral *Torah* constitute an infallible chain of divinely revealed truth. The most prominent of these scholars was Samson Raphael Hirsch who was educated at a German gymnasium and the University of Bonn.

At the age of twenty-two Hirsch was appointed as Chief Rabbi of the Duchy of Oldenburg. In 1846 he published *The Nineteen Letters on Judaism*, a defence of Orthodoxy in the form of essays by a young rabbi to a friend who questioned the importance of remaining a Jew. The work commences with a typical critique of Judaism of this period: 'While the best of mankind climbed to the summit of culture, prosperity, and wealth, the Jewish people remained poor in everything that makes human beings great and noble and that beautifies and dignifies our lives.' (Seltzer, 1980, 586)

In response to such a criticism, Hirsch replied that the purpose of human life is not to attain personal happiness and perfection; rather humans should strive to serve God by obeying His will. To serve as an example of such devotion, the Jewish people was formed so that through its way of life all people would come to know that true happiness lies in obeying God. Thus the people of Israel were given the Promised Land in order to be able to keep God's law. When the Jewish nation was exiled, they were able to fulfil this mission by remaining loyal to God and to the *Torah* despite constant persecution and suffering. According to Hirsch the purpose of God's commands is not to repress physical gratification or material prosperity. Rather the aim of observing God's law is to lead a religious life thereby bearing witness to the messianic ideal of universal brotherhood. In this light Reform Judaism was castigated for abandoning this sacred duty. For Hirsch citizenship rights are of minor importance since Jewry is united by a bond of obedience to God's laws until the time when the 'Almighty shall see fit in his inscrutable wisdom to unite again his scattered servants in one land, and the *Torah* shall be the guiding principle of a state, a model of the meaning of Divine revelation and the mission of humanity' (ibid., 589). Hirsch referred to the synthesis of traditional Judaism and modernity as '*Torah im derekh eretz*' (*Torah* combined with the way of the world). Though uncompromisingly Orthodox, he was committed to harmonizing the Jewish heritage with contemporary life. As a consequence, Hirsch embraced a number of modifications in the synagogue: he wore clerical robes, preached in German, introduced a choir, and stressed the importance of decorum. As far as the liturgy was concerned, Hirsch deleted the *Kol Nidre* prayer on *Yom Kippur* and performed weddings in the synagogue – in his view, such changes did not alter the core of the faith. For Hirsch, there should be no conflict between *Torah* Judaism and the modern age.

Adopting a different approach to the challenge of secularism, nineteenth-century Neo-Traditionalists affirmed that Judaism is incompatible with the values of the modern world. Pre-eminent among such thinkers was Rabbi Moses Sofer (known as the *Hatam Sofer*) who rejected all attempts to adapt the tradition to contemporary life. Born in Frankfort, he served as a rabbi of Dresnitz, Mattersdorf and Pressburg where he founded a large *yeshiva*. Bitterly opposed to the *maskilim*, he interpreted the talmudic dictum 'Hadash asur min ha-Torah' (All that is new is forbidden by the *Torah*) to mean that all innovations are forbidden. Convinced of the perfection of the Jewish way of life and its superiority over the culture of the day, he denounced the Enlightenment as a pernicious threat to Judaism. In particular he opposed the teaching of Moses Mendelssohn and the ideology of the *Haskalah*. Championing the *Shulhan Arukh* as the basis for Jewish living, he urged all Jews to submit to its rulings. As the leader of the rabbis of Europe Sofer attempted to frustrate the Reform movement in Berlin, Hamburg and Vienna.

By the middle of the nineteenth century, the majority of Jews in Eastern Europe continued to live in accordance with the religious tradition. At the margin of Jewish society *maskilim* agitated for religious change – yet most Jews remained unaware of the challenges of modernism. As far as Jewish leaders were concerned, they continued to stress the importance of *Talmud* study and fostered the establishment of the *yeshivot* (rabbinical academies). The first of these talmudic academies was founded in Volozhin by Rabbi Hayyim of Volozhin; during the next century *yeshivot* were established in Lithuania and Belorussia. During this period such figures as Naphtali Zevi Judah Berlin (known as *Ha-Nesiv*), Israel Meir ha-Kohen (known as *Hafez Hayyim*, and Isaac Yitzhak Elhanan-Spektor made significant contributions to the growth and development of Orthodoxy.

A measure of the strength of the tradition was reflected by the opposition of the heads of these *yeshivot* to permit the creation of a progressive *yeshiva* by Rabbi Isaac Jacob Reines. In 1881 he published a critique of the method of study employed in *yeshivot*, advocating a reorganization of eastern European institutions. A more successful attempt to reform the *yeshiva* world, however, was initiated by Israel Salanter who emphasized the need for ethical renewal. Under his leadership, the *Musar* (ethical) movement had a profound impact on the pattern of study in the *yeshiva*: a limited time was allocated for the study of an ethical tract, and weekly talks by moral supervisors were instituted. Another development of this period was the creation of *Agudat Yisrael* which united Orthodox leaders of central and eastern Europe in defence of the tradition. The greatest following of this movement was in Poland where it functioned as a political party after World War I. Through the influence of the Hasidic *rebbe* [spiritual leader] of Ger, Abraham Mordecai Alter, and the leadership of the Lithuanian *yeshivot* including such figures as Rabbi Hayyim Ozer Grodzinski of Vilnus, *Agudat* commanded widespread allegiance.

During World War II, *Agudat* shifted its focus to Israel: with the destruction of the major centres of European Judaism, settlement in Israel became an increasingly desirable option and *Agudat* modified its earlier opposition to Zionism. Among religious Zionists of the period Isaac Breuer became a leading spokesman for the reassessment of the Land of Israel in *Agudat's* programme and ideology. In 1934 he declared 'Do not leave Jewish history of the Zionists' – if *Agudat* wished to prepare the Holy Land for the rule of God, Breuer argued, Orthodoxy had a role to play. Four years later Breuer asked the General Assembly of the *Agudat* to decide whether the Balfour Declaration was part of God's providential scheme or satanic in origin. Although some Orthodox leaders remained antagonistic to this change in policy, many within the *Agudat* movement were prepared to re-evaluate their earlier views. As a result, in succeeding years *Agudat* gained an increasing foothold in the Holy Land.

ORTHODOXY IN ISRAEL

In the pre-Zionistic *yishuv*, both traditionalist Sephardi and Ashkenazi Jews dedicated their lives to following the precepts of the *Torah*. Living apart under the authority of their rabbis and religious courts, they settled in Jerusalem, Hebron, Safed and Tiberius. During this period the supreme religious and judicial authority was vested in the *Rishon le-Zion* who was elected by the Sephardi community. At the end of the nineteenth century this office was held by Raphael Meir Panigel, and then by Jacob ben Eliezer Elyashar. From the Ashkenazi side, Rabbi Samuel Salant was recognized as the head of the Ashkenazi community in Jerusalem; in 1909 he was succeeded by Rabbi Hayyim Berlin. In 1904 Rabbi Abraham Isaac ha-Kohen Kook was appointed rabbi of Jaffa and the surrounding villages; subsequently he became Chief Rabbi of Jerusalem.

Following in the footsteps of such religious Zionists as Judah Solomon hai Alkalai and Zwi Hirsch Kalischer, Kook formulated a vision of messianic redemption integrating the creation of a Jewish state. According to Kook, the centrality of Israel is fundamental to Judaism. In the cosmic scheme of the divine will, he argued, seemingly atheistic and secular actions are absorbed into the unfolding of God's plan for his chosen people. Therefore these pioneers unintentionally contribute to the advent of the Messiah. Thus Kook maintained:

> Many of the adherents of the present national revival maintain that they are secularists. If a Jewish secular nationalism were really imaginable, then we would, indeed, be in danger of falling so low as to be beyond redemption. But Jewish nationalism is a form of self-delusion: the spirit of Israel is so closely linked to the spirit of God that a Jewish nationalist, no matter how secularist his intention may be, must despite himself, affirm the divine. (Hertzberg, 1959, 430)

Opposed to the creation of a centralized rabbinate in Jerusalem with Kook at its head, a number of rabbis organized their own Ashkenazi council which later became the 'Orthodox Community' of *Agudat Israel*. In 1920 the British High Commissioner appointed a committee to consider the creation of a united Chief Rabbinate of the entire country; in the following year Rabbi Kook and Rabbi Yaakov Meir were elected Ashkenazi and Sephardi Chief Rabbis. The Chief Rabbinate, however, was not recognized by the religious zealots of Jerusalem or by non-religious Jews who created their own courts which combined civil and Jewish law. Later the Chief Rabbinate Council was enlarged by the co-option of religious scholars. With the increase in the population first in Jaffa and then in Tel Aviv, hundreds of synagogues, houses of study and *yeshivot* were established and district rabbis appointed.

In 1920 the *Mizrahi* combined its schools with other religious institutions creating a network consisting of 15 primary schools and eight kindergartens with over 2000 pupils. By 1928 the *Mizrahi* had 61 schools and over 5000 pupils. Modern secondary *yeshivot* were founded by the religious movements. Apart from the religious pioneering youth movements which created collective and cooperative settlements, Polish Hasidim founded the first religious *moshav Kefar Hasidim* in the valley of Zebulun. In 1925 *Bene-Berak*, near Tel Aviv, was established by other Polish Hasidim, becoming a city with a large religious majority and a number of *yeshivot*.

With the exception of the ultra-Orthodox *Neturei Karta*, traditional Jews played a central role in the creation of the Jewish state. *Yeshiva* students fought with the *Haganah* and other underground organizations besieging Jerusalem in 1948. *Agudat Israel*, which had initially refused to participate in communal institutions, was represented in the provisional government. At the first elections to the Knesset, four religious parties – *Mizrahi*, *Ha-Poel ha-Mizrahi*, *Agudat Israel*, and *Poalei Agudat Israel* – formed the United Religious Front which joined the first coalition government. The government's statement of Basic Principles presented to the Knesset in 1949 ensures that the state of Israel will provide for the religious needs of the population:

> The state will provide for the public religious needs of its inhabitants but will prevent coercion in matters of religion. The Sabbath and the Jewish holy days will be fixed days of rest in the State of Israel.

With the creation of the State the powers of the Mandatory High Commissioner in matters of religion were transferred to the minister of religious affairs. This ministry deals with *kashrut*, *yeshivot*, synagogues, *mikvaot* (ritual baths), the supervision of burials, and the provision of sacred books. In 1953 the Knesset passed the Rabbinic Courts Jurisdiction Law which provides the Chief Rabbinate and the religious courts jurisdiction in all matrimonial cases. The Chief Rabbinical Council has departments for *kashrut*, the supervision of scribes, and committees for marriage licences; confirmand of rabbinical ordination; and responsa on matters of Jewish law. The Chief Rabbis preside over the Rabbinical Supreme Court which hears appeals from district rabbinical courts. Under the Compulsory Education Law of 1949, the state was to take over the responsibility of providing religious education. Initially there were two types of religious schools: *Mizrahi* and *Agudat Israel*. To cater to the needs of immigrants from Muslim countries, a new religious framework (*Reshet Dati*) was developed by *Ha-Oved ha-Dati*. Because the religious parties objected to this development, there was considerable controversy; however, in 1953 the State Education

Law instituted two types of schools: state and religious. The *Mizrahi* system of education became the nucleus of this network, but the law specified that it should have no connection with any political party, communal or other non-governmental body. A brochure published by the ministry clarifies the objectives of this system:

> In Israel a religious kindergarten, primary school or secondary school is an institution which aims at the religious personality. It does all the work which a kindergarten or an elementary school has to do in general, but it does it in such a manner, with modes of presentation and interpretation of common subject matter, and with classroom and school life organized in such a way, that the pupil may be expected to grow into maturity imbued with ideas, principles and values that mark him as an observer, in deed and in creed, of the Jewish religion.

More intensive religious study was pursued in the *yeshivot ketannot* (for pupils aged 14–15), *yeshiva* high schools, *yeshivot gedolot* (for students aged 18–25), and *kolelim* (for married men).

As far as Hasidism is concerned, early settlements were founded after Israel became a state. The rabbi of Lubavitch who lived in the United States, for example, urged his followers from the Soviet Union to move to the Holy Land where they founded Kefar Habad, the Lydda Yeshiva, and other institutions. Other Hasidic leaders who encouraged such settlements include: Rabbi Jekuthiel Halberstam who established the Kiryat Zanz quarter in Netanyah as well as a section in Jerusalem; the rabbi of Vishnitz who created a quarter in Bene-Berak; the rabbi of Bobova who founded a quarter in Bat Yam; the rabbi of Sasov who established Kiryat Yismah Moshe; and the rabbi of Satmar who built a section for his followers in Jerusalem and Bene-Berak.

As far as modern Orthodox movements in Israel are concerned, the movement for *Torah* Judaism headed by Ephraim Urbach attempted to regenerate religious life on a non-party basis within the framework of *halakhah*. Other religious thinkers such as Yeshayahu Leibowitz and Ernst Simon argued that the *halakhah* was formulated to meet the needs of diaspora life and must therefore be adjusted to the new considerations of statehood. Both of these groups have had an important influence on a number of student groups such as the Yavneh Association which aims to harmonize science and technology with Jewish religious thought. The media have also been instrumental in fostering the Jewish heritage in a contemporary setting through Bible readings, commentaries, talks on rabbinical sources, and the discussion of religious problems. In addition, the Bible Study Association sponsors conventions and arranges study groups; there are also various schemes to facilitate the study of the *Talmud* as well as knowledge of Jewish observances. Yet despite this commitment to spreading the knowledge and practice of traditional Judaism, there has been considerable friction about the authority of Jewish law in the life of the nation.

ORTHODOX JUDAISM IN AMERICA

In the seventeenth and eighteenth centuries, Orthodox Judaism in America was Sephardic in character. Modelled on the Bevis Marks Synagogue in England and the Spanish-Portuguese Synagogue of Amsterdam, services were austere and decorous; preachers recited prayers in Spanish and Portuguese; and the pronunciation of Hebrew followed the Sephardic system. In the colonies a number of such synagogues were established. At first services were held in private houses or stores, but later places of worship were erected in New York, Newport, Savannah, Philadelphia, Charleston and Richmond. The worship was traditional in orientation – men and women were separated and prayers remained unaltered. In this context laity had more power than clergy who served either as ministers or cantors.

These Sephardic congregations founded other institutions including schools which taught religious as well as secular subjects. Originally the Sephardim dominated American Jewish life, but by the 1840s numerous German as well as Latvian and Lithuanian Jews settled in the New World. After 1870 their numbers increased, and from 1881 to 1924 nearly two and a half million Jews largely of Russian origin immigrated to the United States. The impact of these European newcomers was considerable and additional synagogues were established throughout the country.

Initially Jewish scholarship and rabbinic leadership was severely lacking on the American continent. Thus Abraham Rice, the first Orthodox rabbi on American soil, complained about the state of traditional Jewish life: 'I dwell in complete isolation without a teacher or a companion in this land whose atmosphere is not conducive to wisdom' (Rosenthal, 1986, 32). The same malaise affected

Rabbi Abraham W. Edelman, the Orthodox rabbi of B'nai Brith Congregation in Los Angeles, who fought a struggle against the reforming tendencies of his members. Before the 1880s it appeared that Orthodoxy was engaged in a losing battle, yet with the mass immigration of European Jews Orthodox Judaism gained a firm footing in the New World. In 1887 approximately fifteen congregations formed the Association of American Orthodox Hebrew Congregations. According to its charter, its purpose is:

> to encourage, foster, and promote the observance of the Orthodox Jewish religion, to improve and elevate the moral, social and spiritual condition of the Jewish people, to designate, support and maintain a Chief Rabbi and such other officers as may be deemed necessary or advisable, and to do, perform and effect all other charitable and benevolent acts and purposes, as may be specified in the constitution and By-laws.   (Ibid., 35)

In 1888 the Vilna Rav Jacob Joseph arrived in New York to serve as Chief Rabbi, but his policies were bitterly criticized; as a consequence Rabbi Joshua Segal declared himself Chief Rabbi and formed an alternative *Bet Din*. Elsewhere other congregational alliances were formed: in Baltimore 28 Orthodox congregations merged in 1908; after World War I Los Angeles Orthodox synagogues combined together; in Buffalo the Orthodox elected their own Chief Rabbi. These efforts to create communal organizations was also reflected in the field of education. In 1854 seven New York synagogues constructed day schools with 35 teachers and 857 pupils; in 1857 the Downtown *Talmud Torah* was opened; this was followed by the Machziko *Talmud Torah* and the Uptown *Talmud Torah*. By 1898 there were nearly 5000 students enrolled in the Uptown Hebrew Free School Association. During this period community *Talmud Torahs* flourished in New York and elsewhere. In addition, the Etz Chaim Yeshiva was founded in New York in 1886 for the

> improvement of the spiritual, mental, and social condition of Hebrew boys, to provide for their Teachers instructions in Hebrew, to foster and encourage the study of the Sacred Scriptures, the *Talmud*, and the Hebrew language and literature, to hold religious services in accordance with Orthodox Judaism: also to provide teachers and instructors for said Hebrew boys in reading, writing, and speaking the English language'.   (Ibid., 37)

In 1897 the Rabbi Isaac Elchanan Theological Seminary was created on the East Side of New York designed for advanced *Talmud* studies. Its aim was to promote the study of the *Talmud* as well as assist in educating and preparing candidates for the rabbinate. In addition to Hebrew studies secular subjects were included in the curriculum. In 1903 the Union of Orthodox Rabbis endorsed the seminary, designating it as the only legitimate *yeshiva* of higher learning in the country. In the early years the seminary struggled for survival with only one faculty member, insufficient funds, and inadequate facilities. Eventually in 1915 these two institutions combined and a high school programme was added. Under the presidency of Dr Bernard Revel, a teachers' college was established as well as Yeshiva College. The College, Revel declared:

> proposes to establish a College of Liberal Arts and Sciences ... with the double purpose of educating both liberally and Jewishly a number of Jewish young men who have been already imbued with the spirit and the sanctity of Judaism and its teachings, so that these men may not be lost to us ... Secondly, Jewish young men who consider Jewish learning an indispensable part of the moral and mental equipment that they wish to attain through a college education are to have the advantage of such a combined education. (Rosenthal, 1959, 39)

Despite opposition to this proposal, a campus was purchased overlooking the Harlem River, and a graduate school was added in 1937. After Revel's death in 1940, Dr Samuel Belkin was appointed as his successor. During his presidency, the Yeshiva underwent extensive expansion: the school became a university in 1945; a medical college was introduced in 1955; a graduate school, a college of girls, and a West Coast branch were also established. By 1970 Yeshiva University had over 7500 students with 750 in the college alone.

Alongside Yeshiva University, other *yeshivot* and day schools were created throughout the country: New York had four such schools by 1918; in 1895 Chicago's *Etz Chaim* was opened; Baltimore and Philadelphia also established similar institutions. In 1938 the United Yeshivas Foundation was created, followed by the Central Board of Yeshiva Education and eventually *Torah Umesorah*. In 1921 *Beth Ha-Midrash La-Torah* Hebrew Theological College was founded, later adding a preparatory school, Teacher's Institute, and graduate school.

Distancing themselves from such initiatives, the ultra-Orthodox groups erected their own *yeshivot* such as Brooklyn's *Torah Vadaat*, Chaim Berlin, and Lubavitcher *Yeshiva*; Manhattan's Jacob Joseph and *Tifereth Yerushalayim*; Baltimore's *Ner Israel*; Cleveland's *Telse Yeshivah*; Lakewood's *Beth Midrash Gavoha*; and Spring Valley's *Beth Midrash Elyon*. In these institutions only Jewish subjects were studied; in this self-enclosed world, students were educated in rabbinic sources to the exclusion of all other pursuits. As a student at Lakewood's *Beth Midrash Gavoha* explained:

A *yeshiva* ought not to have magazines, newspapers or radios. Guys should not go into New York unless absolutely necessary. The *Torah* is not a course. It requires *kedusha, tahara,* and *amkus* (holiness, purity and depth). Anything that deviates from this doesn't belong in a *yeshiva*. A *yeshiva* is not a college. I'm not saying it's bad to know what's going on in the world. You have to be up to date. You have to know. But not while you're learning. Anybody who thinks differently, I think his *hashkofot* [belief system] is wrong. He doesn't realise what *Torah* is. A *yeshiva* has to be shelter from the world.   (Helmreich, 1983, 139)

Despite the divisions in the Orthodox fold, there have been various attempts to create a national alliance. As early as 1898 a thousand delegates met at New York's *Shearith Israel* in an effort to form a Union of Orthodox Judaism. Affirming its belief in the divine revelation of the Bible and ceremonial law, this body stressed its commitment to the authoritative interpretation of the rabbis as contained in the *Talmud* and Codes as well as Maimonides' thirteen principles of the Jewish faith. Further, they asserted their belief in a personal messiah, circumcision, and baptism for converts. Denouncing Reform Judaism, they stressed their belief in the centrality of Israel in Jewish life. Due to the diversity of the groups making up this body, the Union of Orthodox Jewish Congregations faced serious internal dilemmas but as the years passed it grew in strength, becoming a national body of approximately four million members and 3000 congregations.

Paralleling these attempts to create a Union of Orthodox Congregations, the Orthodox rabbinate made efforts to create a unified body. Thus in 1897 Rabbi Judah Levin of Detroit and Asher Zarchy of Louisville sought to draw their colleagues into a rabbinic body. Similarly at the convention of the Federation of American Zionists,

Rabbi Moses S. Margolies and Rabbi Bernard L. Levinthal, attempted to organize the rabbinate. Subsequently the *Agudat Harabbonim* [the Union of Orthodox Rabbis] was established – initially it rallied the Yiddish speaking rabbis of America and endorsed the Rabbi Isaac Elchanan Theological Seminary. American trained rabbis, on the other hand, developed their own union, the Rabbinical Council of America. Under the leadership of Rabbi Joseph B. Soloveitchik this body has occupied the centre stage of American Orthodox life. Another rabbinic group, *Igud Harabbonim* (Rabbinical Alliance of America) was established in 1944 for graduates of *yeshivot* other than the Isaac Elchanan Seminary and the Hebrew Theological College. Two other Orthodox bodies of importance are the National Council of Young Israel and the Religious Zionists of America who have exerted a significant impact on American Orthodox Jewish life.

THE BELIEFS OF ORTHODOX JUDAISM

In the Hebrew Scriptures the Israelites experienced God as the Lord of history. The most uncompromising expression of His unity is the *Shema* prayer: 'Hear O Israel, the Lord, our God, is one Lord' (Deut. 6.4). According to Scripture, the universe owes its existence to one God, the creator of heaven and earth. Throughout the rabbinic period this belief served as the foundation of the faith. The conviction that God is the source of all continues to animate traditional Jewish life. Maimonides' formulation of this principle at the beginning of his *Code* conveys what has remained the central feature of the Jewish religious tradition:

> The foundation of all foundations and the pillar of wisdom is to know that there is a First Being. He it is who brought all things into being and all the beings in heaven and earth and in between only enjoying existence by virtue of his true being. (Jacobs, 1973, 94)

For the Jew, God has neither beginning nor end. In the Bible the term *olam* is most frequently used to denote the concept of God's eternity; this biblical teaching was elaborated by the rabbis who maintained that God was, is, and for ever will be. Hence in Maimonides' formulation of the thirteen principles of the Jewish faith, the belief that God is eternal is the fourth tenet. 'This means', he wrote, 'that the unity whom we have described is first in the absolute sense. No existent thing outside him is primary in relation to him' (Jacobs, 1988, 135). Again, in the traditional *Ani Maamin* prayer, this cardinal belief is formulated as follows: 'I believe with perfect faith that the Creator, blessed be his name, in the first and the last.' And at the conclusion of the Orthodox synagogue service, Jews voice their commitment that God is eternal:

> He is the Lord of the Universe
> Who reigned ere any creatures yet were formed,
> At the time when all things shall have had an end,
> He alone, the dreaded one, shall reign:
> Who was, who is, and who will be in glory.

The one, eternal creator not only transcends the cosmos, he is conceived within Orthodox Judaism as immanent. Throughout history believers affirmed that God acts in the world, guiding it to its ultimate destiny. In ancient times the Psalmist expressed what has become a central conviction of the faithful:

> Whither shall I go from thy spirit?
> Or whither shall I flee from thy presence?
> If I ascend to heaven, thou art there!
> If I make my bed in *Sheol*, thou art there!
> If I take the wings of the morning
> and dwell in the uttermost parts of the sea,
> even there thy hand shall lead me.
> (Ps. 139.7–12)

From biblical times to the present, the belief in God's omnipotence has also been a major feature of Judaism. Although the rabbis debated whether God could do everything, they universally affirmed that he is almighty in power; similarly, Orthodox Judaism asserts that God's knowledge is not limited by space and time – nothing is hidden from his sight. For this reason the *Mishnah* declares: 'Everything is foreseen' (Avot 3.19), and the *Talmud* asserts: 'No man suffers so much as the injury of a finger when it has been decreed in heaven [Hull. 76]. Such a conviction became a central element of the New Year Service. According to the liturgy, God, the judge of the world, provides for the testing of individuals on the basis of their actions. In the past Jewish thinkers wrestled with the question how human beings could have free will given such a conception of omniscience and providence. Yet, Orthodox Judaism maintains that there is no contradiction between these seemingly incompatible beliefs. As the *Mishnah* declares: 'All is foreseen, but freedom of choice is given.' (Avot 3.16)

According to tradition, the entire Bible was communicated by God to the Jewish people. In Maimonides' formulation of the thirteen principles of the Jewish faith, this belief is the eighth tenet:

> The *Torah* was revealed from heaven. This implies our belief that the whole of the *Torah* was handed down by Moses, and that it is all of divine origin. ˙ (Jacobs, 1988, 216)

In addition, the rabbis maintained that expositions and elaborations of the written law in the Five Books of Moses were also revealed by God to Moses on Mount Sinai; subsequently they were passed from generation to generation, and through this process additional legislation was incorporated. This process is referred to as 'The Oral *Torah*' (*Torah She-Be-Al Peh*). Thus traditional Judaism affirms that God's revelation is twofold and binding for all time. Committed to this belief, Orthodox Jews pray in the synagogue that God will guide them to do his will:

> O our Father, merciful Father, ever compassionate, have mercy upon us. O put it into our hearts to understand and to discern, to mark, learn and teach, to heed, to do and to fulfil in love all the words and instruction in thy *Torah*.

Traditional Judaism is thus committed to the view that the written and the oral *Torah* were imparted by God to Moses on Mount Sinai – this concept of revelation serves as the basis for the entire legal system as well as doctrinal beliefs about God's nature and activity.

The legal system of the *Torah* serves as the background for the understanding of sin and atonement in Orthodox Judaism. In the Bible sin is understood as a transgression against God's law. A sinner is one who has not fulfilled his obligations to God. According to rabbinic Judaism, sins can be classified in terms of their gravity as indicated by the punishments prescribed by biblical law: the more serious the offence the more serious the punishment. Rabbinic Judaism further teaches that there are two tendencies in

every person: the good inclination (*yetzer ha-tov*) and the evil inclination (*yetzer ha-ra*). At all times a person is to be on guard against
the assaults of the *yetzer ha-ra*. In this struggle the *Torah* was perceived as an antidote to the poison of the evil inclination: when
human beings submit to the discipline of the *Torah*, they are liberated from its malign influence. As far as atonement for sin is concerned, Orthodox Judaism teaches that it can be attained after a
process of repentance involving the recognition of sin. It requires
remorse, restitution, and a determination not to commit a similar
offence. Both the Bible and rabbinic sources stress that God does
not want the death of the sinner, but desires that he return from his
evil ways.

For Orthodox Jews, the election of Israel as God's chosen people
is central to the understanding of the law. Through its election
Israel was given a historic mission to bear divine truth to humanity.
Divine choice demands reciprocal response. Israel is obligated to
keep God's statutes and observe his laws. In doing so, Jewry will be
able to persuade the nations of the world that there is only one universal God. Israel is to be a prophet to the nations, in that it will
bring them to salvation. Yet despite this obligation, the Bible asserts
that God will not abandon his chosen people even if they violate
the Covenant. The wayward nation will be punished, but God will
not reject them. As Leviticus declares:

> Yet for all that, when they are in the land of their enemies, I will
> not spurn them, neither will I abhor them so as to destroy them
> utterly and break my covenant with them: for I am the Lord their
> God.   (Lev. 26.44)

Orthodox Judaism hence envisages God's covenant with his people
as enshrined in law as the foundation of the faith. Yet traditional
Judaism is also preoccupied with eternal deliverance and salvation.
According to rabbinic Judaism, the World-to-Come is divided into
several stages. First there is the time of messianic redemption. On
the basis of biblical prophecy, the rabbis believed that the prophet
Elijah would return prior to the coming of the Messiah to resolve all
earthly problems. As the forerunner of the Messiah, Elijah will an-
nounce his coming from Mount Carmel: it will be the King-Messiah
of Israel who will bring about the end of history and the advent of
God's Kingdom on earth. According to the *Talmud* the messianic age
(*yemot hamashiah*) is to take place on earth after a period of decline

and calamity, and will result in a complete fulfilment of every human wish. Peace will reign throughout nature; Jerusalem will be rebuilt; and at the close of this era, the dead will be resurrected and rejoined with their souls, and a final judgment will come upon all mankind. Those who are judged righteous will enter into heaven (*Gan Eden*) whereas those who are judged wicked will be condemned to eternal punishment (*Gehinnom*). Such an eschatological scheme has served as the basis for traditional Jewish life and thought through the centuries to the present day.

Over the centuries, then, the development of Orthodox Judaism rested on a common love of shared belief and practice – biblical and rabbinic teaching about the nature of God and his activity constituted the foundation of the faith. These tenets are best summarized by Maimonides' formulation of Judaism's basic principles which have become authoritative for Judaism and are incorporated into the Orthodox prayerbook:

1. Belief in the existence of God.
2. Belief in God's unity.
3. Belief in God's incorporeality.
4. Belief in God's eternity.
5. Belief that God alone is to be worshipped.
6. Belief in prophecy.
7. Belief in Moses as the greatest of the prophets.
8. Belief that the *Torah* was given by God to Moses.
9. Belief that the *Torah* is immutable.
10. Belief that God knows the thoughts and deeds of men.
11. Belief that God rewards and punishes.
12. Belief in the advent of the Messiah.
13. Belief in the resurrection of the dead.

CRITIQUE

As we have seen, through the centuries the Jewish people have been sustained by a belief in an all-good and all-powerful God who revealed his will on Mount Sinai and exercised providence over all creation – on the basis of such a commitment, the nation was united by a dedication to a shared religious tradition. Yet, the monolithic system of Orthodox Judaism is subject to a number of fundamental criticisms. Arguably the most serious challenge to traditional

Jewish belief is due to the expansion of scientific investigation. Since the Renaissance scientific knowledge has increased in such fields as astronomy, geology, zoology, chemistry and physics. Discoveries in these areas have called into question biblical claims about the origin and nature of the universe.

Increasingly it has become clear that in giving an account of the history of the Jewish nation, the biblical writers relied on a pre-scientific understanding of the world. In the last centuries, scholarly investigations into the culture of the ancient Near East have provided the framework for the thinking of the ancient Israelites. As a result of the expansion of scientific knowledge and a greater awareness of the thought-world of the biblical writers, most Jews are no longer able to accept the biblical depiction of the origin and nature of the world as well as God's action in history. The vast majority of Jews, for example, no longer find plausible the biblical cosmology of a three-storeyed universe with heaven in the sky, hell beneath, and the sun circling around the earth. Moreover, contemporary Jewry has discarded the belief that the world was formed some six thousand years ago, and that human beings and animals came into existence in their present forms at the same time. Further, the notion that at a future date the decomposed corpses of human beings will be resurrected no longer seems credible in the light of a scientific understanding of the laws of nature. In summary, the modern age has witnessed scientific advance on the one hand and the retreat of traditional Orthodox belief on the other.

The climate of thought in the contemporary world is thus one in which scientific explanation has taken the place of theological interpretation. Even though the sciences have not disproved the claims of Orthodox Judaism, they have provided a rational explanation of events that previously would have been understood as the result of God's will. In this light faith has come to be viewed as a personal preoccupation that is destined to be ousted from the central areas of human knowledge. In the future traditional Judaism is likely to be perceived as an antiquated relic of previous ages when scientific knowledge was less extensive. The sciences have thus effectively established the autonomy of the natural world.

A second objection to Orthodoxy stems from the persistence of evil in the twentieth century. For many Jews it is the existence of human suffering that makes the traditional idea of a perfectly loving God utterly implausible. As a challenge to religious belief the problem of evil has usually been formulated as a dilemma: if

God is perfectly loving, he must wish to abolish evil; and if he is all-powerful, he must be able to abolish evil. But evil exists; therefore, God cannot be both omnipotent and perfectly loving. In a post-Holocaust world this religious perplexity has been highlighted by the terrors of the Nazi era. An illustration of the potency of this problem is elucidated by the Jewish writer Elie Wiesel. In his autobiographical memoir *Night* he depicts his transition from youthful belief to disillusionment. At the beginning of the novel the author describes himself as a young boy fascinated with God's mystery, studying *Talmud* and *Kabbalah* in the Transylvanian town of Sighet. Later, he is transported to Auschwitz where the erosion of his faith begins. Shortly after his arrival, he questions God: 'Some talked of God, of his mysterious ways, of the sins of the Jewish people and of their future deliverance. But I had ceased to pray. How I sympathized with Job. I did not deny of God's existence but I doubted his absolute justice' (Wiesel, *Night*, as quoted in Cohn-Sherbok, 1989, 92). In time however his religious rebellion deepens and he feels revolt rise within him. Many modern Jews have shared Wiesel's despair; no longer are they able to subscribe to the Orthodox belief in an all-good, providential Deity who lovingly watches over his chosen people: in the Jewish community traditional theism has been eclipsed by an overwhelming sense that the universe is devoid of a divine presence.

The third challenge to traditional Judaism stems from naturalistic explanations of the origin of religion – sceptics assert that supernatural experience can be adequately accounted for without postulating the existence of God. Pre-eminent among Jewish thinkers who have endorsed such an approach to religious belief is Mordecai Kaplan, the founder of Reconstructionist Judaism. Explaining the evolution of religious belief, he wrote:

> Long before the human being was able to formulate the idea 'God', he was aware that there were elements in his environment, certain animate and inanimate objects, definite places, particular persons upon whose help he depended for the fulfilment of his needs. He ascribed to them power, which he believed he could direct to his advantage by resorting to actions and formulas which we term magic ... As man developed further, he extended the domain of holiness to include not only visible or picturable objects, events and persons, but also customs, laws, social relationships, truths and ideals. (Kaplan, 1967, 317–18)

Here, then, is an interpretation of religion that involves no reference to God as an external Deity who created and oversees human
destiny. Within the Jewish world such a naturalistic interpretation
of religious belief has gained a considerable following.

Another challenge to Orthodox Judaism is based on the critical
findings of biblical scholars. As we have seen, traditional Judaism
maintains that the Five Books of Moses were dictated by God to
Moses on Mount Sinai. This doctrine implies that the entire text –
including precepts, theology and history – is of divine origin: all of
its contents are inerrant. Such a belief guarantees the validity of the
legal system, the Jewish view of God, and the concept of Israel's
pre-eminence among the nations. In the modern period, however,
it has become increasingly difficult to sustain this concept of
Scripture in the light of scholarly investigation and discovery.
Today most biblical scholars contend that the Pentateuch is composed of various separate traditions originating at different times in
the history of ancient Israel which have been combined into a
unified whole. Thus, on the basis of textual criticism, these scholars
conclude that the *Torah* was not written by Moses, but is instead a
mosaic of separate sources.

This theory is further supported by the findings of biblical archaeology. From what is now known of Mesopotamian civilization,
we can see that the Bible reflects various aspects of its cultural
milieu: the physical structure of the universe as outlined in Genesis
parallels what is found in Near Eastern literature: the earth is conceived as a thin disk floating in the surrounding waters; under the
earth is the abode of the dead; like the gods of the ancient litera-
tures, the God of Israel is understood anthropomorphically. In addition to such similarities, there are strong parallels between the
Bible and the literature of the ancient Near East: Genesis appears to
borrow details of the Mesopotamian Epic of Gilgamesh in connection with the legend of the flood; biblical law bears a striking re-
semblance to ancient legal codes such as the Assyrian treaties
between a king and his vassals. The findings of biblical archaeology
thus also call into question the traditional Orthodox doctrine of
Torah MiSinai.

A final challenge to Orthodox Judaism stems from within the
Orthodox camp itself. In theory traditional law goes back consistently and without interruption for thousands of years to the beginning of Jewish history – all the elaborations of *halakhah* in later
Orthodox codes are held to be rediscoveries rather than novelties.

Yet this picture of an eternal developing legal system breaks down when we face its astonishing shrinkages in contemporary society – great areas of Jewish law have disappeared from modern Orthodox life for a wide variety of reasons. Frequently individuals who view themselves as Orthodox have simply ceased to resort to rabbinical courts in numerous spheres of life. Hence there is a large gap between the Orthodox system of practice and the limited observance of Judaism within a major segment of the Orthodox community. Moreover within the Orthodox world Jewish belief has also undergone a process of disintegration: no longer do the majority of Jews who align themselves with Orthodoxy believe in the central theological tenets of the faith. Instead many Orthodox Jews today have rejected such doctrines as the resurrection of the dead, messianic redemption, and final judgment. As a consequence, Orthodox Judaism as it has been understood in the past has ceased to function as an overarching religious system of practice and belief even for those who identify themselves as Orthodox Jews.

3
Hasidism

By the middle of the eighteenth century, the Jewish community had suffered numerous waves of persecution and was deeply dispirited by the conversion of the false Messiah Shabbatai Tzevi. In this milieu Hasidism – grounded in kabbalistic theories about the nature of God's emanation – sought to revitalize Jewish life. The founder of this new movement, the Baal Shem Tov (known as the Besht) attracted a considerable number of disciples who passed on his teaching. After his death, Dov Baer of Mezhirech became the leader of this sect and Hasidism spread to southern Poland, the Ukraine and Lithuania. The growth of this movement engendered hostility on the part of rabbinic authorities. In particular rabbinic leadership in Vilna issued an edict of excommunication – by the end of the century the Jewish religious establishment in Vilna denounced the Hasidim to the state authorities. Yet despite such condemnations, Hasidism was eventually recognized by the Russian and Austrian governments, and in the following years the movement divided into a number of distinct groups under different leaders. In contemporary society Hasidism has become a major force in Jewish life with branches throughout the world. None the less because of its anachronistic attitudes it is inconceivable that this form of Judaism could become a basis for Jewish life in the twenty-first century.

THE RISE OF HASIDISM

Following the massacres of the seventeenth century, many Polish Jews became disenchanted with rabbinic Judaism and through Hasidism sought individual salvation by means of religious pietism. The founder of this new movement was Israel ben Eliezer, known as the Baal Shem Tov (or Besht). According to tradition, Israel was born in 1698 or 1700 in Okop, a small town near Kamenets on the border of Podolia and Moldavia. In his early twenties he journeyed with his wife to the Carpathian mountains; later he travelled to Mezibozh where he performed various miracles and instructed his disciples about kabbalistic lore. By the 1740s he had attracted a considerable number of disciples who passed on his teaching.

Rejecting the asceticism of the *kabbalah*, the Besht emphasized the importance of joy in worship. 'Our Father in Heaven', he stated, 'hates sadness and rejoices when his children are joyful. And when are his children joyful? When they carry out his commandments.' For the Besht worshipping with spontaneity is the keynote to the religious life: thus he stressed that enthusiasm (*hitlahavut*) and ecstasy should replace formalism in prayer. According to the Besht, in each Jew there is a spark of holiness which needs to be kindled. In his view, evil does not exist. Thus once he was asked by a distraught father: 'What shall I do with my son, he is so wicked?' The Besht replied: 'Love him all the more.' Wherever he went, the Besht sought to bring back the wayward of Israel. In this quest, the Besht was anxious to draw Jews back to the tradition through mercy and compassion. 'God does not look on the evil side,' he explained, 'how dare I do so?'

The Besht maintained that he had come into the world to show human beings how to live by three precepts: love of God, love of Israel, and love of the *Torah*. In a letter to his brother-in-law, he declared that this mission was part of God's providential plan:

On Rosh Hashanah 1747, I experienced an uplifting of the soul and I asked the Messiah, 'Let me know, Master, when thou wilt appear on earth,' and the reply was: 'This shall be a sign unto thee, when thy teachings shall become known ... when all other men shall have the power of performing the same mysteries as thyself, then shall all impurity disappear, and the time of great favour and salvation shall arrive.' (*Maggid Devarav L'Yaakov*, 1781).

Initially Hasidism was confined primarily to Podolia, Volhynia and Galicia, however under the influence of the Besht's successor, Dov Baer, the movement spread to Southern Poland, the Ukraine and Lithuania. Because of failing health, Dov Baer was confined mainly to Mezhirech, yet his court attracted disciples who became the founders of distinguished dynasties. Describing Dov Baer's inner circle, Shneur Zalman remarked: 'In the house of my teacher the holy *Maggid* [Dov Baer], you draw up holy spirit by the bucketful and miracles lie around under the benches, only no one had the time to pick them up.' These emissaries spread the teaching of the Besht to remote villages throughout Poland and Lithuania.

In his autobiography, the eighteenth-century Jewish philosopher Solomon Maimon depicted the religious fervour of the *Maggid*'s household. Describing his own visit to the *Maggid*, he wrote:

At last I arrived at Mezhirech, and, after having rested from my journey, I went to the house of the Master (Dov Baer), under the impression that I would be introduced to him at once. I was told, however, that he could not speak to me at this time, but that I was invited to his table on the Sabbath ... Accordingly, on the Sabbath, I went to his solemn meal, and found there a large number of respectable men who had come from various districts. At length, the awe-inspiring Master appeared clothed in white satin ... He greeted every newcomer in turn. After the meal was over, the Master began to sing a melody awesome and inspiring. Then he placed his hand for some time upon his brow, and began to call upon such and such a person of such and such a place. Thus he called upon every newcomer by his own name and the name of his residence .... Each recited, as he was called, some verse of the Holy Scripture. Thereupon the Master began to deliver a sermon for which the verses recited served as a text, so that, although they were disconnected, verses taken from different parts of the Holy Scripture, they were combined with as much skill as if they had been formed as a single whole. What was still more extraordinary, every one of the newcomers believed that he discovered, in that part of the sermon which was founded on his verse, something that had special reference to the facts of his own spiritual life.   (Maimon, 1954, 173–4)

Supplementing the missionary zeal of Dov Baer, Rabbi Jacob Joseph of Polonnoye devoted himself to producing various works containing the teachings of the Besht and Dov Baer. Another important figure of this period was Rabbi Phinehas of Koretz. After meeting the Besht, he became a convert to this new movement, stressing the importance of practical ethics. Like these members of the Besht's inner circle, Levi Isaac of Berdichev profoundly influenced the development of Hasidic thought. Described as 'the merciful one', he undertook to defend Israel before the Heavenly

Tribunal. In addition, he composed prayers infused with the Hasidic belief in God's omnipotence.

> Master of the Universe
> I will sing a song to You
> Where will I find You?
> And where will I not find You?
> Where I go, there are You,
> Where I stay, there are You
> Only You, You only
> You again and only You
> When I am gladdened – You!
> And when I am saddened – You!
> Only You, everywhere You!
> You, You, You!
> Sky is You!
> Earth is You!
> You above! You below!
> In every trend, at every end
> Only You, everywhere You!

The growth of the movement engendered considerable hostility on the part of the rabbinic authorities. Pre-eminent among critics of Hasidism was Elijah ben Solomon, the Gaon of Vilna. Adamant that the minutiae of Jewish law be followed, he castigated the Hasidim for disregarding the fixed hours of worship and believing that spontaneity ranks higher than the punctilious recitation of the liturgy. In addition, he was distressed by the cult of the *zaddik*: instead of poring over the tracts of the *Talmud*, the *zaddikim* expounded the miraculous acts performed by wonder rabbis. In 1772 the *Kahal* of Vilna with the consent of the Vilna Gaon issued a *herem* (decree of excommunication) against this sect. A month after the *herem* was pronounced, a letter was circulated through all the communities of Lithuania and White Russia denouncing this new movement:

Our brethren in Israel, you are certainly already informed of the tiding whereof our fathers never dreamed, that a sect of the suspects has been formed ... who meet together in separate groups and deviate in their prayers from the text valid for the whole people ... The study of the *Torah* is neglected by them entirely and they do not hesitate constantly to emphasise that one should devote oneself as little as possible to learning and not grieve too much over a sin committed ... When they pray according to falsified text, they raise such a din that the walls quake ... and they turn over like wheels, with the head below and the legs above ... Do not believe them even if they raise their voices to implore you.	(Cohen, 1943, 235–7)

In the same year a collection of all the bans issued against the Hasidim, *Uprooting of Tyrants and Flinty Swords*, was published by Aryeh Leib ben Mordecai. In response two of the most distinguished Hasidic scholars, Shneur Zalman of Liady and Menahem Mendel of Vitebsk unsuccessfully sought a personal interview with the Vilna Gaon. As Shneur Zalman recorded:

'We set out towards the saintly Gaon's house to discuss the whole matter with him in order that all misunderstanding might be removed ... But twice the Gaon locked the doors against us ... when his followers started to plead with him, the Gaon left the city and stayed until we returned home.'	(Hielman, 1903, 40)

In 1781 Vilna issued a second *herem* against the Hasidim, and in Shklov and Mogliev in White Russia a circular was issued condemning the Hasidim:

Because of our many sins, worthless and wanton men who call themselves Hasidim have deserted the Jewish community and have set up so-called places of worship for themselves. And thus, as every one knows, they worship in a most insane fashion, following a different ritual which does not conform to the religion of our holy *Torah* ... In addition to this, the works of their teachers have, unfortunately, recently been published, and it is obvious to us that all of their writings are opposed to our holy *Torah* and contain misleading interpretations. The exaggerations and stories of miracles that are described in their books are particularly transparent and obvious lies.	(Marcus, 1938, 276–8)

By the end of the century the Jewish religious establishment had denounced the Hasidim to the government, an act which resulted in the imprisonment of several leaders. Despite such condemnation, the Hasidic movement was eventually recognized by the Russian and Austrian governments; in the ensuing years the movement divided into a number of separate groups under different leaders who passed on positions of authority to their descendants.

FOLLOWERS OF THE BESHT

One of the *Maggid*'s disciples, Shneur Zalman, occupied a position of considerable significance. Born in Liozno, White Russia, he received a traditional Jewish education but became increasingly attracted to Hasidism. At the age of twenty he travelled to Mezhirech where he became a member of the *Maggid*'s inner circle. According to tradition, one evening the *Maggid* passed through the student dormitories and paused at Shneur Zalman's bed. 'Miracle of miracles,' he remarked, 'that so much spiritual strength resides in so frail a dwelling! This young man, sleeping so serenely, will one day become the rabbi of all the provinces of Russia, with multitudes listening to his voice.' (Rabinowicz, 1970, 68). At the *Maggid*'s suggestion, Shneur Zalman completed a new *Shulhan Arukh* at the age of twenty-five. After the *Maggid*'s death in 1773, Shneur Zalman lived in Liozno, later becoming the head of the Hasidic communities in White Russia. Following his imprisonment in St Petersburg, he worked ceaselessly for reconciliation with his opponents. Later he aligned himself with the anti-French faction and was compelled to escape the advancing French armies. In 1812 he fled to Smolensk where he died the same year.

Shneur Zalman's writings include the mystical treatise *Tanya*, which had a profound effect on later Hasidic thinkers. According to Shneur Zalman, the intellect consists of three faculties: *Hokhmah* (wisdom), *Binah* (understanding), and *Daat* (knowledge) – these are the first, second and third of the ten *sefirot* (divine emanations). In his view, God desires both the heart and mind; thus *Hokhmah* and *Binah* act as father and mother, giving birth to the love of God:

It is well known to all who have basked in the fragrant doctrines of the Besht and his disciples that understanding is the mother of children. These 'children' are love and fear, born of knowledge and profound contemplation of the greatness of God (*Tanya*, Chapter XIII).

As a dynamic being, each person must strive to perfect himself; each Jew, he believed, has the potential to become a *zaddik*. With the concept of *Hokhmah, Binah* and *Daat* (*Habad*) the *zaddik* functions as teacher rather than miracle worker. Here the study of *Torah* is conceived as a vital element of the spiritual life, equal to the observance of the commandments. Shneur Zalman's primary aim was to elevate individuals to a knowledge and love of the Divine.

Born in 1722 a year before the *Maggid* of Mezhirech died, Nahman of Bratslav became a kabbalist at an early age. When he was twenty-six he resolved to make a pilgrimage to *Eretz Yisrael*, arriving at Haifa in 1799. In his view, the Holy land 'is the nerve centre of the Jewish people. Each Jew has a share in it as long as he honours the Lord. If he desecrates God's name, he loses the association with the Holy Land and becomes a source of quarrels. I survive only because I have been in the Land of Israel.' (Rabinowicz, 1988, 96–7)

After returning home, Nahman warned against the heretical *maskilim* and the new ideas spread from Germany. Not only his teachings but his prayers were infused with words of caution. Thus he prayed:

> Master of the Universe, help us to resist the temptations that are to be found in the writings and languages of the Gentiles ... Annul the evil decrees, especially the decrees that compel our young people to study ungodly writings.   (Rabinowicz, 1970, 80)

Convinced that the *zaddik* was of transcendent importance, Nahman maintained that only through the *zaddik* could a person attain a true understanding of God. Further, it was the *zaddik* who was able to perform miracles in heaven and on earth. Thus the words of the *zaddik* are more precious than the words of the *Torah* and prophets. But, he explained, people must guard against false *zaddikim*; it was these individuals who were sent by the evil spirit to mislead the people. Such a view gave rise to bitter controversies with other Hasidic masters. In defence of his own teaching, he explained:

> How is it possible that they should not quarrel with me? I am not really of this world, and therefore the world cannot understand me ... All that has been before is as the life within the fruit before it is ripe ... There has never been anyone like me in the world ... I am like a fruitful tree whose branches and foliage are fresh and green ... I have kindled a torch that will never be put out ... The

righteous redeemer will be one of my descendants ... In the world to come all men will be Hasidim of Bratslav. (Rabinowicz, 1988, 100)

In 1802 Nahman settled in Bratslav, Podolia, where he met Rabbi Nathan ben Naphtali Sternherz of Nemirov who recorded his many sayings, designed to elevate listeners to a higher spiritual plane.

Another major figure of this period was Elimelekh of Lyzhansk. Born in 1717 in Lapacha, near Tiktin, he went into exile with his brother Zusya to atone for his sins and seek repentance. Together they traversed Poland reaching as far as Ushpitzin on the German border, spreading Hasidic teachings. In the words of Rabbi Noah of Kobryn: 'You will find Hasidim up to the point that the brothers Rabbi Zusya and Rabbi Elimelekh reach in their long journeyings. Beyond that you will not find Hasidim.' (Rabinowicz, 1970, 88). At the urging of Zusya, Elimelekh visited the *Maggid* of Mezhirech who became his teacher. After the death of the *Maggid* in 1773, Elimelekh's hometown Lyzhansk attracted countless Hasidim who came to him for enlightenment. In addition, Elimelekh visited many villages to preach the virtues of the Hasidic way of life. Drawing up a code of conduct for his followers he counselled moderation in all things and insisted on the study of the *Torah*. Under his influence, Hasidim were encouraged to study Scripture, *Mishnah*, and *Gemara*. Yet despite his erudition and holiness, he was plagued by self-doubt. As he declared:

'I am old. I am nearly sixty years of age, and I have not managed to carry out even one *mitzvah* with proper devotion. A new *Gehinnom* will have to be created for me. The hell that now exists cannot purge my sins and transgressions.' (Rabinowicz, 1970, 90)

When the Vilna authorities excommunicated the Hasidim, Elimelekh like the *Maggid*, counselled his followers to restrain themselves from retaliation. Even when he was assaulted by a *mitnagged* (supporter of rabbinic Judaism), he responded with forgiveness. 'Master of the Universe!', he prayed, 'I forgive him with my whole heart. Let no man be punished on my behalf.' After his death in 1786, his grave became a place of pilgrimage where Hasidim from all over the world would place petitions.

Among Polish Hasidim, Rabbi Israel Hopstein occupied a central role. Initially he studied with the *Maggid* of Mezhirech; after his death, Israel came under the influence of Elimelech of Lyzhansk, eventually becoming *Maggid* of Kozienice where he attracted a large audience. Deeply concerned with the welfare of Jewry, he served as one of 24 delegates who urged the government to abolish the tax on *shehitah* (ritual slaughter). Further, when the state required military service for Jews between 24 and 28, he joined other religious leaders in negotiating for exemption. Renowned for his sanctity, he was revered by his fellow rabbis. As the Rabbi of Rymanov declared: 'I have heard a *Bat Kol* [Heavenly Voice] proclaim that he who lives in the generation of the Maggid [of Kozienice] and has not looked upon his face will not be worthy to welcome the Messiah when he comes.' (Ibid., 96)

Another major Polish figure of this period was Rabbi Jacob Isaac Hurwitz, known as the Seer of Lublin. Born in 1745, he too travelled to the court of the *Maggid* of Mezhirech. After the *Maggid*'s death in 1773, Jacob Isaac became a disciple of Rabbi Shmelke of Nikolsburg. During the lifetime of Elimelekh, Jacob Isaac established his court at Lyzhansk, but later moved to Lublin where his rabbinical academy became a training-ground for future leaders of the Hasidim. Rabbi Uri of Strelisk avowed: Lublin is *Eretz Yisrael*; the court of the *Bet Ha-Midrash* [House of Study] is Jerusalem; the *Bet Ha-Midrash* itself is the Temple; the study of the Seer is the Holy of Holies; and the *Shekhinah* [Divine Presence] speaks from his mouth. (Ibid., 100)

According to tradition, whenever a Hasid arrived, Rabbi Jacob Isaac removed his soul and cleansed it – his followers left him purified and uplifted.

The greatest of Rabbi Jacob Isaac's disciples was also named Jacob Isaac, known as the 'Holy Jew'. Born in 1765 at Przedborz, he was the son of Asher Rabinowicz. He studied at Lissa, Prussia, becoming principal of the Talmudic College at Opatow. Subsequently he wandered from town to town attracting students. Like *Habad* philosophy, the teachings of Jacob Isaac exerted an important influence on later Hasidism. Critical of superficiality, he insisted on sincerity and total involvement in worship, study and all human relationships. Commenting on his master's spirituality, Rabbi Jacob Aryeh of Radzymin stated:

The prayer of Jacob Isaac was like the prayer of the Besht. The prayer of the Besht was like the prayer of Isaac Luria. The prayer of Isaac Luria was like the prayer of Rabbi Simeon ben Yohai, and the prayer of Rabbi Simeon ben Yohai was like the prayer of Adam before he sinned. (Ibid., 106)

Jacob Isaac was succeeded by Simha Bunem, his favourite disciple. Born in 1765, he was initially a timber merchant and later a chemist. However under the influence of Jacob Isaac, Simha surrounded himself with a circle of disciples in Przysucha. Deeply opposed to the *maskilim*, he stressed the importance of the religious life – like the Besht, he recounted numerous parables extolling the life of the spirit.

Another central figure of the late eighteenth century was Menahem Mendel Morgenstern. Born in 1787 in Gorey, near Lublin, he studied at the *Yeshiva* of Rabbi Joseph Hochgelernter at Zamosc. In 1807 he married Glickel Nei of Tomaszow and afterwards made his way to Lublin where he became a Hasid. With the death of Jacob Isaac, Mendel transferred his allegiance to Rabbi Simha Bunem; after Simha's death, Mendel settled in Tomaszow where he attracted a large number of followers. Two years later he moved to Kotzk where he delivered discourses on the religious life. Convinced of his place in the hierarchy of spiritual leaders, he proclaimed:

I am the seventh. I am the Sabbath. Six generations preceded me: the first was Rabbi Dov Baer, the second was Rabbi Shmelke, the third was Rabbi Elimelekh of Lyzhansk, the fourth was the Seer of Lublin, the fifth was the Holy Jew, the sixth was Rabbi Simha Bunem and I, Mendel, am the seventh. (Ibid., 116)

THE NINETEENTH CENTURY

During the nineteenth century Hasidism underwent considerable growth: during this period many Eastern European villages had their own Hasidic courts giving rise to dynasties which continued into the twentieth century. The founder of the Ruzhin-Sadgora dynasty, Israel Friedmann, was born in 1797 in Predzborz near Kiev. At the age of 16 he became a *rebbe*, settling first at Skvira and then in Ruzhin where he established his court. Like the Besht, Israel had lost his father at an early age and was a person of joyous faith. He who does not serve the Lord with joy, he proclaimed, does not serve the Lord at all. For this reason he opposed ascetic practices, believing that such actions endangered the soul. Although he did not write learned books, he had a profound impact on his followers.

In the nineteenth century the town of Belz in the Lvov area of Galicia became the court of the Belz dynasty of Hasidim. Born in 1803, the founder of this dynasty, Rabbi Shalom was known as the *'illui* [genius] of Rava'. Through Rabbi Solomon of Lutzk, Shalom was drawn to the Hasidic movement and dedicated himself to collecting the discourses of the *Maggid* of Mezhirech. At the suggestion of the Seer, he became the rabbi of Belz where he remained for 40 years. Under his leadership, Belz attracted scholars from Galicia, Hungary, and Poland. Convinced that the *Haskalah* would undermine the fabric of Jewish life, Rabbi Shalom declared that the *maskilim* presented a grave danger to Judaism. 'Days are coming', he warned, 'when to rear a son in the *Torah* and in the fear of God will be as hard to accomplish as the Binding of Isaac.' (Rabinowicz, 1988, 162)

Towards the end of his life Rabbi Shalom became blind, and on his death he was succeeded by Rabbi Joshua, his youngest son. Born in Belz in 1825, he was known for his rabbinic knowledge as well as worldly wisdom. Believing that a Jewish spiritual leader is obliged to attract unbelievers to the movement, he offered counsel to many who travelled to meet him; in addition, he established the Mahzikei Ha-Dat organization in Galicia and Bukovina in 1878. In 1882 this body convened a conference attended by 200 rabbis and 800 representatives of different communities – the purpose of this gathering was to protect the religious character of the Jewish communities from the influence of reformers. The third *rebbe* of Belz, Rabbi Issahar Dov, was born in Belz in 1854. Known as the *'illui* of Chernobyl', he succeeded his father in 1894 and revived the Mahzikei Ha-Dat by publishing a proclamation denouncing the influence of nationalism on Jewish life. With the outbreak of World War I, Issahar Dov moved first to Ratzfel, Munkacs and Halshitz, finally returning to Belz. There he hired a personal assistant whose duty was to rebuke him for failing in his duties. Once when they were dining, his assistant declared that the *rebbe* was seated and was unmindful of townfolk who had no food. In response Issahar Dov left the table to collect money for the poor. Under his influence, Sarah Schenirer, the daughter of a devoted Hasid of Belz, founded the Beit Yaakov movement dedicated to the education of Jewish young women. A description of the *rebbe*'s court in Belz was given by Jiri Mordekhai Langer who visited him in 1913:

It is as though an electric spark has suddenly entered those present. The crowd, which till now has been completely quiet, almost cowed, suddenly bursts forth in a wild shout. None stays in his place. The tall black figures run hither and hither round the synagogue flashing past the lights of the Sabbath candles. Gesticulating wildly, and throwing their whole bodies about, they shout out the words of the Psalm.   (Rabinowicz, 1988, 168)

One of the most important advocates of Hasidism in the Ukraine was Rabbi Menahem Nahum of Chernobyl. Born in 1730, he initially served as a teacher, but was increasingly attracted to the Hasidic movement. After visiting the Baal Shem Tov in Medzibozh, he became a disciple of the *Maggid* of Mezhirech. Eventually, Rabbi Nahum settled in Chernobyl where he functioned as a preacher. For Rabbi Nahum, the moral life was of paramount importance. Thus he advised his followers:

Keep yourself from being cross toward your household in any manner. Let your speech be pleasant. Accept whatever portion the Lord gives you in love, whether it be for good or for ill and suffering. Do not glorify yourself, however great your learning or your good deeds, your wealth, or your fine qualities. Do not triumph over any person. If people should come to praise you, do not let it lead you to self-importance.   (Ibid., 174)

Like Rabbi Nahum, Rabbi Dov Baer of Lubavitch, the son of Shneur Zalman (known as the *Mitteler Rebbe*) exerted an important influence on the development of Hasidism in the nineteenth century. Born in 1774, he was named after the *Maggid* of Mezhirech. After his father's death in 1812, he settled in Lubavitch which subsequently became the centre of *Habad* Hasidism. During the reign of Alexander I, Dov Baer endorsed the creation of agricultural settlements for Jews:

My advice is that men, women and children should learn to perform various types of work, such as weaving, spinning, and all skills that are required in factories. The training of artisans should be organized in an orderly manner and should be properly regulated, especially for the children of the poor and the middle class. Furthermore, many Jews should begin to engage in agriculture.   (Ibid., 177)

Like his father, Dov Baer was a supporter of the *yishuv* in Palestine, and he longed to settle in Hebron. In tribute to his piety, his followers stated: 'If you cut his finger you would find that in his veins flowed not blood but Hasidism'. On his death in 1827, he was succeeded by his son-in-law Rabbi Menahem Mendel (known as the *Tzemah Tzedek*). Famous for his diligence in study, he remarked: 'I generally study for eighteen hours a day which includes five hours of writing, and in the past thirty years, I have spent a total of 32,000 hours studying the works of Rabbi Shneur Zalman.' Like his father-in-law, Menahem Mendel, he actively engaged in agricultural settlement; in 1844, he purchased 9700 acres of land at Shezedrin where he founded a settlement for 300 families. Concerning about the growth of the *Haskalah*, Menahem Mendel sent emissaries throughout Russia to counter the arguments of the *maskilim*. In the years that followed, Rabbi Menahem Mendel was succeeded by his youngest son Rabbi Samuel who, like his father, was deeply concerned about the welfare of the Jewish community. Rabbi Samuel's successor, Rabbi Shalom Dov Baer, continued to fight for Jewish rights and was particularly concerned with the Mountain Jews of Uzbekistan.

During this period the Hasidic dynasties of Ruzhin and Sadgora continued to flourish in Galicia. Rabbi Israel of Ruzhin was eventually succeeded in 1851 by Rabbi Abraham Jacob Friedmann, and thousands of followers flocked to his court. Sir Lawrence Oliphant, who journeyed to the *rebbe* in 1850, gave a full account of his visit:

> The whole Jewish community of Sadgora awaited our arrival, lining both sides of the street to see the Gentile coming to their *rebbe*. At the entrance of the *rebbe*'s house his sons and sons-in-law, in Polish dress, greeted us. Inside the *rebbe*'s daughters were hostesses to my wife. I was led into a room, much like a princely court, furnished with precious gold and silver antiques. There I met the *rebbe*, accompanied by two servants. (Dawidowicz, 1967, 197–8)

Another central figure of this period was Rabbi Hayyim Halberstam of Sanz (known as the *Divrei Hayyim*). Known as the *'illui* of Tarnogord', he visited the seer in 1805 who predicted that he would become a leader of his generation. Initially he became the rabbi of Radnick, subsequently serving as rabbi in Zalin, Lalev, and Nowy Sacz. Due to his piety, the Hasidim began to call the town

'Zanz' to indicate that it was the home of the *zaddik*. According to tradition, when Hayyim stood in prayer, light seemed to radiate from him. Among his writings, the *Divrei Hayyim* deals with the laws of the *Shulhan Arukh*; his 729 responsa reflect the social and religious life of Jewry in nineteenth century Galicia.

LATE NINETEENTH AND EARLY TWENTIETH CENTURIES

In the late nineteenth century a number of Hasidic dynasties emerged in Poland. Rabbi Mordekhai Joseph Leiner was the founder of the Radzyn-Izbica dynasty; the rabbis of this dynasty emphasized the importance of informed faith. God, they believed, should be served with intelligence and devotion. Pre-eminent among these rabbis was Rabbi Mordekhai's grandson, Rabbi Gershon Heinokh Leiner (known as the *Baal Hatekheilet*). At the age of eighteen, he began work on his *Sidrei Tohorot*, a compendium of commentaries and interpretations of the sages on the tractate *Tohorot*.

Another important Polish figure of this period was Rabbi Jehiel Meir Lipshitz. Born in 1810, he became a disciple of Menahem Mendel of Kotzk. After Menahem Mendel's death in 1859, Jehiel Meir travelled to various *rebbe*'s courts, eventually becoming a *rebbe* himself. Referred to as a 'miracle worker', his followers had great faith in the power of his prayers. In his religious life, he emphasized the importance of the Psalms. In his will he enjoined his disciples to 'study the Psalms many times with a translation. Let the Psalms be familiar to you. Utilize the commentary of Rashi. Take heed to recite at least five chapters of Psalms daily.' Like other Hasidic leaders, Jehiel Meir was concerned about the influence of secular knowledge. To combat its pernicious influence he signed a public appeal imploring the people not to own or read heretical literature.

Rabbi Isaac Kalish of Warka also had a profound impact on Polish Hasidism. After studying under several great Hasidic masters, he served as a rabbi in Gubartshow, and then in Ruda. After the death of Rabbi Abraham Moses in 1829, he assumed leadership of the Hasidim of Przysucha. When he moved to Warka, many disciples followed him there. Actively engaged in the struggle against the conscription of young Jews for military service, he sought to preserve traditional Jewish life against both external and internal threats. His dedication to his people is epitomized in an encounter between Rabbi Menahem Mendel Morgenstern of Kotzk and Rabbi Jacob David Kalish. 'I have finally found your father, Rabbi Isaac', Rabbi Menahem Mendel declared,

> I searched for him in the Higher Regions but could not find him. I searched for him among the disciples of Rabbi Israel Baal Shem Tov. I looked for him among the *tannaim* and *amoraim*. Eventually I found him gazing sadly at a river. 'What are you doing here?', I asked him. 'The river is full of the tears of the children of Israel and I cannot move from it', he replied.   (Rabinowicz, 1988, p. 201)

Another Polish Hasidic *rebbe* of considerable influence was Rabbi Abraham Bornstein of Sochaczew. Born in 1839, he was known as the '*illui* of Lekish'. After studying with his father-in-law, Rabbi Menahem Mendel Morgenstern of Kotzk, he became a rabbi in Parczew, and than at Krosnowicz, Nasielsk, and Sochaczew where he founded a large *yeshiva*. In 1884 Rabbi Abraham issued a proclamation denouncing heretical writings; in another pronouncement he encouraged rabbis to establish study circles for workers and businessmen.

Rabbi Tzadok Hakohen Rabinowicz was another significant Hasidic personality of this period: born in 1823, he was a prolific author contributing to biblical, talmudic, kabbalistic, halakhic, and homiletic studies. Another Polish luminary was Rabbi Hanokh Heinokh Hakohen. Born in Litomirsk in 1798, he lived in Przysucha, becoming *rebbe* in Alexander at the age of 68. Reluctant to take on the mantle of leadership, he declared: 'Woe to the generation that has me for its leader.' Yet he exercised considerable skills as a *rebbe*. In the years that followed, Hasidim in Poland gravitated to Alexander where a Hasidic dynasty was founded by Rabbi Shragei Feivel. After the death of the Seer, Shragei Feivel became a disciple of Rabbi Simha Bunem, and eventually held rabbinic positions in Gombyn, Grice and Markova. After Shragei Feivel's death in 1849, he was succeeded by his son Rabbi Jehiel. It was said that during prayers Jehiel would weep bitterly. As one Hasid remarked: 'I testify that when I entered the synagogue of the *rebbe*, the entire building seemed to be overflowing with holiness, and the worshippers were weeping.' At his death in 1894, Jehiel was succeeded by Rabbi Jerahmiel ben Isaac. Renowned for his mastery of rabbinic sources, it was said Jerahmiel knew the entire *Zohar* by heart.

Paralleling the dynasty of Alexander, the town of Ger was known for its *rebbes*. The first major Hasidic figure of Ger was Rabbi Isaac Meir, born in 1799. A devoted disciple of the *Maggid* of Kozienice, he later became a follower of Rabbi Simha Bunem. When Simha Bunem died, Isaac Meir transferred his allegiance to Rabbi Mendel of Kotz. After his death, Isaac Meir became a *rebbe* in Warsaw and later in Ger. Together with other leaders, he sought to stem the tide of assimilation and barred secular studies from the *heder* curriculum. 'It is impossible for the words of the *Torah* to enter into the hearts of children,' he wrote, 'when their minds are full of other things.' At his death in 1866, he was succeeded by his grandson Judah Leib. Born in 1847, Judah Leib studied under Rabbi Hanokh Hakohen of Alexander. After the anti-Jewish riots of 1881, he advocated emigration to the Holy Land:

Just as the Jews need the Holy Land so the Holy Land needs the Jews to bring out its intrinsic holiness, the bond pre-ordained and divinely forged between the land and the people, has not been broken despite the fact that the Jews have been driven from its soil.' (Rabinowicz, 1988, 235)

By the end of the nineteenth century approximately six million Jews lived in Europe – after the anti-Jewish outbreaks in 1881, thousands of Jews had fled to other lands. Many Hasidim however were reluctant to uproot themselves. With the Bolshevik revolution and the creation of the USSR three million Jews in Russia obtained emancipation, but the authorities instituted draconian measures aimed at undermining traditional Jewish life: Jewish schools and *yeshivot* were made illegal, synagogues were turned into workers clubs, and *Yiddishkeit* was outlawed. During these upheavals Rabbi Shalom Dov Baer, the fifth *rebbe* of the Lubavich dynasty, dedicated himself to the cause of *Hinukh* (education). Following in his footsteps, his son Rabbi Joseph Schneerson instituted the campaign for Jewish education throughout Russia. In 1927 he was imprisoned in Spalierna Prison and sentenced to death; this decree was commuted and he was banished to Kostrom in the Urals for three years. Eventually he was released and settled in Riga, later returning to Warsaw where he established a *yeshiva*.

Between the two World Wars Poland contained the largest number of European Jews; there Jewry was subjected to frequent attack. More than a third of these Jews were Hasidim associated with the *Aguda* movement. Notable among these figures was Rabbi Meir Yehiel Halevi Halstock of Ostrowiec. Born in 1851 he became rabbi at Skierniewice, eventually settling to Ostrowiec. There he fasted every day; when he died in 1928 ten thousand people gathered for his funeral. Another important Hasidic personality of this period was the Rabbi of Sokolow, Issac Zelig Morgenstern. In 1919 he joined the *Aguda* becoming Vice-President of the Rabbinical Union. Like his father the *rebbe* of Sokolow urged his followers to support the *yishuv* in the Holy Land.

The most important court of Poland at this time was that of Ger where Abraham Mordecai Alter held sway. When the Rabbi of Ger visited a town, it was like a royal visit. As Neville Laski, President of the British Board of Deputies, recorded:

> I heard much talk of the wonder-working rabbi, who is almost worshipped by a section of the population, and I managed to obtain ocular demonstration of his popularity. I went to see his arrival from his cure at Carlsbad and was presented with a spectacle such as I had never imagined. Hundreds and hundreds of, to me, medieval-looking Jews wearing strange hats and kaftans crowded on the platform ... excitement reigned supreme (Rabinowicz, 1970 162–3)

One of the most prominent rabbis of the period was the Rabbi of Novomirsk, Alter Yisrael Shimn Prelov. Born in 1873, he settled in Warsaw where Hasidim of all groups came to pay homage. Although Poland was the centre of *Torah* study, it was not the home of Hasidic *yeshivot* – rather Lithuania attracted students from throughout Europe. In inter-war years, however, Polish *rebbes* began to establish their own *yeshivot*. Rabbi Solomon Henoh Hakohen Rabinowicz of Radomsk, for example, established the *Keter Torah Yeshivot* – subsequently 36 branches were created in Poland and Galicia. The Rebbe of Radomsk's successor was his son-in-law, Moses David Ha-Kohen Rabinowicz. Under his direction, the *yeshivot* of Radomsk set particularly rigorous standards. At Lublin, Rabbi Meir Shapira erected a *yeshiva* of similarly high standards. In Galicia Rabbi Benzion Halberstam established the *Etz Hayim Yeshiva* which eventually developed 46 branches. During these years other sizeable Hasidic groups were established in other lands. Moses Teitelbaum of Ujhely, for example, helped establish Hasidic communities in Hungry; Rabbi Shlomoh Shapira established the Munkacs Hasidic dynasty; and the dynasty of Vishnitz was founded by Menahem Mendel Hager.

CONTEMPORARY HASIDIM

With the outbreak of the Second World War, Hasidim were initially encouraged to join the Polish air force. However once the Nazis were victorious, the Jewish community was helpless – during the war millions of Jews, including many Hasidim, lost their lives. None the less, after the war Hasidism continued to flourish in a number of centres throughout the world. In 1940 the *rebbe* of Ger, Rabbi Israel escaped from Poland to the Holy Land. Located at Rehov Malkhei Yisrael in Jerusalem, he expanded the *Yeshivat Sefat Emat* and encouraged the building of a *yeshiva* in Tel Aviv as well as other educational institutions. At his death in 1977, over 100 000 mourners attended his funeral.

Another Jerusalem *rebbe*, Rabbi Jehiel Joseph Rabinowicz, carried on the traditions of Binla and Przysucha. Arriving in the Holy Land in 1947, he was known as a miracle worker and a servant of the Lord. At his death he was survived by four sons who became *rebbes* at Lugano, Jerusalem and Bnei Berak. Jerusalem was also the residence of Rabbi Abraham Isaac Kahn who continued the dynasty founded by his father-in-law, Rabbi Aaron Roth. Apart from Ger, no other rabbi attracted so many followers. Other Hasidic groups in Jerusalem included the dynasty of Slonim which was established by Rabbi Abraham Weinerberg, as well as the followers of Rabbi Johanan Twersky who founded a *yeshiva* and a *kollel*.

In Tel Aviv Rabbi Aaron Rokeah of Belz established his residence attracting Hasidim from all over the world; in 1957 he was succeeded by Rabbi Issahar Dov Rokeah who made his home in Jerusalem where there is a Belzer *yeshiva*. One of the first *rebbes* of the House of Ruzhin to settle in Tel Aviv was Rabbi Israel of Husyatinulo, who was succeeded by his son-in-law Rabbi Jacob Friedmann. Another resident of Tel Aviv was Rabbi Mordekai Shalom Joseph Friedmann of Sadgora-Pzemysl, who was succeeded by his son Rabbi Abraham Jacob active in the expansion of Hasidic institutions. In 1959 Rabbi Isaac Friedmann of Bohush moved to Tel Aviv where he maintained a small *kollel*. Rabbi Moses Jehiel Epstein of Ozarow was another important figure of the modern period who settled in Tel Aviv and published numerous studies.

The largest concentration of Hasidim in Israel is located at Bnei Berak; there the *rebbe* of Alexander was Rabbi Judah Moses Danziger who was succeeded by his son Abraham Menahem. At Bnei Berak the dynasty of Nadvorna was represented by Rabbi Hayim Mordekhai Rosenbaum who was succeeded by his son Issakhar Baer. In 1976 Rabbi Abraham Hayyim Roth moved to Bnei Berak where he established a *Talmud Torah*. In addition to Bnei Berak, notable among the Hasidic settlements is Kfar Habad, located five miles from Tel Aviv, which was established by the rabbi of Lubavitch, Joseph Isaac Schneersohn. After Kfar Habad, the largest *Habad* settlement is Nahalat Har Habad, near Kiryat Malachi. Near Bnei Berak Kiryzt Vishnitz is the settlement founded by the Romanian rabbi Hayyim Meir Jehiel Hager; by 1973 it housed over 350 families. On the heights of Mount Carmel Ramat Vishnitz is a Hasidic centre established by Rabbi Barukh Hager. Hasidism in Israel is also found at Ramat Gan at a settlement established by Rabbi Hananiah Yom Tov Lippe Teitelbaum of Sasow. As a consequence of the numerous settlements, Hasidic life continues to gain ground on the soil of the Holy Land.

Turning to the New World, Hasidim have also prospered in various centres in the United States, particularly in the Williamsburg area of Brooklyn as well as in Crown Heights, Boro Park and Flatbush. Pre-eminent among American-based Hasidim was Rabbi Joel Teitelbaum of Satmar. Born in 1887 in Sighet, he was a rabbi in Yenice, Orshowa, Nagy Karoly, and Satmar. After escaping to Klausenberg, he was eventually transported to Bergen-Belsen. In 1944 he fled to Geneva and later moved to the Holy Land, eventually emigrating to Williamsburg, to the Satmar community. By the 1980s over 30 000 Hasidim occupied the area, with their own newspaper, welfare services, insurance and pension plans, ambulance service, burial society, synagogues and *yeshiva*. A charismatic individual, the Satmar *rebbe* was an ardent critic of the Jewish state: like other Hasidism he argued that it is an usurpation of God's will for Jews to established a secular homeland without the coming of the Messiah.

Another Hasidic community was established in Rockway County about 40 miles from New York City; similarly New Square was founded in Spring Valley, 30 miles from New York, by Rabbi Jacob Joseph Twersky of Skvira. The son-in-law of Rabbi Mordekhai Hager of Vishnitz is the leader of a small community in Monsey; the Hasidim of Rabbi Raphael Blum of Kashou reside in Irvington;

and Rabbi Jekutiel Judah Halberstam of Klausenberg lives in Union City, New Jersey. Unlike these Hasidic groups who live in virtual isolation, Lubavitch Hasidim have actively launched outreach programmes to draw non-religious Jews back to *Torah* Judaism. Under Rabbi Joseph Isaac Schneerson, the sixth *rebbe* of Lubavitch, a framework for religious education was established throughout the United States and Canada. His successor, Rabbi Menahem Mendel Schneerson, was a major figure in the world of *Torah* Judaism. Born in 1902, he studied philosophy at the Sorbonne, graduating with a degree in electrical engineering. In 1944 he became head of the Kehot publishing house; after the death of his father-in-law in 1950 he became the *rebbe* of the community. From his residence in Brooklyn, the *rebbe*'s words have had a profound impact throughout the Jewish world.

Another important Hasidic figure was Rabbi Solomon Halberstam, the *rebbe* of Bobow. Born in 1907, he was confined to the labour camp at Bochnia near Krakow, but escaped first to Grosswardein and from there to Romania. After the war, he went to Italy and eventually settled in Boro Park, Brooklyn. There he founded a network of education establishments including a large *yeshiva*. In addition he set up a computer studies career development centre for young men and a holiday camp for children. Progressive in approach, he introduced a job scheme whereby courses leading to jobs in industry are taught in a *yeshiva* trade school.

Another leading Hasidic *rebbe* in the United States was Rabbi Moses Halevi. Born in the Holy Land in 1909, he settled in Boston. In 1941 he moved to Williamsburg where he was known as the 'Bostoner *Rebbe*'. Intensively involved in strengthening *Torah* life, he also established various communal institutions. After his death in 1985, he was succeeded by his son Rabbi Hayyim. There are also Hasidic rabbis in other American cities. Rabbi Jacob Israel Twersky for example, lived in Milwaukee, Wisconsin, where he founded the congregation Beit Yehudah in 1939. In Montreal, Canada, Rabbi Samuel Undsorer established *yeshivot* under the auspices of Lubavitch and Satmar and a large Lubavitch day school.

England, too, has witnessed an efflorescence of Hasidic life. In the north-west London suburbs there was a small group of Hasidim under Rabbi Berish Finkelstein, a Hasid of Radzyn. In the Golders Green area there are a number of Hasidic congregations: *Beit Shmuel* under the guidance of Rabbi Elhanan Halpern and a *kollel* and synagogue under Rabbi Gerson Hager. The largest Hasidic concentration is found in the Stamford Hill area – the various *shtibelekh* include Belzer, Bobower, Gerer and Satmarer. In 1973 the Hasidim of Belz obtained a house in the Clapton Common area to serve as a *heder*; the community opened a *Beit Hamidrash*, a *Talmud Torah*, a *yeshiva ketanah*, and a *kollel*. The dynasty of Bobow established roots in north London where it houses a *Beit Hamidrash* and a *yeshiva*. Today these various Hasidic groups co-operate in a number of activities relating to *shehita*, the rabbinate, *mikvaot*, *hevrah kaddisha* and *kashrut*. Outside of London there are also Hasidic groups in Manchester, Glasgow, Leeds and Liverpool.

The post-war years have thus witnessed the revival of Hasidic life following the destruction of Eastern European Jewry. For many Jews Hasidism embodies the most intense spiritual awareness of God's presence. In its quest for the hallowing of everyday exist-ence. It has brought hope to a new generation of Jews in search of the Divine. As observed by Martin Buber:

> The *zaddikim* of ... five generations offered us a number of reli-gious personalities of a vitality, a spiritual strength, a manifold originality such as have never, to my knowledge, appeared to-gether in so short a time span in the history of religion. But the most important thing about these *zaddikim* is that each of them was surrounded by a community which lived a brotherly life, and who could live in this way because there was a leading person in their midst who brought each one near to the other by bringing them all nearer to that in which they believed. (Rabinowicz, 1988, 405)

CRITIQUE

Like Orthodox Judaism, contemporary Hasidism has attracted a wide circle of followers. From New York to Israel to Europe, pious adherents flock to their *rebbes* in search of religious guidance. Not only those born into Hasidic families, but also thousands of con-verts to the Hasidic way of life have been drawn to this new mode of Jewish spirituality. Yet despite the efflorescence of Hasidism in contemporary Jewish society, it is inconceivable that Hasidism could provide an overarching framework for Jewish living in the twenty-first century. Because Hasidism is based on the traditional belief that God revealed the *Torah* to Moses on Mount Sinai, it suffers from the same defects as Orthodoxy. In the light of biblical scholarship, it is no longer possible to believe in the inerrancy of Scripture. Rather, it appears that the *Torah* is a composite work, composed of various strands of tradition originating at different times in the history of ancient Israel. As a consequence, it must be acknowledged that the descriptions of God's nature and activity as well as the hundreds of laws enumerated in the Pentateuch are of human rather than divine origin. Even if one believes that the *Torah* was divinely inspired, it is clear that the Hebrew Scriptures are mediated through human comprehension and reflect the cultural milieu in which the ancient Israelites lived. Hasidism's contention that the *Torah* must be followed because of its divine authority thus crumbles in the light of a contemporary understanding of the Bible and our knowledge of the ancient Near East.

Further, science reveals that the biblical understanding of the origins of the universe, particularly as conceived within kabbalistic Judaism – which has been embraced by Hasidism – has no basis in fact. According to early Jewish mysticism, God created the universe by means of 32 mysterious paths consisting of 22 letters of the Hebrew alphabet together with ten *sefirot* (divine emanations). These recondite doctrines were later developed in the *Zohar*, and by the sixteenth century mystic Isaac Luria. Of primary importance in the Lurianic system is the mystery of creation: for Luria creation was a negative event: the *Ayn Sof* (Infinite) had to bring into being an empty space in which creation could occur since divine light was everywhere, leaving no room for creation to take place. This was accomplished by the process of *tzimtzum*, the contraction of the Godhead into itself.

After this act of withdrawal, a line of light flowed from the Godhead into the empty space and took on the shape of the *sefirot* in the form of *Adam Kadmon*. In this process divine lights created the vessels (the extended spaces of the *sefirot*) which gave specific characteristic to each divine emanation. Yet these vessels were not strong enough to contain such light and they shattered. Following the shattering of the vessels, the cosmos was divided into two parts: the kingdom of evil in the lower part and the realm of divine light in the upper part. According to Luria, God chose the people of Israel to vanquish evil and raise up the captive sparks. On the basis of this cosmological scheme, Hasidim believe that they are living in the final stages of this attempt to overcome evil in which the coming of the Messiah will signify the end of this struggle. In their view, every deed or misdeed has cosmic significance in the quest for deliverance. To the modern mind, however, these notions are nothing more than a concatenation of ancient beliefs far removed from a true understanding of the nature and origins of the universe. For most Jews astronomical investigations rather than kabbalistic speculation as found in Hasidic lore should serve as a basis for an understanding of the origins of the cosmos.

There are also serious difficulties with the Hasidic conception of the *zaddik*. According to Hasidism, the *zaddikim* are spiritually superior individuals who have attained the highest level of *devekut* (cleaving to God). The goal of the *zaddik* is to elevate the souls of his flock to the divine light; his tasks include pleading to God for his people, immersing himself in everyday affairs, and counselling and strengthening them. As an authoritarian figure, the *zaddik* was seen by his followers as possessing miraculous power to ascend to the divine realm. In this context *devekut* to God involved cleaving to the *zaddik*. Given this emphasis on the role of the *rebbe*, Hasidic literature includes summaries of the spiritual and kabbalistic teaching of various famous *zaddikim* as well as stories about their miraculous deeds. For most modern Jews, however, such veneration of saintly figures is misguided and potentially dangerous. The image of black-hatted men dressed in black suits paying homage to patriarchal figures strikes many as a primitive relic of the past: rather than blindly follow the words of the *rebbe*, the vast majority of contemporary Jews would prefer to think for themselves and determine their own fate.

4

Reform Judaism

Since the Enlightenment Jews were no longer required to live in ghettos and *shtetls*. Rather they were increasingly accepted as full citizens in the countries where they resided. In this new milieu a number of reformers encouraged their co-religionists to integrate into the mainstream of Western European life. These advocates of Jewish Enlightenment attempted to modernize Jewish education through the inclusion of secular subjects and called for changes to the traditional liturgy. Despite Orthodox hostility, the early reformers pressed for a revaluation of the Jewish faith, advocating major alterations to both belief and practice. To formulate a coherent policy, a series of Reforms synods were held throughout Germany during the first half of the nineteenth century. Similarly, in the United States Jewish reformers championed emancipation, and in 1885 a formal list of principles – the Pittsburgh Platform – was adopted by the American Reform movement. Subsequently, Reform Judaism underwent various changes which were reflected in a new declaration of principles, the Columbus Platform, endorsed by the movement in 1937. This new statement embraced Zionist ideals, promoted the use of Hebrew, and revived Jewish practices that had previously been set aside. After the Second World War, Reform Judaism continued to evolve – eventually the Central Conference of American Rabbis adopted a new platform (the San Francisco Platform) in 1971. Yet, although Reform Judaism has consistently viewed itself as the most authentic form of Judaism for modern Jewry, it arguably suffers from a number of serious defects of both a theological and practical character.

THE ENLIGHTENMENT

The beginnings of Reform Judaism go back to the seventeenth century when various Jewish thinkers sought to view the Jewish tradition in the light of scientific knowledge and discovery. The

73

Dutch thinker Uriel Acosta, for example, maintained that the *Torah* was in all likelihood not of divine origin since it contains numerous features contrary to natural law. The greatest of these early Dutch writers was Baruch Spinoza who rejected the medieval Jewish synthesis of faith and reason in his *Tractatus Theologico-Politicus*. According to Spinoza, the prophets possessed moral insight rather than theoretical knowledge. Regarding Maimonides' belief that the Bible contains a hidden esoteric meaning, Spinoza argued that the Hebrew Scriptures were designed for the masses. In his view, God can be known from the order of the universe rather than through miraculous occurrences. Concerning Scripture, Spinoza believed that it was not composed solely by Moses; rather the historical books were compilations assembled by generations of scholars. Further, he believed that Ezra was responsible for harmonizing inconsistencies in the biblical text.

Such rational interpretations of the Jewish tradition served as the background to the philosophical investigations of the greatest philosopher of the Enlightenment, Moses Mendelssohn. Born in Dessau, Mendelssohn studied in Berlin where he befriended leading figures of the age, such as Gotthold Ephraim Lessing. Under Lessing's influence, Mendelssohn wrote a number of theological works in which he argued that human beings are able through reason to discover the reality of God, divine providence and the immortality of the soul. In 1783 Mendelssohn produced a defence of the Jewish religion, *Jerusalem, or On Religious Power and Judaism*; in this study, he maintained that no religious institution should use coercion, stressing that Judaism does not coerce the mind through dogma.

In Mendelssohn's view, Jewish law does not empower religious authorities to persecute individuals for holding false doctrines. Nonetheless, Jews should not depart from the tradition. 'Adopt the mores and constitution of the country in which you find yourself,' he declared, 'but be steadfast in upholding the religion of your fathers, too ... I cannot see how those who were born into the household of Jacob can in good conscience exempt themselves from the observance of the law' (Mendelssohn, 1969, 104–5). Hence, despite Mendelssohn's acknowledgement of the links between Judaism and other faiths, he remained an observant Jew, anxious to retain the distinctive features of the Jewish heritage. None the less, by combining philosophical theism and Jewish traditionalism, Mendelssohn sought to overcome ghetto life and enter into the mainstream of European culture as an observant Jew.

To bring about such Jewish modernization, Mendelssohn also translated the *Torah* into German so that Jews would be able to learn the language of the countries where they resided; further, he oversaw the production of a commentary on Scripture which combined Jewish scholarship with secular learning. Following Mendelssohn's example, a number of Prussian advocates of the Enlightenment known as *maskilim* fostered the Jewish Enlightenment (the *Haskalah*) which encouraged Jews to forsake medieval patterns of Jewish life and thought. These *maskilim* also attempted to reform Jewish education by widening the curriculum, producing textbooks in Hebrew and establishing Jewish schools. In addition, *maskilim* produced the first Jewish literary magazine, *The Gatherer*, in 1783; this publication contained poems and fables in the classical style of biblical Hebrew as well as studies of biblical exegesis, Hebrew linguistics and Jewish history.

By the second decade of the nineteenth century the *Haskalah* had spread to Bohemia, northern Italy and Galicia; during this period the journal *First Fruits of the Times* was published in Vienna between 1821 and 1832, and in 1830 the first Hebrew journal appeared which was devoted to modern Jewish learning. From Germany and Galicia, the *Haskalah* spread to Russia. In Lithuania, European fiction and textbooks were translated into Hebrew; in addition, the first Hebrew novel was produced in 1854, and various Hebrew poets published lyrical poetry. Under Tsar Alexander II, several modern Hebrew weeklies were also published and the Society for the Promotion of Culture among the Jews of Russia was established in 1863. Later in the century, a number of Hebrew writers who had abandoned the style of earlier *maskilim* wrote literary and social criticism. The nineteenth century thus witnessed an outpouring of Hebrew literature, advancing the cause of Jewish emancipation. These thinkers, however, were not typical of the Jewish masses: often they lived isolated lives because of their support of the Austrian and Russian government's efforts to alter Jewish education. Moreover, they were virulently critical of rabbinic Judaism and so were viewed with suspicion and hostility by the religious establishment.

During these decades of cultural ferment political developments in central and eastern Europe contributed to this process of Jewish emancipation. After Napoleon's defeat, the map of Europe was redrawn by the Congress of Vienna between 1814 and 1815. At this Congress diplomats issued a resolution instructing the German confederation to improve the status of Jewry. Yet despite this proclamation, the German government disowned the rights of equality that had previously been granted to the Jewish community by the French and instead imposed restrictions on residence and occupation. According to various academics of the period, Jews were Asiatic aliens; consequently they insisted that Jews could not enter into German-Christian culture without converting to Christianity. Due to such xenophobic attitudes, German Jewry was attacked in cities and the countryside. After 1830, however, a more liberal attitude prevailed, and a number of writers advocated a more tolerant approach. The polemicist Gabriel Riesser, for example, argued that the Jews were not a separate nation, and thus were capable of loving Germany as their homeland. Jewish converts to Christianity such as Heinrich Heine and Ludwig Boerne also defended the rights of Jews during this period.

Compared with western Europe, the social and political conditions of eastern European Jewry were less conducive to Jewish emancipation. After the partitions of Poland in the latter half of the eighteenth century and the decision of the Congress of Vienna to place the Duchy of Warsaw under Alexander I, most Polish Jews were under Russian rule. At the beginning of the nineteenth century, Russia preserved its previous social structure; the social classes were legally separated; the aristocracy insisted on its privileges; the peasantry lived as serfs; and the Church was placed under state control. In many towns and villages Jews were in the majority and worked as leasers of estates, mills, forests, distilleries and inns. However, increasingly Jews migrated to larger urban centres where they joined the working class.

At first Catherine the Great was tolerant of her Jewish subjects but in 1804 Alexander I specified territory in western Russia as an area where Jews would be allowed to reside – the Pale of Settlement. After several attempts to expel Jews from the countryside, the Tsar initiated a policy of integrating the Jewish community into the general population by founding a society of Israelite Christians. In 1824 the deportation of Jews from villages began. Alexander I was succeeded by Nicholas I who adopted an even harsher attitude to his Jewish subjects. In 1827 he declared that Jewish boys should be inducted into the Russian army for a 25-year period in order to increase the number of converts to Christianity.

Nicholas I also dispersed Jews from villages in certain areas: in 1827 they were expelled from Kiev and three years later from the surrounding province. In 1835 the Russian government issued a revised code of laws to regulate Jewish settlement in the western border. In order to reduce Jewish isolation the government also set out to reform education, and a young Jewish educator, Max Lilienthal, was instructed to establish reformed Jewish schools in the Pale of Settlement. This instruction encouraged the use of western educational methods and provided a secular curriculum. Initially Lilienthal attempted to persuade Jewish leaders that by supporting this project the Jewish community could improve their lot, but when he discovered that the Tsar's intention was to undermine the *Talmud*, he left the country. Although several of these schools were founded in 1844, they attracted a small enrolment and the Russian government eventually abandoned its plans to eliminate traditional Jewish education.

In the same year, Nicholas I abolished the *kehillot* and placed Jewry under the authority of the police and the municipal government. However, this policy was doomed to failure; it was impossible for the Russian administration to carry out the functions of the *kehillot*, and it was accepted that a Jewish body was needed to regulate Jewish affairs. In 1850–1 the government attempted to forbid dress, men's sidecurls, and the ritual shaving of women's hair. During this period a plan was initiated to categorize all Jews in the country along economic lines – those who were viewed as useful subjects included craftsmen, farmers and wealthy merchants, whereas the vast majority of Jews were liable to further restrictions. However, after the Crimean War of 1853–6, Alexander II emancipated the serfs, modernized the judiciary, and created a system of local self-government. Further, he allowed certain groups – including wealthy merchants, university graduates, certified artisans, discharged soldiers, and all holders of diplomas – to reside outside the Pale of Settlement. As a result, Jewish communities appeared in St Petersburg and Moscow. Furthermore, a small number of Jews were permitted to enter the legal profession and participate in district councils. Government-sponsored Jewish schools also drew more Jewish students, and in the 1860s and 1870s emancipated Jews began to take a more active role in the professions and in Russian economic life.

THE BEGINNINGS OF REFORM JUDAISM

Under the influence of the Enlightenment, Jewish life significantly changed. No longer were Jews insulated from the main currents of

European thought, and such an alteration encouraged many Jews to seek a modernization of Jewish existence. Thus at the beginning of the nineteenth century the Jewish communal leader Israel Jacobson founded a boarding school for boys in Seesen, Westphalia, in 1801; subsequently he established similar schools throughout the kingdom. In these new educational institutions, Jewish teachers gave lessons about Judaism, and secular subjects were taught by Christians. Under Jacobson's leadership, the consistory also introduced reforms to the Jewish worship service including choral singing, hymns and addresses, and prayers in German. In 1810 Jacobson established the first Reform temple next to the school; however after Napoleon's death Jacobson moved to Berlin where he attempted to put these principles into practice by founding a Reform temple.

In 1817 the Hamburg Reform temple was opened – this new institution similarly made a number of changes to the liturgy including prayers and sermons in German as well as choral singing and organ music. In defence of these innovations, Hamburg reformers cited the *Talmud* in support of their progressive ideas. In 1819 the Hamburg Reform community issued its own prayerbook in which traditional prayers related to Jewish nationalism and messianic redemption were eliminated. Israel Jacobson, to whom this prayerbook was dedicated, was successful in obtaining a number of endorsements of these reforms. Thus the Hungarian rabbi Aaron Chorin stated that it was obligatory to free the liturgy from its adhesions, to hold worship services in the vernacular, and to accompany it with organ and song. In response the Orthodox establishment issued a decree condemning the Hamburg reformers.

The major aim of these early progressive Jews was to adapt Jewish worship to modern aesthetic standards. To these innovators, the traditional Jewish service appeared foreign and undignified; as a consequence they insisted on greater decorum, more unison in prayer, a choir, hymns and musical responses, and alterations in prayers and the length of the service. During this period, a number of Jewish intellectuals also founded the Society for the Culture and Academic Study of Judaism. This body encouraged the systematic study of history and a respect for scientific investigation. The purpose of this new approach to the tradition was to gain a true understanding of the origins of Judaism. However, in 1824 the society collapsed and a number of its members – including the poet Heinrich Heine and the historian of law Edward Gans – converted to Christianity.

During this period a number of German rabbis such as Leopold Zunz, influenced by the Enlightenment, undertook a revaluation of the Jewish tradition. As the Reform movement continued to grow, Orthodox authorities vigorously criticized its leadership and ideals. In 1838, for example, the Chief Rabbi of Breslau, Solomon Tiktin, denounced the reform thinker Abraham Geiger as a dangerous radical. In Tiktin's view, anyone who did not subscribe to the absolute truth of the Jewish heritage was unfit to hold a post of rabbinic leadership.

Joining in this protest Tiktin's allies declared Geiger unfit for the position as second rabbi of Breslau, and in 1842 Tiktin published a tract in which he stressed the validity of Jewish law and the authority of the rabbis. In response Geiger's followers published a defence of religious reform. The animosity provoked by this controversy is reflected in the writings of one of Geiger's followers, Joseph Kahn, the Chief Rabbi of Treves:

> We must publicly express our contempt for those who, like Tiktin and company, blindly damn and ban, and in just indignation we must brand them as men who 'some day will have to account for their deeds'.   (Plaut, 1963, 70)

Despite Orthodox hostility to this new movement, the Society of the Friends of Reform was founded in Frankfurt which published a proclamation justifying its innovative approach to Judaism. In the declaration of its principles, the society stated that it recognized the possibility of unlimited progress in the Jewish faith and rejected the authority of the legal code as well as the traditional belief in messianic deliverance. Moreover, members of the society viewed circumcision as a barbaric rite which should be eliminated from Jewish ritual. Alarmed by the danger this group posed to traditional Jewish values, the Rabbi of Prague, Solomon Rapoport warned against associating with any members of this group: 'We must strictly insist and warn our co-religionists not to have any social contacts with members of this Reform association, and especially not to enter into matrimonial union with them' (Ibid., 52).

A similar group, the Association for the Reform of Judaism, was established in Berlin in 1844 under the leadership of Samuel Holdheim. This society produced a prayerbook in German containing little Hebrew and advocated the abolition of what they perceived as outmoded Jewish observances (such as praying with covered heads and blowing the *shofar*). In their declaration of the principles of this association, the Berlin group stated:

> We can no longer recognize a code as an unchangeable law-book which maintains with unbending insistence that Judaism's task is expressed by forms which originated in a time which is forever past and which will never return ... we are stirred by the trumpet sound of our own time. It calls us to be the last of a great inheritance in this old form, and at the same time, the first who, with unswerving courage are bound together as brothers in word and deed, shall lay the cornerstone of a new edifice. (Ibid., 57)

In order to establish a unified policy, the first Reform synod took place in Brunswick in 1844. At this meeting participants pressed for the formulation of a Jewish creed as well as modifications to the Sabbath, dietary laws and Jewish worship. This synod was followed by another conference the next year in Frankfurt which recommended that prayers for the return to Israel and the restoration of the Jewish state be omitted from the prayerbook. At this synod one of the more conservative delegates, Zacharias Frankel of Dresden, expressed his unhappiness with the decision of the synod to regard the use of Hebrew in worship as advisable rather than obligatory. As a result he resigned from the assembly, and later became head of a Jewish theological seminary in Breslau, an institution based on free enquiry combined with a commitment to the Jewish heritage. In 1846 a third synod took place in Breslau. Although the reformers there upheld the rabbinic prohibition against work on the Sabbath, they none the less stated that the talmudic injunctions regarding the boundary for working on the Sabbath were no longer in force. Further, they proclaimed that the second day observance of festivals should be eliminated.

The Revolution of 1848 and its aftermath curtailed the convocation of further Reform synods, and nearly a generation passed before reformers met again. In 1868 twenty-four rabbis led by Ludwig Phillipson and Abraham Geiger assembled in Kassel to lay the foundation for a synodal conference of rabbis, scholars and lay leaders. The next year over eighty congregations were represented when this body met Leipzig under the leadership of Moritz Lazarus. Two years later another conference took place in Augsburg, where the participants formulated a common statement of the principles and tasks of Reform Judaism. First, they declared

that in the past Judaism underwent different phases of development. Reform Judaism, they argued, marks a new and important
beginning. Though the essence and mission of Judaism remains the
same, many ceremonies need to be regenerated. To achieve this
end, the synod saw itself as a vehicle for change. Basing such reforming zeal on a quest for truth, the delegates stated that: 'the
synod intends to labour with clear purpose so that the reform of
Judaism for which we have striven for several decades should be
secured in the spirit of harmony.' (Cohn-Sherbok, 1994, 102)

In England the West London Synagogue was founded in the
1840s by members of the Spanish and Portuguese Synagogue and
the Great Synagogue who sought to adopt a Reform lifestyle. In a
sermon delivered at the opening of this synagogue, the Rev. D. W.
Marks explained his rejection of Orthodox Judaism:

We must (as our conviction urges us) solemnly deny, that a belief
in the divinity of the traditions contained in the *Mishnah* and the
Jerusalem and Babylonian *Talmuds* is of equal obligation to the
Israelite with the faith in the divinity of the Law of Moses. We
know that these books are human compositions, and though we
are content to accept with reverence from our post-biblical ancestors' advice and instruction, we cannot unconditionally accept
their laws. (Ibid., 103)

In subsequent years the Union of Liberal and Progressive
Synagogues was established as an even more liberal interpretation
of Judaism, and both movements were strengthened by the foundation of the Leo Baeck College in 1956 which trains rabbis for both
British and European Jewry.

THE DEVELOPMENT OF REFORM JUDAISM

After 1815 the Jewish population of North America had grown to a
sizeable number as immigrants from Europe sought refuge from
discrimination and persecution. The first signs of Reform appeared
in 1824 when a small Reform congregation was established in
Charleston, South Carolina. Like their German counterparts, these
progressive Jews sought to introduce changes to the traditional
liturgy. According to one of these early Reformers, Isaac Harby, the
aim of this group was to remove anything that might excite the

disgust of the well-informed Israelite. In the period preceding and following the Revolution of 1848, an increasing number of Jews emigrated to the United States: many of these immigrants settled in New York, and by 1842 there were three German congregations there. Three years later Congregation Emanuel was founded and introduced a number of important changes to the traditional worship service. Among these German newcomers were several Reform rabbis who had participated in the early European Reform synods.

Prominent among these early progressive rabbis were David Einhorn of Har Sinai congregation in Baltimore and Samuel Adler and Gustave Gottheil of Temple Emanuel in New York. However, it was not until Isaac Mayer Wise exercised his leadership and organizing skills that Reform Judaism became firmly established on American soil. After serving as a rabbi in Albany, New York, Wise moved to Cincinnati, Ohio, where he published a new Reform Prayerbook as well as several Jewish newspapers. It was Wise's aim to unite American Jewry to meet the challenges of modern life. After several abortive attempts at rabbinic union, the first meeting of the Central Conference of American Reform Rabbis met in 1869 in Philadelphia. This was followed in 1873 by the creation of the Union of American Hebrew Congregations. Two years later Wise founded the Hebrew Union College, the first Reform rabbinical seminary in the United States. Eventually the principles of American Reform Judaism were set out at a gathering of Reform leaders in 1885 in Pittsburgh. Under the chairmanship of Kaufmann Kohler, the Pittsburgh Platform set out the basic principles of the movement:

> First – We recognize in every religion an attempt to grasp the Infinite One and in every mode, source or book of revelation held sacred in any religious system the consciousness of the indwelling of God in man. We hold that Judaism presents the highest conception of the God-idea as taught in our holy Scriptures and developed and spiritualized by the Jewish teachers in accordance with the moral and philosophical progress of their respective ages. We maintain that Judaism preserved and defended amid continual struggles and trials and under enforced isolation this God-idea as the central religious truth for the human race.
>
> Second – We recognize in the Bible the record of the consecration of the Jewish people to its mission as priest of the One God, and value it as the most potent instrument of religious and moral

instruction. We hold that the modern discoveries of scientific researches in the domain of nature and history are not antagonistic to the doctrines of Judaism, the Bible reflecting the primitive ideas of its own age and at times clothing its conception of divine providence and justice dealing with men in miraculous narratives.

Third – We recognize in the Mosaic legislation a system of training the Jewish people for its mission during its national life in Palestine, and today we accept as binding only the moral laws and maintain only such ceremonies as elevate and sanctify our lives, but reject all such as are not adapted to the views and habits of modern civilization.

Fourth – We hold that all such Mosaic and rabbinical laws as regulate diet, priestly purity and dress originated in ages and under the influence of ideas altogether foreign to our present mental and spiritual state. They fail to impress the modern Jew with a spirit of priestly holiness; their observance in our days is apt rather to obstruct than to further modern spiritual elevation.

Fifth – We recognize in the modern era of universal culture of heart and intellect the approach of the realization of Israel's great messianic hope for the establishment of the kingdom of truth, justice and peace among all men. We consider ourselves no longer a nation but a religious community, and therefore expect neither a return to Palestine, nor a sacrificial worship under the administration of the sons of Aaron, nor the restoration of any of the laws concerning the Jewish state.

Sixth – We recognize in Judaism a progressive religion, ever striving to be in accord with the postulates of reason. We are convinced of the utmost necessity of preserving the historical identity with our great past. Christianity and Islam being daughter-religions of Judaism, we appreciate their mission to aid in the spreading of monotheistic and moral truth. We acknowledge that the spirit of broad humanity of our age is our ally in the fulfillment of our mission, and therefore we extend the hand of fellowship to all who co-operate with us in the establishment of the reign of truth and righteousness among men.

Seventh – We reassert the doctrine of Judaism, that the soul of men is immortal, grounding this belief on the divine nature of the human spirit, which forever finds bliss in righteousness and misery in wickedness. We reject as ideas rooted in Judaism the belief both in bodily resurrection and in *Gehenna* and *Eden* (hell and paradise), as abodes for everlasting punishment or reward.

Eighth – In full accordance with the spirit of Mosaic legislation which strives to regulate the relation between rich and poor, we deem it our duty to participate in the great task of modern times, to solve on the basis of justice and righteousness the problems presented by the contrasts and evils of the present organization of society.

This statement of religious beliefs, together with the rabbinical and congregational organizations of Reform Judaism founded in the late nineteenth century, provided a framework for the growth and development of Reform Judaism in the next century.

Fifty years after the Pittsburgh meeting of 1885, the Jewish world had undergone major changes: America was the centre of the diaspora; Zionism had become a vital force in Jewish life; Hitler was in power. The Columbus Platform of the Reform movement of 1937 reflected a new approach to Reform Judaism. Divided into three parts, the Platform begins by defining the essential elements of the Jewish faith.

1. *Nature of Judaism.* Judaism is the historical religious experience of the Jewish people. Though growing out of Jewish life, its message is universal, aiming at the union and perfection of mankind under the sovereignty of God. Reform Judaism recognizes the principle of progressive development in religion and consciously applies this principle to spiritual as well as to cultural and social life. Judaism welcomes all truth, whether written in the pages of Scripture or deciphered from the records of nature. The new discoveries of science, while replacing the older scientific views underlying our sacred literature, do not conflict with the essential spirit of religion as manifested in the consecration of man's will, heart and mind to the service of God and of humanity.

2. *God.* The heart of Judaism and its chief contribution to religion is the doctrine of the One, living God, who rules the world through law and love. In him all existence has its creative source and mankind its ideal of conduct. Though transcending time and space, he is the indwelling Presence of the world. We worship him as the Lord of the universe and as our merciful father.

3. *Man.* Judaism affirms that man is created in the divine image. His spirit is immortal. He is an active co-worker with God.

As a child of God, he is endowed with moral freedom and is charged with the responsibility of overcoming evil and striving after ideal ends.

4. *Torah.* God reveals himself not only in the majesty, beauty and orderliness of nature, but also in the vision and moral striving of the human spirit. Revelation is a continuous process, confined to no one group and to no one age. Yet the people of Israel, through its prophets and sages, achieved unique insight in the realm of religious truth. The *Torah*, both written and oral, enshrines Israel's ever-growing consciousness of God and of the moral law. It preserves the historical precedents, sanctions and norms of Jewish life, and seeks to mould it in the patterns of goodness and of holiness. Being products of historical processes, certain of its laws have lost their binding force with the passing of the conditions that called them forth. But as a depository of permanent spiritual ideals, the *Torah* remains the dynamic source of the life of Israel. Each age has the obligation to adapt the teachings of the *Torah* to its basic needs in consonance with the genius of Judaism.

5. *Israel.* Judaism is the soul of which Israel is the body. Living in all parts of the world, Israel has been held together by the ties of a common history, and above all, by the heritage of faith. Though we recognize in the group the loyalty of Jews who have become estranged from our religious tradition, a bond which still unites them with us, we maintain that it is by its religion and for its religion that the Jewish people have lived. The non-Jews who accept our faith are welcomed as full members of the Jewish community. In all lands where our people live, they assume and seek to share loyally the full duties and responsibilities of citizenship and to create seats of Jewish knowledge and religion. In the rehabilitation of Palestine, the land hallowed by memories and hopes, we behold the promise of renewed life for many of our brethren. We affirm the obligation of all Jewry to aid in its upbuilding as a Jewish homeland by endeavouring to make it not only a haven of refuge for the oppressed but also a centre of Jewish culture and spiritual life. Throughout the ages it has been Israel's mission to witness to the Divine in the face of every form of paganism and materialism. We regard it as our historic task to co-operate with all men in the establishment of

the kingdom of God, of universal brotherhood, justice, truth and peace on earth. This is our messianic goal.

6. *Ethics and Religion*. In Judaism religion and morality blend into an insoluble unity. Seeking God means to strive after holiness, righteousness and goodness. The love of God is incomplete without the love of one's fellow men. Judaism emphasizes the kinship of the human race, the sanctity and worth of human life and personality and the right of the individual to freedom and to the pursuit of his chosen vocation. Justice to all, irrespective of race, sect or class is the inalienable right and the inescapable obligation of all. The state and organized government exist in order to further these ends.

7. *Social Justice*. Judaism seeks the attainment of a just society by the application of its teachings to the economic order, to industry and commerce, and to national and international affairs. It aims at the elimination of man-made misery and suffering, of poverty and degradation, of tyranny and slavery, of social inequality and prejudice, of ill-will and strife. It advocates the promotion of harmonious relations between warring classes on the basis of equity and justice, and the creation of conditions under which human personality may flourish. It pleads for the safeguarding of childhood against exploitation. It champions the cause of all who work and of their right to an adequate standard of living, as prior to the rights of property. Judaism emphasizes the duty of charity, and strives for a social order which will protect men against the material disabilities of old age, sickness and unemployment.

8. *Peace*. Judaism, from the days of the prophets, has proclaimed to mankind the ideal of universal peace. The spiritual and physical disarmament of all nations has been one of its essential teachings. It abhors all violence and relies upon moral education, love and sympathy to secure human progress. It regards justice as the foundation of the wellbeing of nations and the conditions of enduring peace. It urges organized international action for disarmament, collective security and world peace.

9. *The Religious Life*. Jewish life is marked by consecration to these ideals of Judaism. It calls for faithful participation in the life of the Jewish community as it finds expression in home, synagogue and school, and in all other agencies that

enrich Jewish life and promote its welfare. The home has been, and must continue to be, a stronghold of Jewish life, hallowed by the spirit of love and reverence, by moral discipline and religious observance and worship. The synagogue is the oldest and most democratic institution in Jewish life. It is the prime communal agency by which Judaism is fostered and preserved. It links the Jews of each community and unites them with all Israel. The perpetuation of Judaism as a living force depends upon religious knowledge and upon the education of each new generation in our rich cultural and spiritual heritage. Prayer is the voice of religion, the language of faith and aspiration. It directs man's heart and mind Godward, voices the needs and hopes of the community, and reaches out to goals which invest life with supreme value. To deepen the spiritual life of our people, we must cultivate the traditional habit of communion with God through prayer in both home and synagogue. Judaism as a way of life requires in addition to its moral and spiritual demands, the preservation of the Sabbath, festivals and Holy Days, the retention and development of such customs, symbols and ceremonies as possess inspirational value, the cultivation of distinctive forms of religious art and music and the use of Hebrew, together with the vernacular, in our worship and instruction. These timeless aims and ideals of our faith we present anew to a confused and troubled world. We call upon our fellow Jews to rededicate themselves to them, and, in harmony with all men, hopefully and courageously to continue Israel's eternal quest after God and his kingdom.

REFORM JUDAISM IN THE MODERN WORLD

Prior to the Second World War, Reform Judaism had undergone a major transformation. In contrast with the Pittsburgh Platform, the Columbus Platform of 1937 embraced Zionist ideals, endorsed the use of Hebrew and encouraged the retention of observances that had previously been rejected by Reformers. After the Second World War Reform Judaism continued to develop. On the far right of the movement a number of rabbis advocated a personalist basis for religious faith. Thus Bernard Martin, Professor at Case Western Reserve University, stated that God 'is personal ... in the sense that he lives, acts, is conscious, and enters into personal relationships with man, addressing him and demanding his personal response'. Again, Emil Fackenheim, Professor of Philosophy at the University of Toronto, wrote: 'God surely resembles a human person far more closely than he does an impersonal force ... the most exalted picture we can make of God is a person.' In the view of Eugene Borowitz, Professor of Religious Thought at the Hebrew Union College, a personal God is whom we meet and confront: 'He hears us ... [He] is always ready for prayer.' Such personalist terminology was also employed by Jacob Petuchowski, Professor at the Hebrew Union College: 'Tradition does speak of God's will, and of God's concern. And to have a will, love and concern means that one is so constituted as to have them, and in our human language, that kind of constitution is called "personality"' (Raphael, 1984, 56–7).

Other more radical thinkers, however, conceived of God in a less personal way. Roland Gittelsohn, rabbi of Temple Israel in Boston, for example, emphasized that increasing numbers of Jews were unable to accept the traditional understanding of God's nature and activity. 'I do not conceive of God as a Person,' he wrote, 'but as a process of Power or Thrust within the universe ... [God] is the active spiritual seed of the universe – the Energy, the Power, the Force, the Direction, the Thrust ... in which the universe and mind find their meaning.' According to Gittelsohn, prayer is therefore not directed to a God who hears, but inwards to oneself. Thus he declared: 'It is a reminder of who I am, of what I can become, and of my proper relationship to the rest of the universe' (Raphael, 1984, 58). Other Reform thinkers offered a similar interpretation. Henry Smolinsky, Professor of Theology at the Jewish Institute of Religion, for example, denied God's perfection and unlimited power – in his view God combats evil and is dependent on human beings for help.

Although there has been a similar response to the traditional conception of the *Torah*, there has in recent years been an increased use of it in worship. *Bar* and *Bat Mitzvah* ceremonies, for example, have become commonplace in which boys and girls read from the *Torah* and recite the traditional *Torah* blessing ('Blessed art Thou, O Lord our God who has given us the *Torah*'). Even such radical thinkers as Roland Gittelsohn, who has produced naturalist liturgies, employed the following blessing in his Prayerbook: 'Praised be the Eternal our God, Ruling Spirit of the universe, who has chosen us from among all peoples to give us the *Torah*.' None the less, Reform rabbis in line with both the Pittsburgh and Columbus Platforms continue to reject the traditional doctrine of *Torah MiSinai*. Rather, they subscribe to a belief in progressive revelation. As Maurice Eisendrath, President of the Union of American Hebrew Congregations explained: 'God is a living God – not a God who revealed himself and his word once and for all times at Sinai and speaks no more' (Ibid., 59).

Paralleling this renewal of interest in the *Torah*, a number of Reform rabbis have also become preoccupied with *halakhah*. After the Second World War, Solomon Freehof, rabbi of Rodef Shalom in Pittsburgh, issued Reform responsa based on traditional sources. In several books he sought to uncover the legal background to current Reform Jewish practice – these collections of halakhic precedents have offered Reform rabbis and laity a basis for reconstructing ceremonies and observances within a Reform Jewish framework. In addition, David Polish and Frederick A. Doppelt produced in 1957 a guide which attempted to regulate Reform Jewish conduct; this was followed in 1972 by a code of Jewish observance for the Sabbath. This compendium contains specific recommendations for Reform Jewry: 'It is proper to prepare for *Shabbat* ... to light *Shabbat* candles ... to recite or chant the *kiddush* ... to maintain and enjoy the special quality of *Shabbat* throughout the afternoon ... [it is best not to] engage in gainful work on *Shabbat* ... perform housework on *Shabbat* ... shop on *Shabbat* ... participate in a social event during *Shabbat* ... [or engage in] public activity which violates [the *Shabbat*].' (Raphael, 1984). More recently a new association was founded to encourage the formulation of a Reform code of Jewish law.

Despite such a return to *halakhah* contemporary Reform Judaism has abandoned a number of important features of the tradition. In 1973, the Central Conference of American Rabbis (CCAR) discussed the issue of rabbinic participation in interfaith marriages; although a resolution against such participation was passed in 1909, a growing number of rabbis have recently participated in such ceremonies. After a heated debate a resolution was passed opposing such activity, yet many Reform rabbis continued to officiate at such marriage services. Of even greater consequence was the decision taken in 1983 by the CCAR expanding the determination of Jewishness to include patrilineal as well as matrilineal descent. By altering Jewish law in this way, the Reform movement defined as Jews individuals whom the other branches of Judaism regard as gentiles. This means that neither these persons nor their offspring can be accepted as Jews by the other branches of Judaism.

In recent years the Reform attitude toward Israel has also undergone a dramatic change. Following the Second World War, the State of Israel was endorsed by Reform Judaism despite its earlier reluctance to countenance the creation of a Jewish homeland. As a consequence, the study of Hebrew as well as Israeli culture has become a central element of the curriculum of Reform religion schools; in addition, the Sephardic pronunciation of Hebrew currently in use in Israel has been introduced into the liturgy. The Reform movement has also encouraged the growth of Reform Judaism in Israel: congregations were established in the Jewish state, and since 1970 Reform rabbinic students have been required to spend the first year of their training at the Jerusalem campus of the Hebrew Union College. For many Reform Jews Israel has been pivotal in their understanding of Jewish history and the survival of Judaism. Such attitudes are reflected in the writings of a number of Jewish thinkers such as Emil Fackenheim. In Fackenheim's view, diaspora living is no longer viable – Jews must make Israel their home. Today the *Oleh* (immigrant to Israel) has taken the place once occupied by *Torah* students: 'What the Jew by birth can do in our time is to recognize that just as one kind of Jew – the *Torah* student – set the unifying standard for all Jews, so this standard is set today by another kind – the *Oleh*.' Such an individual makes *aliyah* because of love: thus the Zionist enterprise serves as the paramount act of Jewish loyalty in a post-Holocaust world.

In recent years Reform synagogues have also undergone significant change, becoming increasingly democratic; in particular women have moved into positions of leadership, serving as presidents, members of the board of directors, and youth group leaders. Today the Reform synagogue serves as the centre of communal life and recreational, cultural and social activities have been added into its programme of religious worship. Simultaneously, Reform Jewish commitment has been strengthened by summer camps staffed by rabbis, rabbinic students and others. From the 1970s Reform Jewish Day Schools have also been created in many cities, providing students with a more intensive Jewish education. Alongside such activities, small groups of Reform Jews (*havurot*) have been formed outside the synagogue to meet, study and pray together in one another's homes.

The nature of the Reform liturgy has also undergone important modifications. In many synagogues cantors have replaced choirs, contemporary Israeli melodies have been introduced and rabbis have adopted a more informal preaching style. In the 1960s creative liturgies were used, and in the 1970s a new Reform prayerbook was introduced which altered the content as well as the format of worship. The *New Union Prayerbook* eliminated sexist language, included special services for Israel Independence Day, and adopted a positive attitude toward Israel. Unlike previous prayerbooks, this volume presents ten distinctly different Sabbath services reflecting a variety of religious standpoints. In this way the new Reform prayerbook gives expression to a diversity of religious positions ranging from traditionalist to non-theist.

Like the synagogue, the role of the rabbi has also undergone considerable change in the post-war years. During the period between the Pittsburgh and Columbus Platforms, a number of rabbis gained recognition as Jewish scholars. But by the 1960s and 1970s their place had been taken by academics in universities. Further, the male-dominated nature of the rabbinate had significantly altered since the first woman rabbi was ordained in 1972: by the 1980s more than seventy-five women had entered the rabbinate. In the 1960s and 1970s those entering the Reform rabbinate were more likely to have come from Reform backgrounds, and the majority of rabbinic students were married. Paradoxically many of those ordained were agnostic, an attitude which has caused considerable dilemmas for those pursuing the congregational rabbinate.

A CENTENARY PERSPECTIVE

In 1971 the Central Conference of American Rabbis sponsored a study of the nature of Reform Judaism. Published in 1971 *Rabbi and Synagogue in Reform Judaism* provides an overview of the state of Reform belief and practice in the latter half of the twentieth century. According to this survey, Jewish consciousness was identified by most Reform Jewish congregants in terms of living a moral life. Although Jewish identification was an important factor in the lives of most Reform Jews, many declared that they remained Jews 'because it is simply the most convenient thing to do'. Even the most traditional were not particularly observant. More had a family Thanksgiving dinner, for example, than observed the High Holy Days at home; almost as many exchanged Christmas gifts as attended Friday night services. In addition, 17 per cent stated that they believed in God 'in the more or less traditional sense of the term'; 49 per cent qualified their belief in terms of their own religious views; 8 per cent maintained that they were non-religious believers; 21 per cent said they were agnostics; and 4 per cent identified themselves as atheists. A religiosity index constructed on the basis of response patterns to 'belief in God' and 'being an ethical person' showed the following distribution: Reform congregants who are religious, 48 per cent; marginally religious, 24 per cent; non-religious, 28 per cent. Within the Reform rabbinate, 10 per cent stated that they believed in God 'in the more or less traditional Jewish sense'; 62 per cent believed in God 'in the more or less traditional sense' but qualified this conviction in terms of their own views of what God is and what he stands for; 14 per cent saw themselves as non-traditionalists; 13 per cent were agnostics; and 1 per cent atheists. In terms of belief in God as well as other aspects of religiosity, Reform rabbis were categorized as: traditionalists, 10 per cent; moderates, 62 per cent; and radicals, 28 per cent (Lenn, 1972).

In 1976 the Reform movement produced the San Francisco Platform; like the Pittsburgh and Columbus Platforms, this declaration seeks to provide a unifying framework which would bring a sense of order into the movement. Although it avoids taking a theological position, it affirms God's reality without defining what is meant by this expression. *Torah,* it explains, resulted from 'the relationship between God and the Jewish people' and Israel was viewed as an 'uncommon union of faith and peoplehood'. *Mitzvot* are interpreted as 'claims made upon us'. Although vague and equivocal, the San Francisco Platform none the less did provide a sense of unity despite the divisions within modern Reform Jewry.

The Platform itself commences with a statement explaining that the centenaries of the founding of the Union of American Hebrew Congregations and the Hebrew Union College – Jewish Institute of Religion offered an opportunity to depict the spiritual state of Reform Judaism. This is followed by an account of the evolution of Reform Judaism in North America, the lessons learned during this period, and the importance of diversity within the movement:

> Reform Judaism does more than tolerate diversity, it engenders it
> … We stand open to any position thoughtfully and conscientiously advocated in the spirit of Reform Jewish beliefs. While we may differ in our interpretations and applications of the ideas enunciated here, we accept such differences as precious and see

in them Judaism's best hope for confronting whatever the future holds for us.

Following this introduction, the text is divided into seven sections:

1. *God*. The affirmation of God has always been essential to our people's will to survive. In our struggle through the centuries to preserve our faith we have experienced and conceived of God in many ways. The trials of our own time and the challenges of modern culture have made steady belief and clear understanding difficult for some. Nevertheless, we ground our lives, personally and communally, on God's reality and remain open to new experiences and conceptions of the Divine. Amid the mystery we call life, we affirm that human beings, created in God's image, share in God's eternity despite the mystery we call death.

2. *The People Israel*. The Jewish people and Judaism defy precise definition because both are in the process of becoming Jews by birth or conversion and so constitute an uncommon union of faith and peoplehood. Born as Hebrews in the ancient Near East, we are bound together like all ethnic groups by language, land, history, culture and institutions. But the people of Israel are unique because of its involvement with God and its resulting perception of the human condition. Throughout our long history our people has been inseparable from its religion with its messianic hope that humanity will be redeemed.

3. *Torah*. *Torah* results from the relationship between God and the Jewish people. The records of our earliest confrontations are uniquely important to us. Lawgivers and prophets, historians and poets gave us a heritage where study is a religious imperative and whose practice is our chief means to holiness. Rabbis and teachers, philosophers and mystics, gifted Jews in every age amplified the *Torah* tradition. For millennia, the creation of *Torah* has not ceased and Jewish creativity in our time is adding to the chain of tradition.

4. *Our Obligations: Religious Practice*. Judaism emphasizes action rather than creed as the primary expression of a religious life, the means by which we strive to achieve universal justice and peace. Reform Judaism shares this emphasis on duty and obligation. Our founders stressed that the Jews' ethical

responsibilities, personal and social, are enjoined by God. The past century has taught us that the claims made upon us may begin with our ethical obligations but they extend to many other aspects of Jewish living, including: creating a Jewish home centred on family devotion; life-long study; private prayer and public worship; daily religious observance; keeping the Sabbath and holy days; celebrating the major events of life; involvement with the synagogue and community; and other activities which promote the survival of the Jewish people and enhance its existence. Within each area of Jewish observance, Reform Jews are called upon to confront the claims of Jewish tradition, however differently perceived, and to exercise their individual autonomy, choosing and creating on the bases of commitment and knowledge.

5. *Our Obligations: The State of Israel and the Diaspora.* We are privileged to live in an extraordinary time, one in which a third Jewish commonwealth has been established in our people's ancient homeland. We are bound to that land and to the newly reborn State of Israel by innumerable religious and ethnic ties. We have been enriched by its culture and ennobled by its indomitable spirit. We see it providing unique opportunities for Jewish self-expression. We have both a stake and a responsibility in building the State of Israel, assuring its security and defining its Jewish character. We encourage *aliyah* for those who wish to find maximum personal fulfilment in the cause of Zion. We demand that Reform Judaism be unconditionally legitimized in the State of Israel. At the same time we consider the State of Israel vital to the welfare of Judaism everywhere, we reaffirm the mandate of our tradition to create strong Jewish communities wherever we live. A genuine Jewish life is possible in any land, each community developing its own particular character and determining its Jewish responsibilities. The foundation of Jewish community life is the synagogue. It leads us beyond itself to co-operate with other Jews, to share their concerns, and to assume leadership in communal affairs. We are, therefore, committed to the full democratization of the Jewish community and to its hallowing in terms of Jewish values.

The State of Israel and the diaspora, in fruitful dialogue, can show how a people transcends nationalism even as it affirms it, thereby setting an example for humanity which remains largely concerned with dangerously parochial goals.

6. *Our Obligations: Survival and Service.* Early Reform Jews, newly admitted to general society and seeing in this the evidence of a growing universalism, regularly spoke of Jewish purpose in terms of Jewry's service to humanity. In recent years we have become freshly conscious of the virtues of pluralism and the values of particularism. The Jewish people in its unique way of life validates its own worthwhile working toward the fulfilment of its messianic expectations.

Until the recent past, our obligations to the Jewish people and to all humanity seemed congruent. At times now these two imperatives appear to conflict. We know of no simple way to resolve such tensions. We must, however, confront them without abandoning either of our commitments. A universal concern for humanity unaccompanied by a devotion to our particular people is self-destructive: a passion for our people without involvement in humankind contradicts what the prophets have meant to us. Judaism calls us simultaneously to universal and particular obligations.

7. *Hope: Our Jewish Obligations.* Previous generations of Reform Jews had unbounded confidence in humanity's potential for good. We have lived through terrible tragedy and been compelled to reappropriate our tradition's realism about the human capacity for evil. Yet our people have always refused to despair. The survivors of the Holocaust, on being granted life, seized it, nurtured it, and, rising above catastrophe, showed humankind that the human spirit is indomitable. The State of Israel, established and maintained by the Jewish will to live, demonstrates what a united people can accomplish in history. The existence of the Jew is an argument against despair; Jewish survival is warrant for human hope. We remain God's witness that history is not meaningless. We affirm that with God's help, people are not powerless to affect their destiny. We dedicate ourselves, as did the generations of Jews who went before us, to work and wait for that day when 'They shall not hurt or destroy in all my holy mountain for the earth shall be full of the knowledge of the Lord as the waters cover the sea'.

CRITIQUE

Reform Judaism seeks to provide a modernized and relevant form of Judaism for the modern age. But is such a liberal interpretation of the Jewish faith truly viable for the twenty-first century? The central difficulty with Reform Judaism is its lack of uniformity and consistency. As we have seen, regarding religious belief Reform rabbis and congregants have held – and continue to hold – widely divergent views about the nature of the Divine. The Lenn Report of 1972, for example, reveals that the range of religious opinion within the movement varied from traditionalist to atheistic: hence there is no common ground within contemporary American Reform Judaism about the central tenets of the faith. Subsequent to this sociological study, I designed a similar questionnaire concerning Jewish belief which I distributed to Reform and Liberal rabbis in the United Kingdom. Assuming that the responses to this questionnaire reflect the attitudes of Reform Judaism generally, it is obvious that there continues to be no general consensus about religious doctrine within the movement.

Regarding belief in God, progressive rabbis were asked their view about the claim: 'There is such a being in reality to which the traditional notion of God corresponds.' In response, the majority of rabbis agreed (85 per cent), 6 per cent were uncertain, and 9 per cent disagreed. Similarly, nearly all rabbis (94 per cent) agreed with the view: 'God is the ultimate source of good', and 97 per cent believed that 'the biblical prophets were inspired by God'. However there was no such uniformity about belief in God's activity: 73 per cent concurred that 'God has revealed himself on Mt. Sinai', where 15 per cent were uncertain, and 12 per cent disagreed. Again, there was no common accord about the occurrence of miracles: 15 per cent agreed, 35 per cent were uncertain, and 50 per cent disagreed with the statement that: 'Divine miracles which can be defined as violations of the laws of nature have occurred as a matter of historical fact.' Finally, there was a lack of uniformity of belief that 'God is concerned with the affairs of each person': 60 per cent agreed, 20 per cent were uncertain, and 20 per cent disagreed.

Turning to the Afterlife, 68 per cent agreed, 26 per cent were uncertain, and 6 per cent disagreed that 'there is life after death'. Though no rabbis believed that 'in the Afterlife people will have bodies', 33 per cent were uncertain, and 67 per cent disagreed. Similarly no rabbi disagreed with the assertion that 'after death the soul lives on apart from the body'. But here too there was a lack of unanimity: 72 per cent agreed as against 28 per cent who were uncertain. Only 7 per cent maintained that 'in the Afterlife we will recognize those whom we have known in our present lives', yet 61 per cent were uncertain, and 33 per cent disagreed. 'Belief in a personal Messiah who will arise at some time in the future to bring about the Messianic Age' also gave rise to a wide range of opinion. 24 per cent agreed, 30 per cent were uncertain, and 46 per cent disagreed. Finally, concerning the belief that 'one is either rewarded or punished in the Afterlife', 12 per cent agreed, 46 per cent were uncertain, and 42 per cent disagreed (Cohn-Sherbok, 1991, 66–7).

As in the area of Jewish theology, there is a parallel divergence of views within Reform Judaism regarding Jewish law. Although Reformers have been anxious to provide a basis for Jewish living in contemporary society, they are unable to reach any agreement about the principles for selecting those aspects of the tradition which are spiritually significant for modern Jewry. One common suggestion – enshrined in the various platforms propounded by the movement – is that Jews should seek to ascertain what God's will is. In this way they would be able to establish an ultimate authority for their adherence to Jewish law. But what has God revealed? As we have seen, most Reform Jews maintain that the Hebrew Scriptures contain God's revelation – but where is it to be found? In the past there has been an attempt within the movement to distinguish between ritual and moral law. But is this distinction valid as far as God's will is concerned? These are unanswerable questions since there is simply no basis within Reform Judaism for knowing what God's intention is. Since the inception of Reform Judaism, some rabbis have stated categorically that they have an apprehension of God's disclosure to his chosen people, but an examination of the fundamental diversity of opinion among Reform Jews illustrates that such claims are nothing more than subjective beliefs based on personal disposition and judgement.

What can be said about the claims of personal conscience? At synods and in numerous publications Reform rabbis have asserted that conscience can serve as a reliable guide for formulating a modern system of Jewish law. Yet this criterion is beset with difficulties. No doubt many Reform Jews do follow their consciences when making decisions, but how can one ascertain if their views are in fact morally correct? The dictates of one person's conscience often differ from someone else's: when there is a direct conflict, there is simply no way to determine whose conscience is on the right track. And if in adjudicating between competing positions an external standard is employed, conscience then ceases to function as the final arbiter for moral action.

What about the concept of relevance? This is a principle often advanced by Reform rabbis for establishing a contemporary code of Jewish law, but it too is problematic. It is obvious that what one individual considers relevant may not be seen in the same way by someone else. Similarly, the notion of contemporary appeal is equally ambiguous. How can one decide what is of true worth when change is so constant? The same applies to such a standard of selection as moral sensitivity which has been recommended. From daily experience it is clear that what is morally offensive to one person can be totally acceptable to another. Nor does aesthetic sensitivity provide a solution. Some laws, like ritual immersion, might commend themselves on such grounds. Indeed there is a growing number of Reform Jews who maintain that such symbolism is highly important for those converting to Judaism. Other rabbis, however, believe that ritual immersion is aesthetically offensive because it involves the personal indignity of the convert who must be interrogated naked. This example illustrates the inevitable subjectivity of such principles of selection.

Some Reform rabbis have suggested that psychological considerations should be taken into account when formulating a modern Code of Jewish Law. On this basis certain laws should be eliminated because of a modern understanding of human psychology. For example, it could be argued that homosexuality, which is forbidden in the Bible, should be tolerated today because of a more enlightened understanding of human sexuality. However, in a well-known decision, the most prominent Reform halakhist, Rabbi Solomon Freehof, declared in *Contemporary Reform Responsa*:

> Homosexuality runs counter to the sancta of Jewish life. There is no sidetracking the fact that from the point of view of Judaism, those who practice homosexuality are to be deemed sinners. (Freehof, 1974, 24)

Here, too, we can see that subjective judgement is unavoidable in applying such nebulous concepts.

What then about common sense? In the past a number of Reform rabbis maintained that it is vitally important to consider whether Jewish law legislates beyond such limits. For example, various reformers stated that Sabbath laws transcend the boundary of common sense. However, there are other Reform thinkers who advocate a strict observance of Sabbath law. It is common sense, they contend, for Jews to differentiate themselves from non-Jews in precisely this fashion in order to perpetuate Judaism as a religious civilization. In this regard, it is equally hopeless appealing to the notion of reasonableness as a criterion for the selection of Jewish law. How could Jewish ritual and practice be regarded as reasonable? Jewish observances may be desirable on other grounds – but not because they are inherently reasonable.

Another standard of selection is what has been deemed by various rabbis as 'the good of the community'. Here what is important is the significance of traditional law for Progressive Jewry. Yet, who can say what is good for the Reform Jewish community as a whole? A disagreement among English Reform Jews some time ago illustrates this point. Rabbi Dow Marmur argued the case for ritual immersion for converts, however he stressed that the decision of the Reform Synagogues of Great Britain was not welcomed by many English Reform Jews (Marmur, 1978, 7). Due to a failure of communication, he wrote:

> the decision of the Reform rabbinate was badly received in the movement. So far most of the arguments among the laymen have been primarily about the rabbis' right to decide, and not about the intrinsic merits of the decision made. (Ibid., 36–7)

Such a conflict between rabbis and laity demonstrates the difficulties of establishing law for the community as a whole – such a lack of agreement about what is best for Reform Jews exemplifies the perplexity of deciding which aspects of Jewish law are applicable to the movement.

Finally, it has been suggested by some rabbinic authorities that traditional laws should be retained out of a commitment to the wider Jewish community. On this ground Marmur defended the implementation of circumcision and ritual immersion for converts as well as a bill of divorce by Reform rabbinical courts to divorcees. This concern for the community, he stated:

> is not a matter of expediency but a religious principle ... [We] are, therefore prepared to act to further the unity of the Jewish people, out of a sense of responsibility and concern ... Out of our concern for the Jewish people of Israel we are able to provide an acceptable forum, which, at some future time, may really become the authentic rabbinical court of Anglo-Jewry. (Ibid., 43–4)

Yet, given this commitment to the unity of the Jewish people, where is one to draw the line? If ritual immersion, circumcision and Jewish divorce are obligatory, what about the other laws contained in the *Code of Jewish Law*. Regrettably, Marmur did not provide any explanation how to decide which traditional laws need to be retained for the community's sake.

What can be seen, therefore, is that there appears to be no way to determine what the central beliefs of Reform Judaism are, or what traditional law ought to be included in a modern Reform system of law. All that can be said is that although Reform Jews are heirs to a vast religious system, they do not possess any well-defined, coherent and consistent method for sorting out which elements of the Jewish heritage should be retained and which discarded, despite the numerous pronouncements of various rabbinic authorities. This is not a temporary difficulty which can be resolved in the future – it is rather an inevitable consequence of the rejection of the divine authority of the tradition.

5

Conservative Judaism

Conservative Judaism emerged from the ranks of the Reform movement as a reaction against its radical tendencies. In 1845 Zacharias Frankel broke ranks with other Reformers, and subsequently became the head of the Jewish Theological Seminary in Breslau. In the United States a number of like-minded adherents of the positive-historical approach to Judaism established the Jewish Theological Seminary in New York which was later headed by the Cambridge scholar Solomon Schechter. As Conservative Judaism expanded in the 1920s and 1930s, a degree of uniformity was instituted within the movement, yet there was a general reluctance on the part of most thinkers to enunciate a comprehensive philosophy of the movement. In consequence, there is considerable uncertainty within Conservative Judaism about religious principles as well as observances: as in Reform Judaism, Conservative thinkers have advanced a wide variety of interpretations of the central teachings of the faith. Similarly there is considerable variance with regard to Jewish practice. Such a lack of coherence constitutes Conservative Judaism's central weakness – despite its promotion of traditional values, Conservatism is deeply divided over the central features of the Jewish heritage.

THE RISE OF CONSERVATIVE JUDAISM

The founder of what came to be known as Conservative Judaism was Zacharias Frankel. Born in Prague, he was ordained and received a doctorate in Classical Philology at the University of Pesth in 1831. Subsequently he held rabbinic positions in Teplitz, Bohemia and Dresden, before becoming president of the Jewish Theological Seminary in Breslau. An advocate of moderate reform, he was committed to a historically evolving dynamic Judaism. The aim of such an approach (positive historical Judaism), he believed, would be to uncover the origins of the Jewish people's national spirit and the collective will. Both the past as enshrined in tradition and the present as embodied in the religious consciousness of the people should determine the nature of Jewish life.

In 1845 Frankel left the Reform rabbinical conference in Frankfurt because a majority of the participants had voted that there was no need to use Hebrew in the Jewish worship service. At this synod one of the Reform leaders, Abraham Geiger, maintained that since Hebrew was simply a national element in the service which Reform Judaism sought to replace with universal symbols, it could be eliminated. In response, Frankel stated that Hebrew is a vital historical feature of the Jewish heritage – it is the sacred tongue in which Jews have expressed their beliefs and ideals through the centuries. Following the conference, Frankel wrote a letter to a Frankfurt newspaper, stressing his commitment to positive historical Judaism. Although he agreed with other reformers that Judaism needed to be revised, he disagreed with them over the legitimate criteria for religious change. None the less, he broke with Orthodoxy in asserting that the Oral law was rabbinic in origin, that the *halakhah* had evolved over time, and that the source of religious observance was not divine.

In 1854 Frankel became the head of the Jewish Theological Seminary in Breslau which eventually became the most important rabbinical college in Europe. Frankel insisted that the seminary was not to be identified with the Reform movement, yet neither was it to be Orthodox in orientation. Committed to free inquiry, Frankel rejected Samson Raphael Hirsch's request that the Seminary endorse the traditional doctrine of *Torah MiSinai*; instead he stressed the importance of historical research into the origins of rabbinical teachings. Although Hirsch denounced the Seminary as heretical, it attracted numerous students who subsequently served as rabbis and scholars throughout Germany.

In the first year of its existence, Frankel appointed Heinrich Graetz to the faculty. Born in the eastern part of Prussia, Graetz studied in a *yeshiva* under a rabbi opposed to secular learning; however, on his own he studied Latin and French and read history and modern literature. Initially, Graetz wrote to Hirsch to express admiration for his *Nineteen Letters on Judaism*. In response Hirsch invited Graetz to be his student and assistant. In 1840 Graetz returned home where he took a position as a tutor; two years later he was admitted to the University of Breslau where he obtained a doctorate. For several years he taught in various Jewish schools, publishing essays on Jewish history until he was appointed to the Jewish Theological Seminary.

Graetz's conception of Judaism was first formulated in an essay. 'The Construction of Jewish History', written in 1846. Here his aim was to illustrate that the essence of Judaism does not reside in an abstract idea, but in the concrete manifestations of the Jewish faith. Like Hirsch, Graetz believed that all aspects of Judaism should be perceived as the unfolding of a religious system. In his view, this was not simply a logical process, but a historical development that emerged over time as Jews coped with challenges posed by social, economic and cultural conditions in which they lived. Such a construction of Jewish history endeavoured to demonstrate how both the laws and the beliefs of Judaism manifest themselves in history. According to Graetz, the Jewish tradition can be divided into three stages. The first period began with the conquest of the land and ended with the destruction of the first Temple in 586 BCE. The second stage took place after the Babylonian exile and lasted until the destruction of the second Temple in CE 70. During this cycle of history the struggle against Greek paganism culminated in the emergence of the Pharisees who introduced doctrines concerning the afterlife into Jewish thought. For Graetz the third stage was the diaspora in which Jews attempted to attain intellectual self-perfection and rationalize their religious faith. This scheme of Jewish history was elaborated in his *History of the Jews* published between 1854 and 1876.

In the United States a similar approach to the tradition was adopted by a number of leading figures. The German-born *hazzan* of Mikveh Israel, Issac Lesser, for example, pioneered the introduction of the sermon in English and advocated liturgical change. Although a staunch traditionalist in other respects, he co-operated with Isaac Mayer Wise in attempting to organize rabbinic and congregational union. Although such efforts were unsuccessful, he did succeed in creating a rabbinical school, Maimonides College in 1867. Even though it ceased to function in 1873, it graduated four men trained for the American rabbinate. Benjamin Szold, another moderate reformer, came to Baltimore where he founded the first Conservative group in the United States. Two other scholars, Marcus Jastrow and Alexander Kohut, also advocated change to the Orthodox worship service. When the Reform rabbinate published the Pittsburgh Platform in 1885, Kohut took issue with Kaufmann Kohler (the principal author of this document) and together with another conservative reformer of this period, Sabato Morais, encouraged the creation of a rabbinical school dedicated to the knowledge and practice of historical Judaism. In 1887 this institution was founded by Morais, Mendes and Kohut, as well as a number of prominent laymen. In its Articles of Incorporation the Jewish Theological Seminary of America declared its dedication to 'the preservation in America of the knowledge and practice of historical Judaism as ordained in the law of Moses expounded by the prophets and sages in Israel in biblical and talmudic writings'.

In 1902 the Cambridge scholar Solomon Schechter became president of the Seminary; his Romanian background, traditional Jewish education and strict adherence to Jewish law made him an ideal head of this new institution. According to Schechter, 'the observance of the Sabbath, the keeping of the dietary laws, the laying of *tefillin*, the devotion to Hebrew literature, and the hope for Zion in Jerusalem are all things as absolutely necessary for maintaining Judaism in America as elsewhere' (Raphael, 1984, 88).

It was Schechter's desire to combine Jewish traditionalism with a commitment to the scientific study of Judaism so as to build 'a school of Jewish learning, which should embrace all the departments of Jewish thought … which alone deserve the name of research' (Schechter, 1959, 232). Yet despite his adherence to traditional practices, the Union of Orthodox Rabbis issued a writ of excommunication against the Seminary in 1904. In response, Schechter began to delineate the nature of what came to be regarded as Conservative Judaism. In a letter written in 1907 he stated what he believed to be the task of this movement: 'Conservative Judaism can only be saved in this country by giving to the world trained men on scientific lines, and proving to the world that *Wissenschaft* and history are on our side' (Raphael, 1984, 89). Several years later, he emphasized that Conservative Judaism should combine elements of both traditional and non-traditional Judaism: 'Conservative Judaism unites what is desirable in modern life with the previous heritage of our faith … that has come down to us from ancient times' (Raphael, 1984, 89).

Disdainfully, Schechter rejected both Reform ('Lord forgive them, for they know nothing'), and Orthodoxy ('A return to Mosaism would be illegal, pernicious and indeed impossible.') Instead Schechter emphasized the importance of traditional rituals, customs and observances, as well as belief, while simultaneously stressing the need for a historical perspective. In contrast with the Orthodox,

Schechter admired modern scientific biblical scholarship. In line with contemporary biblical criticism, he maintained that the Pentateuch was not of divine origin – what is required, he stated, is the continual reinterpretation of the tradition. 'The *Torah*', he wrote, 'is not in heaven; its interpretation is left to the conscience of Catholic Israel' (Raphael, 1984, 90). As a champion of such an evolutionary understanding of Jewish civilization, he pressed for the establishment of a union of congregations sympathetic to Conservatism. In February 1913, a union of 22 congregations was founded, committed to maintaining the Jewish tradition in its historical continuity. In the preamble to its constitution the United Synagogue stated its intention to separate from Reform Judaism – it was committed to a heterogenous, traditional mode of belief and practice through the observance of ritual in the home and the synagogue.

The distinctiveness of this new movement was reflected in Schechter's rejection of a European form of tradition; rather he insisted that Conservative Jews should be thoroughly American in habits of life and mode of thinking and imbued with the best culture of the day. In this light, Conservative Jewry was obliged to demonstrate to east European immigrants that secular education and the traditional mode of Jewish life are fully compatible. To accomplish this goal, ordinands were trained in scientific research at the Jewish Theological Seminary, encouraged to preach in English rather than Yiddish, and urged to publish modern textbooks about Judaism. Convinced that the survival of the tradition depended on fostering such an approach, the congregations that joined this new movement endorsed the fusion of ancient practice and modern life. Typical among these congregations was Birmingham's K'nesseth Israel that consisted of 'gentlemen whose devotion to Judaism has never permitted them to diverge from its most Orthodox aspects'; Chicago's Anshe Emeth where there prevailed a 'mode of worship that would reflect somewhat the modern tendencies and still retain the essential features of the old Orthodoxy'; and St. Paul's Temple of Aaron in which 'Conservatism was absolutely necessary to promote modern American Judaism (and where) the old traditional form of the Jewish ritual should be followed, omitting such portions of it that would not interest the younger folks and the coming generation' (Ibid., 92).

As Conservative Judaism expanded in the 1920s and 1930s, a degree of uniformity emerged in congregational worship: services normally commenced late Friday evening and early Saturday morning; men were required to wear head coverings; prayer shawls were obligatory on Sabbath morning; rabbis conducted the service and preached sermons in English; prayerbooks other than the Union Prayer Book of the Reform movement were used; many congregants joined the rabbi for afternoon study. Further, many synagogues had organs, mixed choirs and family pews, as well as *minyans* that met three times a day for prayer. Others had a junior congregation where younger members elected their own officers and board of trustees as well as conducted their own High Holy Day and Sabbath services.

Such departures from traditional Judaism frequently caused dissension; occasionally those of a more Orthodox inclination attempted to restore Orthodox practices to communal life. Such diversity of practice caused some leaders of the movement to seek a clearer definition of the nature and task of Conservative Judaism. Thus, in 1919 a group of six rabbis and professors from the Jewish Theological Seminary urged their colleagues to formulate a statement of principles. Opposed to such an action, a prominent professor of the Jewish Theological Seminary, Louis Ginzberg, refused to allow these men to meet at the Seminary. In the 1940s the Conservative thinker, Robert Gordis bemoaned that 'many of our most distinguished scholars and thinkers have declined to formulate a specific programme' or to 'enunciate the philosophy of Conservative Judaism' (Raphael, 1984, 95). Similarly, Moris Adler, rabbi of Sharre Zedek in Detroit, deplored the fact that: 'our members sense that they are not Orthodox, they are not moved by Reform, but they have yet to learn that they are Conservative'. (Adler, 1964, 25)

In the 1970s, Hillel Silverman, rabbi of Sinai Temple in Los Angeles, characterized Conservative Judaism as 'a "catch-all" for the dissatisfied, a conglomeration of many needs, pluralistic in approach to the extreme, boasting a left, a centre, and a right a tepid Orthodoxy at the same time a timid reform'. In his view, Conservative Judaism *'is nisht a hin and nisht a her'*, a synthesis that avoids extremes and yet stands for little that is novel and authentic (Raphael, 1984, 95). Later in the 1970s, Benjamin Z. Kreitman of Brooklyn's Sharre Torah in Brooklyn, pleaded for a clarification of Conservative principles, and David Lieber, President of the University of Judaism, urged the Conservative movement to formulate a definition of Conservatism which was intelligible and unambiguous, a clear and persuasive definition. Yet despite these appeals, Conservative Judaism never produced an official statement of its cardinal tenets like the Pittsburgh, Columbus and San Francisco Platforms issued by the Reform movement. As a result, Conservative Judaism has remained ambiguous in character.

None the less, the Conservative movement endorsed a general policy regarding the tradition. From its beginnings in the nineteenth century, Conservatism emphasized that east European immigrants should adjust to the social, economic and cultural conditions of America while preserving their Jewish identity. For this reason, Conservative Jews were anxious to conserve the essential customs, beliefs, traditions and rituals of the faith. As Max Arzt of Temple Israel in Scranton and later Vice-Chancellor of the Jewish Theological Seminary explained: 'We are anxious to conserve those tangible and visible and time-honoured elements of Jewish life which make for continuity with our past and which have intrinsic value and content.' (Arzt, 1955, 63)

In advocating this approach, Conservative Jews viewed the Jewish faith as an evolving organism that remained spiritually vibrant by adjusting to environmental and cultural conditions. In consequence, Conservative Jewish thinkers strove to preserve those elements of the tradition which they believed to be spiritually meaningful while simultaneously setting aside those observances which actually hindered the continued development of Judaism. Such obsolete practices were not abrogated, but simply ignored. In a similar spirit, Conservative Jews in contrast with the Orthodox felt no compulsion to accept theological doctrines which they believed were outmoded – hence Conservative Judaism distanced itself from Orthodoxy concerning the belief that the *Torah* was disclosed to Moses on Mount Sinai. In its quest to provide a modernized interpretation of the faith, Conservative scholars attempted to create an authoritative body whose purpose was to adapt Judaism to contemporary society; as early as 1918 it was felt desirable to establish 'a body of men learned in the law who will be able to advise us concerning the great questions that arise in our present day religious life.' (Raphael, 1984, 97). Hence, even though the Conservative movement was unwilling to formulate a coherent platform or series of creedal statements, these features of Conservative Judaism provided a coherent and imaginative approach to the Jewish heritage.

THE INSTITUTIONS OF CONSERVATIVE JUDAISM

The Conservative movement is composed of three major institutional structures. The first consists of the Jewish Theological Seminary of America. Founded in New York in 1886, it was reorganized and recharted in 1920. The New York Seminary sponsors the following:

1.　The Seminary College of Jewish Studies offers undergraduate programmes in a variety of areas including Bible, Jewish literature, Jewish history, philosophy, rabbinic literature and Jewish education. A joint programme with Columbia University enables candidates to earn two bachelor's degrees – one at Columbia and one at the Seminary in virtually any subject. In addition, the Seminary faculty also provides support for educational and religious supervision at Camp Ramah and offers a Leaders Training Fellowship for high school students enrolled in a formal programme of Jewish studies.
2.　The Seminary College of Jewish Music provides undergraduate programmes in Jewish music for men and women in coordination with the Cantors Institute.
3.　The Rabbinic Department is designed for rabbinic candidates; it offers a graduate programme in both academic and professional courses leading to ordination.
4.　The Graduate School offers MA, DHL and PhD programmes in a wide variety of subject areas within the fields of Jewish studies and Jewish education.
5.　Summer programmes for both undergraduate and graduate courses are held for students of other universities and seminaries who seek to broaden their understanding of Judaica and Jewish education.
6.　The high school department of the Seminary is designed for younger students with evening and Sunday classes at the Seminary and at five branches in the Greater New York area.

On the West Coast of the United States, the University of Judaism in Los Angeles under the aegis of the Jewish Theological Seminary offers a parallel series of programmes:

1.　The University College of Jewish Studies provides an undergraduate curriculum in a variety of Jewish subjects including

Bible, contemporary Jewish life, Hebrew literature, Jewish history, philosophy, rabbinic literature, and Jewish education. Through a joint programme with UCLA, students are able to earn two BA degrees majoring in virtually any subject area.

2. The Graduate School of Judaica sponsors courses for the first two years of rabbinical school; in addition, candidates are able to follow MA programmes in specific areas of Jewish studies as well as doctoral programmes in conjunction with the Seminary.

3. The Adult College of Jewish Studies is an undergraduate programme leading to the AA or BA degree focusing on Jewish history, thought and literature.

4. Summer programmes at both undergraduate and graduate level are held for students of the University of Judaism and other universities who wish to supplement their studies.

5. The Department of Continuing Education offers courses at the University and on an extension basis at many Conservative synagogues in the Los Angeles area. Further, the Earl Warren Institute of Ethics and Human Relations sponsors seminars for business men and women.

6. Camp Ramah in California is affiliated with the National Ramah Commission under the educational and religious supervision of the University.

7. The Centre for Arts in Jewish life sponsors classes, exhibits and performances in Jewish theatre, dance, art and music.

8. The Centre for Contemporary Jewish life concentrates on research, conferences, publications and classes on modern Judaism.

In Israel, the Seminary supports the American Student Centre at Neve Schechter. Based in Jerusalem, this Centre provides a one-year academic programme for Seminary students on various levels. In addition, the Schocken Institute for Jewish Research at the Schocken Library in Jerusalem holds exhibitions and public lectures and sponsors publications and research institutes in medieval Hebrew poetry and Jewish mysticism.

In addition to these institutions and programmes located in the United States and Israel, the Seminary oversees a number of other miscellaneous activities:

1. The National Ramah Commission supervises six overnight camps in Wisconsin, Pennsylvania, Massachusetts, California,

New York and Ontario which stress Hebrew and Jewish living. Further the Seminary supervises Ramah programmes in Israel for the summer and the spring semester after high school graduation, a Camp Leadership Programme for counsellors and specialists, and a *Tikvah* programme for teenagers with learning disabilities.

2. Under the Seminary's auspices, the Jewish Museum of New York houses the most comprehensive collection of Jewish ceremonial art and artefacts in the world and offers courses on Jewish art, workshops in Jewish arts and crafts, as well as films, lectures, concerts and children's programmes.

3. The Institute for Religious and Social Studies is a scholarly fellowship of clergy, theologians and teachers of all religions; it holds a variety of lectures, conferences and seminars.

4. The Melton Research Centre is the Seminary's centre for research in education. It produces texts on Judaica and trains teachers and principals.

5. The Bernstein Centre and the Brand Foundation are the Seminary's two counselling centres, providing short-term counselling, referral and assistance to rabbis and rabbinic students.

6. The Universal Brotherhood Programme of the Seminary encourages leaders to discuss current moral and social issues.

The second major institutional structure is the Rabbinical Assembly, an international association of Conservative rabbis with over 1100 members. Founded in 1901 as an alumni association of the Seminary, its revised constitution of 1962 states its major aims:

> To promote Conservative Judaism; to cooperate with the Jewish Theological Seminary of America and with The United Synagogue of America; to advance the cause of Jewish learning; to promote the welfare of its members; and to foster the spirit of fellowship and cooperation among the rabbis and other Jewish scholars.

In addition to promoting the educational, social and professional welfare of its members, the Rabbinical Assembly engages in four major spheres of activity:

1. Subsidizing Conservative institutions and publications in Israel.

2. Working to protect Jewish interests in political and social issues.
3. Publishing books and other materials including the journal *Conservative Judaism*.
4. Making decisions on contemporary issues in Jewish law through its Committee on Jewish Law and Standards.

The third major institutional structure of Conservative Judaism is the United Synagogue of America. Founded in 1913 by Solomon Schechter, it serves as the organization of Conservative synagogues in the United States and Canada. Having established the Seminary as a first rank scholarly institution, Schechter was anxious that all synagogues devoted to the cause of the conservation of Judaism should unite in common cause. Today the United Synagogue has a membership of over 800 congregations, and its work extends to the fields of Jewish education, youth affairs, congregational standards, social action and Israel affairs. Such affinity is accomplished through the publication of the *United Synagogue Review*, its network of regional branches and its international office. The United Synagogues support numerous bodies as institutions:

1. The professional organizations of the Conservative movement include the Cantors Assembly, the Educators Assembly, the Jewish Youth Directors Association, and the National Association of Synagogue Administrators. These bodies sponsor programmes to augment the skills of their members and ensure the highest standards for professionals serving congregations.
2. The National Academy for Adult Jewish Studies offers direction and information about a broad range of programmes aimed to stimulate adults to increase their level of Jewish knowledge. The Academy's publications include textbooks as well as resource material.
3. The Israel Affairs Committee encourages and aids congregations in establishing closer ties with Israel through conferences, publications, films, special events and information programmes. In cooperation with the Israel Affairs Department the United Synagogue supports an Aliyah Department and a Jerusalem Centre for Conservative Judaism.
4. The Youth Commission and the Department of Youth Activities aims to draw Jewish youth closer to Judaism; it now includes

three subdivisions. United Synagogue Youth; a college-age programme; and a pre-teen unit – all these bodies seek to communicate the Jewish way of life to children and young adults.

In addition to those organizations, the Conservative movement
also embraces a number of other bodies:

1. The Women's League for Conservative Judaism, established by
   Mathilde Schechter in 1818, now contains 800 affiliated groups
   numbering over 200 000. Today this organization serves as the
   overseeing body for sisterhoods in the diaspora and Israel; each
   of its branches conducts an annual conference, programmes in
   co-operation with local synagogues, workshops and study
   groups.
2. The National Federation of Jewish Men's Clubs is composed of
   over 400 men's Clubs affiliated with Conservative synagogues;
   these organizations promote an active appreciation of the
   Jewish tradition. The Federation trains laymen for leadership
   roles and also issues pamphlets and magazines as part of its
   programme of adult education.
3. The Conservative movement supports a number of commis-
   sions including: The Joint Commission on Jewish Education;
   the Joint Commission on Social Action; the Joint Placement
   commission; the Joint Prayer Book Commission.
4. The World Council of Synagogues is concerned with the advancement of the Conservative approach to the Jewish heritage;
   it consists of Conservative synagogues and synagogue organ-
   isations in 26 countries.

THE BELIEFS OF CONSERVATIVE JUDAISM

Although the Conservative movement has not issued a statement of
its central tenets, it is possible to isolate a number of its core beliefs.
Regarding the doctrine of God, Conservative writers have generally subscribed to the Orthodox understanding of God as omnipotent, omniscient, and all good. Thus, Seymour Siegel, Professor of
Theology at the Seminary, described God as a transcendent person
who gave the *Torah* to Israel and who 'is addressed and ... addressed us ... reveals himself ... and tells man what he wishes and
what he expects of mankind' (Siegel, 1980, 398–402).

Through its history such a view of the Deity dominated Conservative thought. Conservative thinkers have also generally endorsed the traditional belief in divine revelation. In the words of Louis Finkelstein, Professor of Talmud and Chancellor at the Seminary:

> The codes of law in Exodus, Leviticus and Deuteronomy, though expressed in prosaic form ... can only be recognized as prophetic and divine, in the same sense that the fiery words of Isaiah and Jeremiah are prophetic and divine. (Finkelstein, 1948, 45)

Yet in contrast with Orthodox Judaism, there is considerable uncertainty about this process of divine disclosure. Unlike Orthodox writers who conceive of revelation as verbal in nature and Reform theologians who conceive of the *Torah* as the product of human reflection, the Conservative movement has generally attempted to bridge these two positions. As to what constitutes the nature of such a divine–human encounter, Conservative Jews vary: some maintain that human beings correctly recorded the divine will as disclosed at Sinai; others contend that the writers of the Scriptures were divinely inspired. Yet despite such differences of interpretation, most Conservative thinkers recognize that there was greater divine involvement in the *Torah* compared with the other books of the Hebrew Scriptures even though they reject the Orthodox belief that God literally revealed the *Torah* in its entirety to Moses on Mount Sinai.

The theological extremes within the Conservative movement are represented by various leading thinkers who have wrestled with this issue. For example, Abraham Heschel, Professor of Ethics and Mysticism at the Seminary, viewed God as an overwhelming presence. In his view 'the speech of God is not less, but more than literally real ... If God is alive then the Bible is his voice' (Heschel, 1966, 244–5). According to Heschel, revelation is not simply inspiration, even though those who heard God recorded more what they understood than what they actually heard. Revelation, he argued, is the transmission of thought and will from heaven to earth. However, since heaven remains heaven and what is earthly remains earthly, such divine disclosure must be translated into human thought-patterns. In a similar vein, Gilbert S. Rosenthal, rabbi of Temple Beth El in Cedarhurst, New York, affirmed that the 'biblical kernel of Jewish law ... is divine – the revealed will of God'

(Rosenthal, 1980, 376). Again, Ernst Simon, Visiting Professor at the Seminary, depicted the Hebrew Bible as a 'human echo of the divine voice ... a human translation of God's word' (Simon, 1958, 3–4). In contrast with this notion, Ben Zion Bokser, rabbi of the Forest Hills Jewish Centre in Long Island, New York, maintained that revelation should be understood essentially as inspirational in character. For Bokser, revelation is the power behind oneself that brought new visions of truth and beauty to the world; it is the breathing in by humans of the message they felt compelled to record. In the opinion of more radical Conservative writers, on the other hand, the Hebrew Scriptures are devoid of divine inspiration: the Bible, they insist, is simply the product of human creativity.

Regarding *halakhah*, most Conservative thinkers emphasize the importance of keeping traditional Jewish law, including dietary observances; Sabbath, festival and liturgical prescriptions; and ethical precepts. Nonetheless, Conservative writers have encouraged change and renewal. On the whole they have emphasized the historical importance of the Jewish heritage. In the words of Ben Zion Bokser:

> Conservatism admits the propriety of change. It admits the divine origin of the *Torah*; but it asserts that, as we encounter it, every divine element is encumbered with a human admixture, that the divine element ... rests in specific forms which are historically conditioned. These historically conditioned forms are ... subject to adjustment.   (Bokser, 1964, 12–13)

Guided by such an approach to Jewish law, the Conservative movement resorted to what Schechter called the 'conscience of the Catholic Israel' in determining the status of both biblical and rabbinic law. In the early years of the United Synagogue, such leaders as Ginzberg urged Conservative Jews to reach consensual agreement. As a consequence 'Catholic Israel' came to signify the vast majority of the membership of Conservative synagogues. Further, a body of representative rabbis selected by the Rabbinic Assembly of America (the rabbinical body of the movement) established a Committee on Jewish Law; later this body was expanded into a Committee on Jewish Law and Standards. This Committee rules on issues of Jewish law in the light of past needs and present conditions. As Alexander Kohut explained, the teaching of the ancients serves as the starting point, yet the Committee was anxious not to lose sight of the needs of each generation. Initially the Committee was criticized for its conservatism, however, when the committee was expanded the new chairman, Morris Adler, resolved no longer to halt between 'fear of the Orthodox and danger to Reform'. Instead, he sought to articulate 'positive and unambiguous affirmations' and to 'introduce into our thinking this revolutionary fact – the impact of an entirely changed world both outer and inner' (Raphael, 1984, 102).

Unless the Committee made unanimous recommendations, congregational rabbis were at liberty to rely on their own authority: although this resulted in charges of inconsistency, this approach allowed individual rabbis freedom of decision-making. In establishing its attitude to *halakhah*, Conservative Judaism stressed that halakhic change does not emanate from God's revelation on Mount Sinai, but from Catholic Israel. The Conservative movement thus based its decisions on human reflection rather than God's will. In the words of the rabbi and writer, Harold Kushner, the authority of the law is based on *Torah Mitoldot Ameinu* rather than *Torah MiSinai*. By this he meant that 'generations of our people have found holiness in performing them [laws] and continue to do so today' (Raphael, 1984, 104). In expounding this approach the Conservative movement has in general viewed the main outlines of the Jewish legal system as binding but has permitted individuals to fill in the amount of detail they wish to follow: this is the sphere where personal choice is paramount.

Because of its dedication to the peoplehood of Israel, the Conservative movement has from its inception been dedicated to the creation of a Jewish state. Religion and nationality, Conservative thinkers maintain, are inseparably related. According to Louis Ginzberg, Jewish nationalism without religion is a tree without fruit; Jewish religion without Jewish nationalism is a tree with no roots. In the late nineteenth and early twentieth century, Conservative leaders were ardent Zionists, and as early as 1927, Israel Goldstein, rabbi of New York's Bnai Jeshurun, reported that the Zionist Organization of America viewed the Conservative rabbinate as a bulwark of American Zionism. Nearly twenty years later, Solomon Freehof, a leading Reform rabbi, observed that nearly the entire Conservative rabbinate as well as the membership of Conservative congregations were pro-Zionist. By 1983 more than a hundred rabbis ordained at the Seminary had settled in Israel.

Related to its endorsement of Jewish peoplehood, the Conservative movement under the influence of Mordecai Kaplan,

Professor at the Seminary, embraced the notion of Judaism as a civilization. As early as the First World War, Kaplan stressed that Judaism was 'the *tout ensemble* of all the elements of what is usually termed the cultural life of a people, such as language, folkways, patterns of social organization, social habits and standards, creative arts, religion' (Kaplan, 1916, 170). In Kaplan's view, the totality of Jewish activities – not simply religious acts – should be considered aspects of Judaism. During this period Kaplan's writings began to have an impact on Seminary ordinands, and there was an increase in the establishment of synagogue-centres which combined religious and secular activities. In 1916, Kaplan founded the first synagogue-centre in New York City; in 1920 Israel Levinthal created the Brooklyn Jewish Centre, the most important of these institutions. Such centres were developed to serve as the focus of Jewish communal life: 'In our community all the Zionist, all the work for Hebrew culture, for philanthropy, for every phase of Jewish life, is being done through the centre' (Levinthal, 1928, 65).

Similar synagogue centres were later founded in Cleveland, Philadelphia, Newark, Chicago, Manhattan and Jacksonville, as well as several Long Island communities. These new Jewish institutions not only conducted religious services but also showed films, housed orchestras, organized athletic teams, encouraged drama clubs, and held adult educational programmes. Some employed rabbis to direct these social and educational activities: others hired full-time recreational leaders. This new Jewish establishment was organized to include all dimensions of Jewish life. As Israel Goldstein explained, these synagogue centres were 'built on the theory that there should be no cleavage between the religious and secular activities of man [and] to give full expression to all interests, physical, social, intellectual, within the province of the synagogue' (Goldstein, 1928, 32). In the 1930s and 1940s fewer of these centres were created, but after the Second World War a number of Conservative leaders urged the movement to remake the synagogue into a synagogue-centre.

A final dimension of Conservative ideology concerns the status of women. In 1947, Mordecai Kaplan distinguished between three distinct attitudes in the movement towards Jewish law. On the right, traditionalists were reluctant to make changes to ritual law. Centrists, on the other hand, no longer believed in the revelation at Sinai as a historical event but viewed it as a process continuing into the twentieth century. As a result, they permitted change in ritual and law if it were sanctioned by legal precedent. Finally, radicals, including Kaplan, did not hesitate to advocate modification to the Code of Jewish Law if it were necessary in the light of contemporary circumstances. In 1948 the Rabbinical Assembly Law Committee attempted to represent these three tendencies in its ruling about the status of women, but subsequently the leftists along with centrists issued rulings which attempted to remove traditional legal distinctions based on gender.

In 1955, the Committee on Jewish Law and Standards voted in favour of women being called to the reading of the *Torah* and added a clause to the *ketubah* (the Jewish marriage document) which granted equal rights to men and women; in addition, the Committee decreed that women should be counted as equal with men in the quorum necessary for communal prayer. Further, the United Synagogue recommended that married women have a vote equal to their husbands, single women be entitled to membership, and women be eligible for any congregational office. Although initially there was considerable reluctance to ordain women as rabbis, in 1978 a commission of lay and professional Conservative Jews decreed that there is no direct halakhic objection to training and ordaining women to be rabbis, preachers and teachers. Although the Seminary at first rejected this proposal, in 1983 the Faculty approved the admission and ordination of women.

AUTHORITY IN CONSERVATIVE JUDAISM

As we have seen, the Conservative movement – unlike Orthodox Judaism which affirms that God revealed his will to Moses on Mount Sinai – has adopted a range of theological positions regarding the nature of divine authority. The most traditional view asserts that God revealed himself to Moses and at other times in the history of the nation; these revelations, however, were recorded by human beings and as such provide a variety of interpretations of this encounter with God. Nonetheless, the revelation to Moses was the fullest and most public disclosure – it is the most authoritative record of God's will. From Sinai on, Jewish law and theology are to be conceived as individual perceptions: hence the authority of Jewish law is based first on the fact of God's revelation, and second on the amplification of this legislation by reliable rabbinic commentary. Modifications of the law are acceptable, but only with extreme caution.

According to this position, all the laws of the *Torah* are authoritative in character – yet there is an acknowledgement that divine law is mediated through human comprehension. In this light, the historical investigation of Judaism is a viable enterprise since the tradition is perceived as subject to historical change. Modern exponents of this view hold that the Bible is divine even though it has been fashioned through human comprehension. Thus Abraham Joshua Heschel, Professor of Jewish Ethics and Mysticism at the Seminary, stated with regard to the prophets:

> The prophets bear witness to an event. The event is divine, but the formulation is done by the individual prophet. According to this conception, the idea is revealed; the expression is coined by the prophet. The expression 'the word of God' would not refer to the word as a sound or a combination of sounds. Indeed, it has often been maintained that what reached the ear of man was not identical with what has come out of the spirit of the eternal God. For 'Israel could not possibly have received the Torah as it came forth from the mouth of the Lord, for ... the word of God in itself is like a burning flame, and the Torah that we received is merely a part of the coal to which the flame is attached' ... The Bible reflects its divine as well as its human authorship. (Levine, 1977, 292–5)

On such a view, God spoke at Sinai – his will is authoritative for all time. Yet such a belief does not preclude a historical and literary analysis of the biblical text since it was written down by human hands.

An alternative understanding of divine authority is based on a number of different assumptions. On this view, the *Torah* was composed by human beings at various times and places: hence the *Torah* contains diverse documents, laws and ideas. None the less those who wrote down these words were divinely inspired and their words carry the insight and authority of God. In this light, Jewish laws and ideas can be altered since the *Torah* is a combination of divine inspiration on the one hand, and human articulation on the other. Moreover, divine inspiration did not occur once and for all at Sinai – it continues on in the form of new interpretations for future generations. Changes to the law are permissible, but they must take place through rabbinic decisions and communal custom.

One of the most eloquent advocates of this quasi-traditionalist position is Ben Zion Bokser; in his book, *Judaism, Profile of a Faith,* he wrote:

> The partnership between God and man is ... at work in bringing forth the truth on which our souls are nourished. Man receives a divine communication in the moment when the divine spirit rests on him, but man must give form to that communication; he must express it in words, in images, and in symbols which will make his message intelligible to other men. Out of this need to give form to the truth that is revealed to him the prophet places the stamp of his own individuality upon that truth. He draws upon his own experience, upon the idiom current in his time; he creates images that will be familiar to his people. Thus the truth becomes personalized; it takes upon itself the robes of the world in which it is to enter to perform its work of moral and spiritual transformation. In the process of expression and transmission truth takes on a historical dimension, which the historian can examine by the tools of historical investigation. (Bokser, 1963, 273–4)

Supporters of this position stress that there is an important distinction between such a notion of inspiration and revelation. Revelation presupposes a verbal transmission of a specific message from God: inspiration however denotes an experience of divine contact mediated though human understanding. For this reason, it is necessary to disentangle those aspects of the tradition which emanate from a divine source and those which stem from human reflection and are thereby susceptible of radical modification. Most advocates of this position would hold that we must listen to the tradition and try to apply it appropriately to modern life. But they would claim, as do traditionalists, that decisions about the status of Jewish law should be made for the community by its religious leaders.

An alternative notion of authority within the Conservation movement is that revelation should be understood as the disclosure of God himself, rather than a series of propositions. It is not revelation or inspiration which takes place, but instead a meeting of God and man. On this view, the *Torah* is a record of the human response to God – Jewish law thus has authority for the Jewish people because Jews are members of a covenanted community. As such, they have obligations to follow God's law. However, since the *Torah* was composed by human beings, it is necessary to employ the techniques of biblical scholarship to uncover the origins and meanings of Scripture. Further, since the Bible is a human product it reflects the social and cultural milieu of its authors. It follows that Jewry today must alter the tradition so that it most effectively expresses God's will in the modern world. Finally, this understanding of authority emphasizes the communal character of Jewish law: it is God's encounter with the Jewish people as a whole which is fundamental. Changes in laws of the Jewish faith must be made by rabbis on behalf of the entire community rather than by specific individuals independent of the rabbinic establishment.

One of the most important advocates of this view, Louis Jacobs, rabbi of the New London Synagogue, emphasized the non-propositional character of divine revelation:

> According to the traditional view, God revealed certain propositions all at once, whereas according to 'progressive revelation' theory, he revealed them gradually. In more recent times, a very different (and to many minds far more satisfactory) view of revelation has gained ground. On this view, revelation does not mean that God conveys to man detailed propositions at all, but rather that he enables men to have an encounter with him of a specially intense form. It is God himself who is disclosed in revelation. Revelation is an event, not a series of propositions about God and his demands.   (Jacobs, 1973, 202)

Despite this reorientation in perspective, Jacobs argued that traditional law is binding upon the Jewish community:

> Revelation can thus be seen as the disclosure of God himself. The rules and regulations, the *Torah* and precepts, provide the vocabulary by which the God who is disclosed is to be worshipped, in the broad sense of the term. They are a repertoire which has evolved in response to the impact of the original disclosure ... The precepts of the *Torah* are binding because they provide the vocabulary of worship – always understanding worship in its widest sense. God did 'command' them, but not by direct communication – as in the traditional view – but through the historical experiences of the people of Israel.   (Ibid., 202–10)

Those who subscribe to this position tend be more willing to countenance change in the legal code. In the words of Seymour Siegel,

Chairman of the Committee on Jewish Law and Standards of the Rabbinical Assembly and Professor of Theology and Ethics at the Seminary:

> The process of reevaluating the *mitzvot* through interpretation goes in the living community of the people of Israel. The *mitzvot* are not to be seen as a group of Platonic ideas existing for all time in their perfect and unchanging character. They are the demands of God upon the community of Israel, which lives in time, and they are therefore subject to change, growth, and (all too frequently) decay. (*The Condition of Jewish Belief*, 1989, 224)

A final standpoint in the Conservative movement concerning authority has been profoundly influenced by Reconstructionist ideology. According to this position, human beings wrote Scripture without supernatural intervention – hence the Jewish way of life is not superior to the patterns of living found in other faith communities. None the less Jewish law is authoritative for the people of Israel; it should be observed so as to give the nation a sense of continuity and coherence. As explained by Mordecai Kaplan, the founder of Reconstructionist Judaism:

> Instead of assuming the *Torah* 'to be divine revelation', I assume it to be the expression of ancient Israel's attempt to base its life on a declaration of dependence upon God, and on a constitution which embodies the laws according to which God expected Israel to live ... Our position is that those *mitzvot* which, in tradition, are described as applying 'between man and God' should be observed, insofar as they help to maintain the historic continuity of the Jewish people and to express or symbolize, spiritual values or ideals, which can enhance the inner life of Jews. (Kaplan, 1956, 265–6)

THE FUTURE OF CONSERVATIVE JUDAISM

The summer 1977 issue of *Judaism* was devoted to a consideration of the future of the Conservative movement. In their reflections contributors focused on a number of key problems facing Conservatism. First, there was considerable debate about the nature of the movement. In his contribution Arthur J. Levine, Past

President of the United Synagogues of America, pointed out that there were valid reasons why Solomon Schechter avoided defining Conservative Judaism. Today however, he argued, there is a pressing need to formulate a clear purpose as well as a delineated role for the individual Jew:

> We make commitments only to what we perceive and feel, and our philosophy has been too ill-defined to create such a feeling-tone in the individual adherent. We must see ourselves in more precise terms, and define the minimal obligations for those who will join with us.   (Dorff, 1979, 212)

Viewing the Conservative movement from an Orthodox perspective, Schlomo Riskin, the Orthodox rabbi of Lincoln Square Synagogue and Dean of Manhattan Hebrew High School, was critical of such a lack of theological clarity. Conservative Judaism, he observed, is unable to create Jewish communities which are committed to the tradition in accordance with Conservative principles. Most Jews, he maintained, perceive Conservative Judaism as guided by compromise. Generally the statement 'I belong to a Conservative Synagogue' becomes an excuse for religious inconsistency and pragmatism. The problem, he wrote, 'is rooted in the lack of clear ideology which will define the movement and help its adherents to define themselves *vis-à-vis* our [Orthodox] tradition.' (Ibid., 214)

Responding to such criticism, Benjamin Z. Kreitman, Executive Vice-President of the United Synagogue of America and former Chairman of the Rabbinical Assembly Committee on Jewish Law and Standards, urged his co-religionists to attain a greater understanding of the Bible, the history of Jewish law, and the evolution of other movements to which Conservative Judaism reacted. In this way, Conservative Jews would be able to comprehend more fully their role in the Jewish community. 'It is our hope that,' he wrote, 'by the resolution of the problems faced by Conservative Judaism, it will become, in the near future, what Solomon envisaged for it in his day – the mainstream of Jewish life.' (Ibid.)

A second area of concern within the movement has been its lack of clarity over a number of institutional issues. According to Jacob Stein, Past President of the United Synagogue of America, Conservative Judaism has not defined criteria for standards of service that the synagogue should offer: educational goals are undeveloped; communal practices in the fields of *kashrut* and funerals have received little attention: the synagogue has failed to make an impact on other Jewish organizations in the community. To meet these deficiencies, new thinking is required. Thus Mordecai Waxman, rabbi of Temple Israel of Great Neck, New York, and Past President of the Rabbinical Assembly, stressed that Conservative ideology must be translated into concrete action through the intervention of national bodies. Over the past few decades, he noted, the autonomous synagogue was loosely related to the national organization. During this period there was relatively little need for its services, but the situation had now radically changed:

> Synagogues which were growing yesterday are declining today. Changing neighbourhoods and a diminishing birthrate have made it clear that very few institutions last more than a generation or two in American Jewish life. The result is that the organized bodies of Conservative Judaism, and the United Synagogue most of all, are called upon to perform tasks with which hitherto, they have only toyed. If old congregations are to be maintained, they will often need financial help from a regional or national body. Schools with decreasing populations will have to be merged – but they ought to be merged by Conservative bodies rather than by federations of charities. If it is to deal adequately with a mobile population, the Conservative movement must establish and fund new synagogues where needed ... new patterns of education, an expansion of camping facilities for school and adult use, the manpower to staff them, part-time and travelling personnel for small regional or national intervention ... The national and regional organizations must expand to meet the tasks.   (Ibid., 215–16)

A further major dilemma facing Conservative Judaism is the place of law and ethics in the movement. Philip Segal, former member of the Rabbinical Assembly Committee on Jewish Law and Standards, noted that there are a number of crucial modern areas to be discussed including:

1.   The status of mixed marriages where the non-Jewish partner is a monotheist who plans to live a Judaic life-style.
2.   The *halakhah* of *kashrut*.
3.   The equalization of rites and rights for men and women from the admission of an infant into Judaism through the life-cycle events at home and in the synagogue.

4. The point at which life-sustaining measures may be terminated.
5. Transvestism.
6. Homosexuality and lesbianism.
7. Cloning.
8. The meaning of work on the Sabbath.
9. Honour and power in the Jewish community.
10. The question whether money obtained through white-collar crime can be accepted by charitable groups.
11. The status of a child.

As Conservative Judaism stands on the threshold of the twenty-first century, Segal emphasized the importance of facing these and other dilemmas:

> As the Conservative movement, dated from the birth of its Seminary enters into the last decade of its first century, it should establish halakhic goals to reach before the centennial celebration. These should include, first of all, a more comprehensive articulation of a theology of *halakhah* that has hitherto been produced and should encompass doctrines concerning revelation, authority and methodology.   (Ibid., 217)

In a similar vein Ben Zion Bokser called for a return to moral and ethical ideals in the movement; given the increasing secularization of the modern age, Conservative Judaism, he believed, should aim to draw Jews back to the principles of the faith:

> Our culture is contaminated with opportunism, in which material gain supersedes all other values, and Jews have often been drawn into the whirlpool of general corruption. From the highest circles in government, business and the professions there comes an ever-recurrent manifestation of the betrayal of integrity and a surrender to the lowest forms of self-seeking ... One misses a prophetic strain in the preoccupation of contemporary Jewish religious leadership. Instead the focus falls on sociological aspects of Jewish religious institutions and on the ritualistic aspect of tradition. These is little evidence of a stress on the ethical and moral ideals of our heritage in order to challenge the waywardness of our society generally, or of the Jewish constituency particularly ... Conservative Judaism needs to

redress this imbalance if it is to meet fully the claims of the original insight that inspired its emergence as a distinctive movement. (Quoted in ibid., 218–19)

A final area of concern relates to the Conservative movement's identity. In the view of David Shapiro, the Orthodox rabbi of Congregation Anshe Sfard in Milwaukee, Conservative Judaism should never have separated itself from Orthodoxy. Under the influence of Mordecai Kaplan, he argued, there has been a reversal of attitudes within Conservatism: the time-honoured principles of Judaism were relegated to a secondary status. Conservative Judaism ceased to be interested in encouraging Jewry to be loyal to Jewish observance. The movement, he wrote, should never have left the mainstream of Jewish life:

Had it remained within it, it would have checked itself and been kept from meandering. The rift was created by giving itself a new name which, as Conservatism is now taught and practised, is misleading. Conservatism has, thereby, brought itself danger-ously close to an alliance with Reform Judaism, against which it had originally taken up the cudgels. (Ibid., 220)

Agreeing with Shapiro about the direction of Conservatism, Roland B. Gittelsohn, Reform Rabbi of Temple Israel in Boston, encouraged the leaders of the movement to acknowledge that they have much more in common with their Reform colleagues than with the Orthodox. 'There are', he wrote, 'only two thoroughly consistent religious positions: that of the rigidly intransigent Jew who will change nothing, and that of the totally "emancipated" Jew who rejects everything ... Conservative Judaism will be happier within itself and able to offer the rest of us even more if it accepts itself as a variant version of modernity, committed to the truth that tradition can survive only if it changes, and that change must sometimes be both painful and bold.' (Ibid., 221)

Responding to these observations, Gerson D. Cohen, Chancellor of the Jewish Theological Seminary, maintained that Conservative Judaism has a distinct identity and aim. Contemporary Conser-vatism, he asserted, has recovered from the Kaplanian challenge and is beginning to grapple with the halakhic tradition. In his view, the Conservative movement is seeking to articulate both in theory and in practice its deep-seated commitment to tradition as interpreted by the tools of critical scholarship. Those who see only the dilemmas faced by Conservative Jews fail to perceive its strengths:

> Critical observers of Conservative Judaism ... have on occasion remarked that Conservative Judaism has no genuine constituency but only a rabbinate and scholarly class. I certainly think it is fair to say that Conservative Judaism has determined the dominant styles and postures of contemporary American Jewish life ... Conservative Judaism remains ... the pacesetter, at least for positive adherence to historic forms and values ... Whatever may be said of the Conservative synagogue ... it has become the centre of Jewish communal activity on the local level for the overwhelming majority of affiliated Jews in the United States. (Ibid., 222–4)

CRITIQUE

Like Reform Judaism, the Conservative movement has distanced itself from the traditional understanding of divine revelation: the *Torah* is perceived as a composite work containing various strands of tradition dating from different periods in the history of ancient Israel. As a result, there is considerable uncertainty about the status of both Jewish belief and observance. As we have seen, some traditionalists assert that Scriptural and rabbinic law remains authoritative for the community; others press for halakhic change. The existence of such divergent groups within the Conservative movement embracing radically distinct philosophies has made it impossible for Conservative Judaism to formulate a coherent platform of beliefs – thus there is a profound lack of clarity within the movement about its underlying religious principles.

Regarding the doctrine of God, for example, some Conservative leaders believe in a personal, supernatural God who is active in human history. According to Solomon Schechter, God is not a mere idea but a spirit who is present everywhere. Other thinkers, such as Ben Zion Bokser, however, maintain that God should be understood in non-personal terms: his nature transcends human categories of conceptualization. Adopting a mystical approach, Abraham Heschel believed that we should not try to prove God's existence; instead we should attempt to experience his spirit in the order of the universe and the moral law. According to Heschel, we are capable of such perception when we confront the glories of nature and history – an amazement that cannot be expressed in words. At the other end of the spectrum, there are many Conservative thinkers who reject the notion of a supernatural deity altogether. For Robert Gordis, God is creative power in the world; he is the force behind social, political and scientific progress. Such a broad range of opinion highlights a fundamental lack of theological coherence within the movement.

Similarly, Conservative thought is equally divided concerning the doctrine of revelation. As we have seen, both Orthodox and Hasidic Judaism subscribe to the conviction that God gave every word of the *Torah* to Moses on Mount Sinai. Reform Judaism generally rejects this doctrine, preferring to see God's inspiration behind the moral law. Conservative Judaism, on the other hand, contains a vast range of opinion regarding the nature of God's disclosure. Some traditionalist thinkers contend that God revealed the *Torah* to Israel even though they do not accept that every word in the Pentateuch is of divine origin. Other writers believe in the doctrine of divine inspiration, holding to a notion of progressive encounter. Some more radical theologians, on the other hand, deny God any role in this process. In their view, the entire corpus of Jewish law is rooted in human experience. Such a broad spectrum again emphasizes the subjective nature of Conservative belief.

The same lack of agreement is found in the sphere of halakhic interpretation. In general Conservative Jews accept that the *halakhah* has a pivotal role to play in the modern world. Yet within the movement there are widely discrepant patterns of observance. Initially Solomon Schechter insisted that law is basic to Judaism, but he believed that the living body of people (including prophets, psalmists, sages and rabbis) should have the final word in altering Jewish law. Subsequently Louis Ginzburg stressed the importance of understanding the development of each law; however he wished that the modernization of the system of *halakhah* be undertaken by religious authorities. His position on Jewish law had a profound impact on later thinkers; none the less there is today no universal agreement within Conservative Judaism about the process of such legal revision. Instead there is deep-seated uncertainty about which traditional laws should be discarded and which retained, as well as the method to be employed in making such decisions.

Another area of dispute concerns the doctrine of chosenness. On the one hand, the Sabbath and High Holy Day prayerbooks have retained the traditional formula: 'You have chosen us from all the nations.' For many Conservative Jews, such a belief implies that God singled out the Jews from all nations for his special purposes because of their inherent spiritual and moral qualities. However, in the view of others the doctrine of chosenness must be understood in the light of God's purposes. Thus Robert Gordis claimed that Israel is the chosen people in the sense that it was elected in order to serve humanity. Again, Simon Greenberg wrote that the Jews are not inherently superior, but rather have a greater obligation to obey the *Torah*. Ben Zion Bokser also sought to avoid claims of tribalism; in his opinion, all groups are equally God's chosen – they are unique vehicles of his revelation and the instruments of his purposes in history (Raphael, 1984, 105). The language of the prayerbook therefore reinforces the traditional conception of election even though there is widespread disagreement in the movement as to its meaning in the modern world.

As far as religious observance is concerned, there is a similar diversity of opinion. Officially Conservative Judaism insists that its members uphold the *mitzvot* and lead a life based on *halakhah*. In reality, however, few Conservative laypeople live up to this ideal. Moreover, the movement itself has officially sanctioned practices that deviate from the tradition. For example, Conservative Jews are permitted to use electricity on the Sabbath and Festivals; the observance of the second day of Passover, *Shavuot*, and *Sukkot* is regarded as optional; Conservative Jews are permitted to discard skull-caps outside the synagogue; women are not obliged to cover their hair or go to the *mikvah* [ritual bath]. Hence there is considerable ambiguity about acceptable patterns of observance within the movement: no uniformity exists, nor is it conceivable that a coherent Jewish life-style could emerge within Conservative Judaism given the lack of agreement about the essential features of the faith.

Finally regarding interfaith activities Conservatism is similarly divided. In the opinion of a number of leading rabbis, it is important for Jews and non-Jews to come to understand one another and co-operate in building a better world. Louis Finkelstein, for example, attempted to bring together religious dialogue as did Abraham Joshua Heschel. Yet within the movement other leaders have regarded such interfaith activity as fruitless – in their view, Jews should remain aloof from such exchange. What is required instead is intensive study of the Jewish heritage and unceasing effort to educate Jewry in the faith.

The Conservative movement is hence riddled with disagreement. Although there is a universal acceptance of the need for historical investigation of the origins and development of Judaism, no consensus exists concerning the acceptable lifestyle for the Conservative community. Instead Conservative Jews accord for themselves the right to make decisions about which aspects of the faith they wish to observe. This, of course, runs counter to the desire of the movement to legislate for its adherents. From its inception in the mid-nineteenth century to the present day Conservative rabbis have insisted that those who belong to the movement should be bound by *halakhah*, and that any alterations to the Code of Jewish law should be determined by proper authorities: change was to emanate from Catholic Israel, and Conservative Jews were to respect the authority of the Committee on Jewish Law and Standards.

The central weakness of Conservatism then is its lack of consistency, and internal disharmony over the fundamentals of the faith. While seeking to conserve traditional Judaism, it has dramatically departed from Orthodoxy. In so doing, it has sought to invest authority in official committees empowered with the responsibility to determine Conservative practice for the community as a whole – yet the vast majority of Conservative Jews generally ignore their pronouncements if they conflict with their personal preferences. It is difficult to see how such a chaotic state of affairs could serve as a recipe for Jewish living in the next century.

6

Reconstructionist Judaism

Under the influence of Mordecai Kaplan, Reconstructionist Judaism has emerged as an important force on the Jewish religious scene. Based on the concept of Judaism as a civilization, Reconstructionism hallows the *sancta* of Jewish life: language, history, culture, folkways, social organization, and dedication to Israel. Yet for Reconstructionists there is no longer any basis for believing in a supernatural Deity – instead Reconstructionist Judaism has redefined God as the highest possible fulfilment of human beings; God is understood as a complex of forces manifest in the universe and in individuals that makes salvation possible. In this light the *Torah* should be conceived as the creation of the Jewish people in its search for divine illumination.

Today this radical interpretation of the Jewish faith has its own rabbinical seminary, federation of synagogues, and assembly of rabbis. Though smaller than Orthodox, Hasidic, Reform or Conservative Judaism, this new denomination has had a profound impact on American Jewish life. Yet given its non-theistic orientation, it is difficult to envisage Reconstructionism as an all-embracing ideology for world Jewry.

THE ORIGINS OF RECONSTRUCTIONIST JUDAISM

Unlike the Reform and Conservative movements, Reconstructionist Judaism developed out of the thinking of an individual Jewish scholar. Born in Lithuania in 1881, Mordecai Kaplan had a traditional education in Vilna and emigrated to New York City as a child in 1889. After graduating from the City College of New York, he was ordained at the Jewish Theological Seminary; subsequently he obtained a master's degree from Columbia University in 1902. He then served as an associate minister of Rabbi Moses S. Margolis at New York's Orthodox congregation, *Kehilath Jeshurun*. Although formally Orthodox in observance, Kaplan became increasingly disenchanted with traditional Jewish theology. In 1909 he was invited by Solomon Schechter to head the Teachers' Institute of the Jewish Theological Seminary; in the following year he was appointed Professor of Homiletics at the Seminary's rabbinical school where he taught philosophy of religion.

During the 1910s and 1920s Kaplan engaged in wide-ranging congregational activity. At this time, together with several former *Kehilath Jeshurun* members who had moved to the Upper West Side, Kaplan organized the New York Jewish Centre where he experimented with the concept of Judaism as a civilization. Two years later the first stage of a synagogue-centre was completed on West 86th Street where Kaplan officiated as rabbi. In addition to overseeing Jewish worship, he introduced a programme of wide-ranging activities including study, drama, dance, song, basketball and callisthenics. During these years, Kaplan endorsed a number of controversial political policies and challenged traditional Jewish beliefs. When the board of Directors insisted on strict Orthodoxy in 1921, Kaplan resigned and established the Society for the Advancement of Judaism which he led for the next 20 years.

According to some scholars, Reconstructionism began in 1922 when Kaplan initiated a programme of reconstructing Judaism to meet the demands of contemporary life; another interpretation traces the origins of this movement to the publication of Kaplan's *Judaism as a Civilization* in 1934. Kaplan himself, however, maintained that Reconstructionist Judaism emerged in 1935 when, as a result of the publication of this work he and others founded the Reconstructionist magazine. In any event, *Judaism as a Civilization* provided the basis for Reconstructionist ideology. In this work, Kaplan began by assessing the main religious groupings of American Jewry. In his opinion, Reform had correctly acknowledged the evolving character of Judaism as a religious system, yet it ignored the social basis of Jewish identity as well as the organic character of the community. Neo-Orthodoxy, on the other hand, recognized Judaism as a way of life and provided an intensive programme of Jewish education; none the less, it mistakenly viewed the Jewish religion as static. In contrast, Conservative Judaism was committed to the scientific study of the development of the Jewish faith while upholding the unity of the Jewish people. Yet Conservative Judaism was too closely bound to Jewish law and thus unable to respond to changing circumstances. All of these movements, he believed, failed to accommodate the Jewish heritage to the modern age; what was needed, Kaplan insisted, was a definition of Judaism as an evolving religious civilization. Hence the title of his book.

In the light of this new conception of Judaism, Kaplan called for the re-establishment of a network of organic Jewish communities that would insure the self-perpetuation of the Jewish tradition. Membership of this new movement, he argued, should be voluntary; leaders should be elected democratically, and private religious opinions respected. In addition, Kaplan proposed a world-wide Jewish assembly which would adopt a covenant defining the Jews as a transnational people. This formulation was based on a combination of the Jewish historian Simon Dubnow's concept of an autonomous global Jewry with the Jewish essayist Ahad Ha-Am's stress on the land of Israel as the spiritual centre of the Jewish nation. For Kaplan, religion constitutes the concretization of the collective self-consciousness of a group which is manifest in spiritual symbols such as persons, places, events and writings. Such *sancta* inspire feelings of reverence, commemorate what the group believes to be most important, provide historical continuity, and strengthen the collective consciousness of the nation. In order for the Jewish people to survive, Kaplan believed, it must eliminate its authoritarian, dogmatic characteristics.

In *Judaism as a Civilization* Kaplan argued for a new approach to Judaism; in his view there was a pressing need to reinterpret the Jewish faith so that it could meet the challenges of rationalism and modernism. According to Kaplan, all the branches of contemporary Judaism had failed to provide a sufficient basis for Jewish identification, nor had they offered a viable basis for communal loyalty. Reform Judaism, for example, was inadequate because it repudiated the notion of Jewish peoplehood and narrowed the law to moral demands. Neo-Orthodoxy had also failed because it had supernaturalized the concept of Jewish rationalism, replacing it with the conception of Jewish mission. As a consequence, Orthodoxy was incapable of modifying the faith to conform to modern expectations. Conservatism, too, was insufficient for the modern age since it had been unable to establish a coherent religious ideology. Finally, secular nationalism which ignored the spiritual dimension of the Jewish tradition presented a distorted image of Judaism and was therefore unsatisfactory for Jews who sought spiritual sustenance from the Jewish heritage.

What was now required, Kaplan urged, was a reconstruction of the religious foundations of Judaism and a new vision of the Jewish community in a pluralistic society. For Kaplan, Judaism was something far more comprehensive than the Jewish religion. It included the nexus of a history, literature, language, social organization, folk sanctions, ethics, social and spiritual ideals, aesthetic interests which in their totality formed a civilization. Given this conception of the character of Jewish experience, Kaplan maintained that only in Israel was it possible to live a fully Jewish life; none the less, it was possible to sustain a Jewish way of life in the diaspora. The programme of Reconstructionist Judaism – as represented by a wheel – placed Israel at the hub of Jewish history from which all dynamic forms of Judaism radiated. The philosophy of such an Israel-centred movement was based on ten fundamental tenets:

1. *Judaism as an Evolving Religious Civilization*
    Judaism, or that which has united successive generations of Jews into one people, is not only a religion; it is an evolving religious civilization. In the course of its evolution, Judaism has passed through three distinct stages, each reflecting the conditions under which it functioned.
2. *What the Present State Calls for*
    During those stages the Jews constituted a people apart. Now, the Jewish people, like every other, must learn to live both in its own historic civilization and in the civilization of its environment. That will usher in the democratic stage of Judaism during which the reconstitution of the Jewish people, the revitalization of its religion, and the replenishment of its culture will be achieved.
3. *Unity in Diversity*
    Jewish unity should transcend the diversity among Jews, which is the result of geographical dispersion and of differences in cultural background and in world outlook.
4. *The Renewal of the Ancient Covenant*
    Jews the world over should renew their historic covenant binding themselves into one transnational people, with the Jewish community in Israel, henceforth to be known as 'Zion', as its core.
5. *Eretz Yisrael the Spiritual Homeland of World Jewry*
    Eretz Yisrael should be recognized as the home of the historic Jewish civilization.

6.   *Outside Israel, The Foundation of Organic Communities*
     Outside Israel, Jewish peoplehood should lead to the estab-
     lishment of organic communities. All activities and institu-
     tions conducted by Jews for Jews should be interactive and
     should give primacy to the fostering of Jewish peoplehood, re-
     ligion and culture.
7.   *Prerequisites to the Revitalization of Religion*
     The revitalization of religion can best be achieved through its
     study in the spirit of free inquiry and through the separation
     of church and state.
8.   *How the Belief in God is to be Interpreted*
     The revitalization of the Jewish religion requires that the belief
     in God be interpreted in terms of universally human, as well
     as specifically Jewish experience.
9.   *What Gives Continuity to a Religion*
     The continuity of a religion through different stages, and its
     identity amid diversity of belief and practice, are sustained by
     its *sancta*. These are the heroes, events, texts, places and
     seasons, which that religion signalizes as furthering the
     fulfilment of human destiny.
10. *Torah as Synonymous with Ongoing Jewish Culture*
     The traditional concept of *Torah* should be understood as
     synonymous with Jewish religious civilization and should,
     therefore, embrace all the ongoing ethical, cultural and spiri-
     tual experiences of the Jewish people.

THE IDEOLOGY AND GROWTH OF RECONSTRUCTIONIST JUDAISM

According to Kaplan, the Jewish people should not be understood
primarily as a religious denomination – rather the nation had produced a civilization. Religion, Kaplan wrote, was a quality inherent
in the very substance of a civilization which included non-religious
ingredients such as law, language, literature, art, history and folk
traditions. All of these elements were vital for Jewry: they were
the symbols whereby an individual was able to express his
identification with the community. For Kaplan Jewish rituals
should be perceived as *minhagim* (customs) rather than *mitzvot*
(commandments). Such practices served as the means whereby a
group was able to externalize the reality of its collective consciousness. These observances were 'poetry in action' expressing a mood,

functioning as ideas, or creating a bond between the individual and the community. Seen in this light, the notion of sin ceased to be relevant: religious ceremonies should be understood as folkways rather than divine immutable laws. Thus Orthodox Jews might wish to adhere to the Code of Jewish Law, yet there was no reason for other Jews to feel the same compulsion. Instead, non-Orthodox Jews should seek to formulate a basis for determining which traditional laws should be retained in contemporary society.

In propounding this theory about the nature of Jewish rituals, Kaplan made a number of suggestions about various aspects of the Jewish heritage. In addition to stressing the significance of religious folkways, festivals and worship, he proposed the use of Jewish names to demonstrate an identification with the tradition. In the diaspora, he argued, first names should be distinctively Jewish whereas surnames should conform to the names used by the general community – in this way, a person was able to express his attachment to Judaism while affirming his membership of the secular community. Kaplan also recommended that the traditional Jewish calendar should be altered: rather than numbering the Jewish year from creation – which can no longer be sustained by the findings of science – Jews should count the years from the destruction of the Second Temple. This turning point in the history of the nation would remind the Jew of his ancestral roots. Such a reconstruction of Jewish life, he believed, was called for in the modern world – it was no longer advisable to wait for an authoritative body to modify Jewish law. Instead changes to the tradition should be undertaken by groups of scholars attuned to modern circumstances.

In advancing this new conception of Jewish existence, Kaplan drew on various sources. From the Jewish side, he was deeply influenced by the writings of Ahad Ha-Am who devised the concept of spiritual nationalism. For Ahad Ha-Am, the salvation of Jewry could only be attained through spiritual renewal in Israel. In his view, a self-governing Jewish community in the Jewish homeland should serve as a means for the resurrection of the Jewish spirit. Yet despite the centrality of Israel, Ahad Ha-Am believed that spiritual rebirth could also occur in communities outside the Jewish state. Drawing on Ahad Ha-Am's ideas, Kaplan similarly maintained that Jewish survival could be assured by a regulation of spiritual life in Israel and elsewhere.

A second source of Kaplan's thought was the teaching of the American pragmatist, John Dewey. For Dewey reality was constantly changing and evolving. Hence there was a need to re-consider and reconstruct prevailing opinions. The first task of reli-gion, he believed, was to make life more meaningful and raise the individual to a higher spiritual realm. Yet this could not be accom-plished by means of traditional Jewish theology. Instead these beliefs must give way to a naturalistic understanding of revelation and supernatural divinity. This reversal has serious implications for Reconstructionist thought: espousing a similar form of pragmatism, Kaplan stressed that to be effective modern Judaism must divest itself of the supernatural trappings of the past.

A final influence on Kaplan was the writing of the French-Jewish sociologist Emile Durkheim. As a consequence of his investigation of the society of primitive groups, Durkheim discovered that such communities were dominated by the collective consciousness of the tribe. On the basis of this observation Durkheim argued that an in-dividual's mental life and his religious experience were condi-tioned primarily by his social environment. Religion therefore embraces the values, interests, beliefs and aspirations of tribal society – it sanctifies the ideas and institutions it values as a means of preserving them. Such features become the *sancta* of the group. According to Kaplan, *sancta* are found in advanced religions as well: in Judaism they are exemplified by the Bible, the festivals and other observances. Religion, therefore, is essentially a social phe-nomenon, reflecting the outlook, history and traditions of a given society. From this perspective, Kaplan's understanding of Jewish reality is grounded in the social life of the nation.

In the light of this conception of Judaism, Kaplan argued that God is not a supernatural being but the power that makes for salva-tion. 'God', he wrote, 'is the sum of all the animating, organizing forces and relationships which are forever making a cosmos out of chaos (Kaplan, 1962, 36). In his view, the idea of God must be understood fundamentally in terms of its effect:

> We learn more about God when we say that love is divine than when we say that God is love. A veritable transformation takes place...Divinity becomes relevant to authentic experience and therefore takes on a definiteness which is accompanied by an awareness of authenticity.   (Kaplan, 1970, 73)

In Kaplan's view, God is a 'trans-natural', 'supra-factual' and 'super-experiential' transcendence which does not infringe the laws of nature. Such a notion is far removed from the biblical and rabbinic concept of God as the creator and sustainer of the universe who chose the Jewish people and guides humanity to its final destiny. Such an interpretation of the nature of God calls for a reformulation of the spiritual dimension of the faith. Thus Kaplan argued that salvation must be understood in humanistic terms:

> When religion speaks of salvation it means in essence the experience of the worthwhileness of life. When we analyse our personal experience of life's worthwhileness we find that it is invariably based on specific ethical experiences – moral responsibility, honesty, loyalty, love, service. If carefully pursued, this analysis reveals that the source of our ethical experience is found in our willingness and ability to achieve self-fulfilment through reciprocity with others. This reciprocity in turn is an expression of a larger principle that operates in the cosmos in response to the demands of a cosmic force, the force that makes for creativity and interdependence in all things. (Ibid., 70).

Given this naturalistic conception of religion, what is the role of prayer in Reconstructionist thought? For Kaplan, religious worship is necessary for subjective reasons – it is as essential as the release of emotions. Through prayer human beings are able to become aware of the force that operates in one's inner consciousness, human relationships, and the environment. Further, through worship one is able to focus on the spiritual goals of a religious community. The petitioner, for example, is able to gain spiritual nourishment in times of crisis as well as consolation for bereavement. Worship, therefore, offers considerable psychological benefits and is able to shape an individual's ideals. Many of the ideas found in Kaplan's writings were reflected in the religious literature that appeared during the early period of Reconstructionism's development. The *New Haggadah*, edited by Kaplan, Eugene Kohn and Ira Eisenstein, for example, applied Kaplan's theology to liturgical texts, subordinating miracles and plagues in the traditional *Haggadah* to the narrative of Israel's redemption from Egypt and its contemporary significance. Again, the Sabbath Prayer Book was designed for those who were dissatisfied with synagogue worship – its aim was to arouse emotion by eliminating theologically untenable passages and adding inspirational material drawn from the tradition. This new prayer book deleted all references to the revelation of the *Torah* on Mount Sinai, the Jews as God's chosen people, and the doctrine of a personal Messiah. In response, a number of Kaplan's colleagues denounced him and the Union of Orthodox Rabbis excommunicated him for expressing atheism, heresy and disbelief in the basic tenets of Judaism.

In the 1940s and 1950s the leaders of Reconstructionism insisted that they were not attempting to form a new branch of Judaism. As Jacob Agus, rabbi of Chicago's North Shore *Agudas Achim* stated: 'Reconstructionism is not a sect but a movement to concentrate and give organizational form to the elements of strength within all sections of American Judaism.' (Raphael, 1984, 185). Throughout this period Reconstructionists hoped to be able to infuse the three major groups within North American Judaism (Orthodoxy, Conservative Judaism, and Reform Judaism) with its ideas. However, by the end of the 1960s the Reconstructionist movement had become a denomination – it established a seminary to train Reconstructionist rabbis and instituted a congregational structure. Regarding *halakhah*, the Reconstructionist Rabbinical Association issued a statement of its 1980 convention that placed authority in the Jewish people (as opposed to the rabbis) and created a process whereby each congregation would be free to evolve its own *minhagim* (customs). Three years later the Association produced guidelines on intermarriage, encouraging rabbis to welcome mixed couples (a Jew and a non-Jew), permit them to participate in Jewish synagogue life, and recognize their children as Jewish if raised as Jews. In addition, the Association decreed that rabbis could sanctify an intermarriage as long as it was accompanied by a civil, rather than a religious, ceremony.

RELIGIOUS BELIEFS AND PRACTICES

The central principle of Reconstructionism is that Judaism is an evolving religious civilization: in the biblical period the Jews constituted a people; later they became a religious congregation; eventually they entered the rabbinic era when the legal system ruled their lives; in modern times individual Jews are free to adapt the tradition to their own needs. Because of this continual development, ideas about God, humanity, sin, miracles, laws, prayer and the afterlife have all undergone considerable change over the centuries. In Kaplan's view, Judaism is therefore more than a religious denomination; it is a total civilization embracing art, music, language, folkways and customs whose purpose is to ensure the survival of the Jewish nation.

Within this framework, Reconstructionists have adopted a humanistic and naturalistic understanding of the nature of the Divine based on the teachings of Mordecai Kaplan. Kaplan was a humanist because he discerned the presence of God in human experience. For Kaplan human potential and striving to improve life reflected the power of God. Kaplan also found evidence of design in the universe because nature follows specific laws. In his opinion, the regularity of nature was devised to enable human beings to achieve their highest goals. In this light, Kaplan believed that faith in God should be grounded in scientific knowledge and on a faith in humanity. As noted previously, such a humanistic perspective is based on a radically new definition of God as the power that makes for human salvation and fulfilment. In his works, Kaplan repeatedly expressed his faith that human beings have the capacity to strive for such ideas as justice, truth, goodness and peace. Just as gravity is an invisible force in nature, he asserted, so there is a power in human beings which makes humans strive for perfection. That power is what we call 'God'. Reconstructionism thus does not teach that God is a person residing in Heaven; such a notion, Kaplan believed, is a childlike fantasy. It is thus a mistake to strive to experience God through mysticism, nor should we think of God as a miracle-worker or judge. In this connection Reconstructionists insist that God, as defined in Kaplan's system, is limited. According to Reconstructionism, God's power extends only to certain spheres, yet Reconstructionists believe that one day God's spirit will fill the entire world: our task as human beings and as Jews is to bring about the realization of such a utopian vision.

Turning to the doctrine of revelation, Reconstructionism differs markedly from Orthodox Judaism. Accepting the findings of modern biblical scholars who view the *Torah* as composite, Kaplan stressed that the Bible was not a record of God's dealing with his chosen people; rather it reflected the Jewish search for God. Hence whenever a great teaching or moral truth is uncovered in Scripture, this is a revelation of God's will. As a consequence of this view, Reconstructionists do not regard Jewish law as holy and unchanging. Since the Jewish community can no longer enforce an acceptance of the *mitzvot*, it is misleading to retain the legal terminology of the past. In place of traditional language, Reconstructionists utilize the terms 'folkways' and 'customs' to designate traditional observances, expressions which reflect the fact that throughout history all peoples have created their sacred events, holy days, and religious objects. In the same way Jewry has its heroes (the patriarchs, Moses, the prophets, the rabbis); sacred events (birth, marriage, death); holy days (Sabbath, *Rosh Hashanah*, *Yom Kippur*, Pilgrim Festivals); and holy objects (*Torah*, *tefillin*, prayer shawls). Such folkways bring Jews closer to God, help individuals to lead more meaningful lives, and bring the community together as a united people.

In Kaplan's view, folkways and customs help to sustain the Jewish nation and enrich the spiritual life of Jewry. Yet Kaplan argued that such observances should be accepted voluntarily; in the modern world there is no role for coercive authority. In this regard, Kaplan endorsed the concept of democratic decision-making in determining which laws are relevant for the community. The past, he declared, should have a vote, but not a veto. In this spirit Kaplan believed that the Jewish legal code should be consulted, but previous rulings should not determine contemporary practices. For Kaplan, anachronistic laws as well as those regulations which conflict with the highest ideals of Judaism have no place in a modern Code of Jewish Law unless new meaning can be given to them. Further, Kaplan stressed the importance of formulating new customs to take the place of those that had ceased to give meaning to contemporary Jewish life. Initially it was feared that such freedom of choice might lead to anarchy, but Kaplan suggested that such a difficulty could be avoided if legal guides were produced by the movement – as a result the *Guide to Ritual Usage* was created in 1941. Such resources, he believed, should be perceived as guidelines rather than obligatory rules. In his opinion, it should be the people, rather than the rabbis, who determine appropriate patterns of observance.

One of the most important features of Reconstructionist ideology is its emphasis on Jewish peoplehood. For Kaplan, the purpose of Jewish civilization was to ensure the continuation of the group; moreover, in his view the *Torah* existed for the sake of the nation. It was a great *mitzvah* for any people to survive, create and flourish, he believed, but for the Jews this was an even greater obligation since the Jewish people were created in the image of God. The purpose of Reconstructionist Judaism is therefore to revive the Jewish people's will to identify with tradition. To promote this goal, Kaplan recommended that representatives of world Jewry gather together each year in Jerusalem to renew the sacred covenant. Yet despite this focus on Jewish solidarity Kaplan did not believe that the Jewish community was chosen by God: such a idea, he argued, was racist in character. In place of this notion, Kaplan propagated the concept of mission:

> The purpose of Jewish existence is to foster in ourselves as Jews, and to awaken in the rest of the world, a sense of moral responsibility in action … When that comes about, the Messianic Age will have arrived.   (Rosenthal, 1978, 134)

Reconstructionists therefore believe it is necessary to live in two spheres simultaneously: as a Jew in secular society. It is the responsibility of modern Jewry to strengthen Judaism by blending together the positive features of contemporary culture and the most important values of the Jewish heritage.

Despite Kaplan's endorsement of Zionism and his belief that a full Jewish life could only be led in Israel, Kaplan was a realist, recognizing that it was unlikely that most Jews would in fact settle in the Holy Land. As a consequence he rejected the standard Zionist conviction that Israel should be a religious state characterized by *Torah* Judaism. Instead he asserted that the Jewish homeland should be governed by spiritual principles in line with Ahad Ha-Am's teaching about spiritual ideals. According to Ahad Ha-Am, *Eretz Yisrael* should be a cultural and spiritual centre; similarly Kaplan believed that the state of Israel could inspire world Jewry and draw the community back to tradition. What is required, he maintained, is a creative partnership between Israel and diaspora Jewry.

In accord with this policy, Kaplan endorsed the creation of community centres designed to bring together all the various factions within the Jewish population. Continually he urged Jews to establish organic communities, based like the *kehillot* of Europe on voluntary membership. These American *kehillot*, he argued, should include Jewish community councils or organizations to which all Jews would be encouraged to belong regardless of their religious and political differences. In Kaplan's view such organic communities should undertake to:

1. Keep records of vital statistics.
2. Encourage Jews to join local and national Jewish organizations.

3. Set a budget for Jewish organizations to spend on Jewish needs.
4. Develop guidelines of ethical and moral behaviour.
5. Strengthen Jewish education and culture.
6. Work to improve the health and welfare of Jews and to eliminate poverty within the Jewish community.
7. Encourage culture and the arts.
8. Fight discrimination and anti-Semitism.
9. Work with non-Jewish groups for the common good.   (Ibid., 136)

In line with these communal goals, Kaplan taught that the aim of religion was to bring fulfilment to the Jewish people as a whole rather than to its individual members. This could take place, he believed, only if religious principles were translated into action. Embracing this policy of social involvement, Reconstructionism from its beginnings engaged in socialist action. In the 1930s, for example, Kaplan and Ira Eisenstein (one of the leaders of the movement) supported the socialist idea that government should be responsible for major American industries. More recently, Reconstructionist Judaism has supported labour unions in their struggle to improve working conditions and defend civil rights. In addition, the movement advocated birth control, opposed the death penalty, and endorsed the work of the United Nations. Paradoxically, however, Reconstructionism has not been in the forefront of interfaith activity largely because Kaplan did not believe that religious dialogue would lead to religious tolerance. Instead, the movement has focused primarily on Jewish concerns, believing that the future of Judaism is dependent on the recognition of the multi-faceted dimensions of the Jewish heritage. According to Reconstructionism, what is required today is a commitment to sustain the *sancta* of Jewish life in the face of increasing secularism and assimilation in contemporary society.

RECONSTRUCTIONIST PRACTICES AND PROGRAMMES

As we have seen, Reconstructionism is more than a religious ideology: it embraces a wide range of activities:

1. *Worship and Ritual*. Central to the Reconstructionist interpretation of Judaism, public worship served to unite the community and

draw it back to traditional values. As leaders of the movement, Kaplan and supporters published prayer books for the Sabbath, festivals, the High Holy Days, and daily use. Explaining the philosophy of Reconstructionism, the editors of the *Sabbath Prayer Book* – Kaplan, Eugene Kohn, Milton Steinberg, and Ira Eisenstein – stated that they wished to retain the classic framework of the service and to adhere to the fundamental teachings of the tradition concerning God, man and the world. However, ideas or beliefs in conflict with what has come to be regarded as true or right should be eliminated.

In these liturgical works, Reconstructionists insisted on the validity of their perspective. Thus in the *New Haggadah*, the editors assert that all references to events, real or imaginary, in the Exodus story which might conflict with our highest ethical ideals have been omitted. In reply to the criticism that such a non-supernatural standpoint rendered prayer a meaningless activity, Kaplan argued that worship:

> should intensify one's Jewish consciousness... It should interpret the divine aspect of life as manifest in social idealism. It should emphasize the high worth and potentialities of the individual soul. It should voice the aspiration of Israel to serve the cause of humanity.   (Liebman, 1975, 228)

The purpose of prayer is therefore to affirm one's commitment to an ongoing religious heritage that extols human values.

As far as the *Guide to Jewish Ritual* is concerned, Reconstructionists emphasize that the legal system is no longer binding on all Jews. Rather the *Guide* extols Jewish observances as a means to group survival and the enhancement of human existence. According to Reconstructionist ideology, each Jew should feel at liberty to determine which rituals and folkways should be practised:

> The circumstances of life are so different for different Jews, their economic needs and opportunities, their cultural background, their acquired skills and inherited capacities are so varied that it is unreasonable to expect all of them to evaluate the same rituals in the same way.   (Ibid.)

Such a liberal outlook provides individual Jews with a broad latitude in their departure from traditional law. The *Guide* explains the significance of a set of rituals for the various Jewish holidays and recommends their adoption – yet it affirms that the ultimate criterion for deciding which observances should be retained is the self-fulfilment of the individual. Thus, for example, the *Guide* suggests that work permitted on the Sabbath includes all enjoyable activities which a person is unable to engage in during the week excluding the means of making a living. For Reconstructionists, what matters is not the ceremonial observance of the Sabbath, but the extent to which these ceremonies help one to live and experience Sabbath joy. Consistent with Kaplan's early writing, the *Guide* stresses that Jewish folkways should be observed if they enhance modern life – thus Reconstructionists seek to provide a social rationale, rather than a theological justification, for obeying the commandments.

2. *Zionism.* The establishment of a Jewish homeland in Palestine has also been a major focus of Reconstructionist concern. For Kaplan, Jewish civilization is able to flourish most fully in Palestine: therefore a fundamental precondition for the revival of Jewish life in the diaspora entails a dedication to the building of the state of Israel. Later he reformulated this idea in terms of a Jewish collective consciousness which arises out of the struggle to create a national identity.

From the earliest period Kaplan and his supporters advanced a Zionist policy: in the 1920s, 1930s and 1940s they campaigned on behalf of a Jewish state despite considerable opposition from various quarters such as those who were aligned with the American Council for Judaism, Jewish Communists, and the American Jewish Committee. For Kaplan the building of Palestine was a matter of faith: Zionism, he believed, was a modern expression of Jewish religiosity, and Kaplan sought to give this religious expression a philosophical basis. The Zionist programme of Reconstruction grows out of its adherents' Jewish commitment.

Nonetheless Kaplan's Zionism was American in character: he rejected the necessity of emigrating to Palestine, the ingathering of the exiles in Israel, and the negation of the diaspora. Hence he wrote an editorial in the *Reconstructionist* attacking the Chief Rabbi of Israel for giving religious sanction to the policy of associating the call for return of Jews to Zion with the state rather than with some vague messianic period. Kaplan announced, however, that Israel must be a haven of immigration for all Jews who were unable to feel at home in the countries where they lived. Jews, he believed, should be permitted to constitute a majority within a Jewish commonwealth even though they need have no exclusive responsibility for military defence or foreign policy. Prior to the creation of the

Jewish state, many other Zionists were similarly prepared to accept these conditions.

THE ORGANIZATIONS, INSTITUTIONS AND LITURGY OF RECONSTRUCTIONIST JUDAISM

In its development from the post-First World War period to the present, Reconstructionist Judaism founded a number of institutions and organizations to further its ideology and also produced liturgical material for public worship.

Society for the Advancement of Judaism

In 1922 Mordecai Kaplan along with other supporters of Reconstructionism established the Society for the Advancement of Judaism (SAJ) in New York City. From its inception this body stressed the religious character of the movement: in addition to regular celebrations of festivals and holidays, worship took place on Friday afternoons and Sunday mornings and the main service was held on Saturday morning when Kaplan delivered a lecture. Unlike Conservative Judaism, Reconstructionism insisted on the complete equality of men and women in worship. Initially traditional prayer books were used with loose-leaf inserts of songs and readings; subsequently these were replaced by Reconstructionist prayer books.

In addition to the worship services, a variety of activities were fostered by the SAJ. In the 1920s Palestine, extra-mural and cultural programmes took place under its auspices as well as an assortment of cultural events including Jewish music concerts, Jewish plays, Friday and Monday morning lectures, Saturday afternoon history lessons, Sunday and Wednesday evening forums, Saturday Sabbath study circles, current events discussions, and youth education. In addition, the SAJ sponsored a sewing circle and library foundation. Athletics also played a role in this new centre. Very early in its history the SAJ had a director of athletics, and the top storey of its building was used for basketball, volleyball, and other recreational programmes.

Although Reconstructionist Judaism did not produce an organizational body in its early years, a number of Conservative synagogues affiliated with the SAJ usually these congregations were led by former students of Kaplan who were influenced by his ideas. In the

1930s Rabbi Ira Eisenstein served as Kaplan's assistant; when Kaplan retired in 1945 Eisenstein became leader of the SAJ. Eventually Eisenstein left to encourage the growth of Reconstructionism in Chicago; later he oversaw the development of the Jewish Reconstruction Foundation, directed the Fellowship of Reconstructionist Congregations and *Havurot*, and edited the *Reconstructionist* magazine. From 1961 Alan W. Miller served as the rabbi of the SAJ.

The Jewish Reconstructionist Federation and the Federation of Reconstructionist Congregations and *Havurot*

In the 1940s the Jewish Reconstructionist Foundation (JRF) was established to continue the Reconstructionist programme which had been initiated and sustained by the Society for the Advancement of Judaism – this body was the successor to the Friends of Reconstructionism composed of SAJ and Park Avenue Synagogue supporters of the movement organized in the 1930s by Rabbi Milton Steinberg. This new body encouraged the publication of the *Reconstructionist* magazine as well as books, pamphlets and educational material; in addition it was responsible for the co-ordination of the movement's activities including the Reconstructionist Youth Institute of Study. In the 1940s Kaplan and his associates supported the founding of *havurot* (fellowships) within existing congregations to further the aims of Reconstructionism. These *havurot* were subsequently co-ordinated by the Jewish Reconstructionist Fellowship; through their activities Reconstructionist ideology was put into practice without competing with the existing branches of contemporary Judaism. By 1945 there were four Reconstructionist fellowship chapters under the direction of local rabbis as well as 41 study groups.

In most cases the *havurot* consisted of a rabbi and lay people who met to discuss Reconstructionist literature; the members were individuals affiliated to Reform, Conservative, and Orthodox congregations as well as non-affiliated Jews,and at this stage more than twenty Reform and Conservative rabbis participated in the study groups. As the number of these fellowships grew, congregations in Buffalo, Los Angeles and Skokie [in addition to the SAJ] declared themselves to be Reconstructionist, and the Reconstructionist Federation of Congregations was established in 1945. This body – including synagogues and fellowships – became the Federation of Reconstructionist Congregations and Fellowships in 1961, the change in name reflecting a growing awareness that the movement was developing into a separate denomination. By 1983 the Federation, which was no longer a subsidiary of the JRF, included 46 member units consisting of about ten thousand members in the United States and Canada; synagogues and fellowships numbered twelve in New York, and six in California and Pennsylvania, and Reconstructionist synagogues in Montreal and Toronto. In the last ten years Reconstructionist Judaism has increased in strength and numbers, becoming an important Jewish presence on the North American continent.

Reconstructionist Rabbinical College

In the 1960s Reconstructionist leaders became convinced that the movement needed to train its own rabbis. At the Montreal conference in 1967, the JRF was given the responsibility of establishing a rabbinical college. Although a number of supporters of Reconstructionism did not wish to see the movement evolve into a separate branch of Judaism, there was an increasing recognition that a new curriculum should be devised for Reconstructionist rabbinical students. Under the influence of Ira Eisenstein, it was decided that the Reconstructionist Rabbinical College be established in Philadelphia. On 13 December 1968 the College was dedicated with Eisenstein as president. The course of study consisted of a joint programme with Temple University leading to a doctorate from the university, and a doctorate in Hebrew literature and ordination from the Reconstructionist Rabbinical College. Both men and women were accepted as rabbinical students, and today over 100 rabbis have been ordained. These graduates serve as rabbis and educators in Reconstructionist congregations as well as in Reform and Conservative synagogues. In 1981 Ira Silverman succeeded Eisenstein as president; during his tenure the college offered a five-year curriculum in which each year was spent studying each of the major periods of Jewish civilization: biblical, rabbinic, medieval, modern and contemporary. The purpose of this course of study was to communicate the evolving character of the Jewish heritage.

Reconstructionist Rabbinical Association

In the 1950s the Reconstructionist Rabbinical Fellowship (RRF) – consisting of about a hundred Conservative and Reform rabbis sympathetic to the philosophy of Reconstructionism – was created; its aims were to encourage creative synagogue worship and education as well as the establishment of local and national organic communities. Those who belonged to this body were simultaneously members of the Central Conference of American Rabbis and the Rabbinical Assembly; at this stage it was hoped that the ideas of Reconstructionist Judaism could be communicated without creating a separate denomination. However, with the founding of the Reconstructionist Rabbinical College, a Reconstructionist Rabbinical association of Conservative and Reform rabbis appeared inconsistent with the aims of the movement. In consequence, a rabbinical association of Reconstructionist rabbinical alumni was founded. In 1975 its first conference was held, and six years later it began to publish its own journal, *Raayonot*.

Reconstructionist Liturgy

Many of Kaplan's ideas as expressed in his writings were embodied in a corpus of creative liturgical material that began to appear in the 1930s. These works included Kaplan's *Supplementary Prayers and Readings for the High Holy Days* (1934), a *New Haggadah* (1941), a reconstructed *Sabbath Prayer Book* (1945), a *High Holy Day Prayer Book* (1948), and a *Festival Prayer Book* (1958). The *New Haggadah*, edited by Kaplan, Eugene Kohn and Ira Eisenstein, applied Kaplan's teaching to Jewish worship – it subordinated the miracles and plagues of the traditional Passover *Haggadah* to the account of Israel's redemption from Egypt and its significance for both contemporary Judaism and humanity. In addition, it added new material written in an attempt to give the *Haggadah* contemporary appeal. The *Sabbath Prayer Book* was similarly composed for those who were unable to empathize with the traditional *siddur* – it was designed to evoke religious sentiment in those seeking a modern form of spirituality. This new volume eliminated anachronistic and religiously offensive prayers and all references to supernaturalism and divine revelation; further, all allusions to the doctrine of the chosen people, Gods's encounter with Moses on Mount Sinai, bodily resurrection, miracles and a personal Messiah were discarded. Other prayers which Kaplan and his associates viewed as central to the tradition but problematic in character were supplemented with commentaries and modern interpretations.

RECONSTRUCTIONIST POLICIES

For Reconstructionist Jews the concept of an organic Jewish community is based on the notion of *Kelal Yisrael* (the community of Israel). This doctrine implies that Jews should feel a sense of identification with Jews world-wide. In previous centuries Jews regarded themselves as a community in exile, separated from their ancestral homeland. Today, however, Jews no longer regard themselves in such negative terms; rather they perceive themselves as fully integrated in the countries where they dwell. Further, traditional Judaism in the post-Enlightenment age no longer has the capacity to bind all Jews into a single collectivity. Such altered conditions arguably call for a radical redefinition and reformulation of the covenant. According to Kaplan, covenantal obligation should now be conceived as a basis for reinvigorating contemporary Jewish life.

A new concept of covenant, Kaplan suggested, should be initiated by a Covenant Assembly to be held in Jerusalem including all segments of world Jewry: it should formally acknowledge that a new stage in Jewish life had been inaugurated by the creation of a Jewish homeland. Given this recognition, the covenant should serve as a stimulus for the transformation of the principle of Zionism to extend to the idea of a 'Greater Zionism' grounded in the concept of a transnational Jewish community with its core in *Eretz Yisrael*. Such a notion would transcend national boundaries, providing a foundation for the creation of moral and spiritual links between all Jews. The covenant conceived in this fashion would provide a common bond among all sectors of Jewry despite their ideological orientations.

Central to this vision of a revitalized Judaism is the notion of organic communal life. As early as 1908 Kaplan proposed a comprehensive programme of Jewish institutional activity combining religious, cultural, social and recreational interests. In his view, the synagogue should become a *Beit Knesset* (a House of Assembly). Ten years later Kaplan organized a synagogue-centre in New York along these lines, and a decade later, Dr Israel H. Levinson founded a similar centre in Brooklyn. This new interpretation of Jewish communal existence attracted a wide circle of supporters from the ranks of Conservative Judaism, and similar centres were established in the following decades.

For Kaplan, such Jewish social entities could best maintain and further Jewish civilization: it was not the congregational unit that would ensure the survival of the Jewish people, but a structure that encompassed the entire range of communal affairs. Such a Jewish centre, Kaplan believed, should function as a coordinating body, responsible for the administration of all religious, educational, philanthropic and social activities. Within this context, special attention should be given to religious and educational agencies since they formed the nucleus of Jewish life, yet there must be a general recognition that Jewish existence is multi-faceted, and all interests should be included. One important advantage of this type of institutional framework is that the duplication of organizational bodies in the Jewish community would be eliminated. To achieve greater efficiency such communal agencies should be prepared to function on the local, regional and national levels.

Membership in this consolidated communal body would be open to all those who wished to identify with the Jewish people. This overarching communal agency would replace the synagogue as the primary focus of Jewish identification, extending its influence to all spheres of Jewish life – it would be responsible for regulating marriages, divorces and deaths, and also be concerned with the religious, cultural, economic and social welfare of Jewry. In promoting this conception of Jewish existence Kaplan drew attention to the presence of similar structures in Europe. In the past, he noted, the European *kahal* existed because of external pressure, but this new conception of the *kahal* would be a voluntary association, based on democratic principles.

As far as Reconstructionist policies are concerned, Kaplan stressed that central to Reconstructionism was the role of public worship; in his view, it served to unite the community and draw it back to traditional values. In line with this policy Kaplan and his supporters published prayer books for the Sabbath and festivals, the High Holy Days, and daily use. Explaining the philosophy of the movement, the editors of the Sabbath Prayer Book – Kaplan, Eugene Kohn, Milton Steinberg, and Ira Eisenstein – stated that they wished to 'retain the classic framework of the service and to adhere to the fundamental teachings of that tradition concerning God, man and the world. However, ideas or beliefs in conflict with what has come to be regarded as true or right should be eliminated' (Liebman, 1975, 227).

In addition to such liturgical publications, the movement also issued a *Guide to Jewish Ritual*. According to Reconstructionist policy, the legal system should no longer be regarded as binding on all Jews. For this reason the *Guide* extols Jewish observances as a means to group survival and the enhancement of human existence. In the Reconstructionist view, each Jew should feel at liberty to determine which rituals and folkways should be practised.

Finally, in line with the Reconstructionist focus on Israel's centrality to Jewish life, Reconstructionist policy has been Zionistic from its early beginnings. For Kaplan, Jewish civilization was able to flourish most fully in Palestine; therefore, a fundamental precondition for the revival of Jewish life in the diaspora entailed a dedication to the building of the state of Israel. 'Take Palestine out of the Jew's life,' he wrote, 'and the only spheres of influence that remain to him as a Jew are the synagogue and the cemetery' (Liebman, 1975, 230). Later he reformulated this idea in terms of a Jewish collective consciousness arising out of the struggle to create a national identity.

CRITIQUE

Despite the fact that Reconstructionist Judaism has attracted a significant following, its ideology is beset by a number of serious defects. First, the Reconstructionist quest to embrace secular standards while remaining loyal to the Jewish heritage is an incoherent policy. As we have seen, Kaplan and his followers endorsed the democratic values of American society – for this reason they opposed day schools because they fail to prepare students for democracy. According to Kaplan, Jewish day schools are neither feasible nor desirable. For similar reasons the leaders of Reconstructionism viewed the doctrine of chosenness as undemocratic and unegalitarian. As Ira Eisenstein explained:

We Jews have a remarkable history. In some respects we have been more preoccupied than other peoples with the belief in God and with the conception of God, with problems of life's meaning and how best to achieve life's purpose. But we should not boast about it. Humility is more befitting a people of such high aspirations. We ought not to say that God gave the *Torah* to us and to nobody else, particularly at a time when mankind seeks to foster the sense of the equality of peoples. We should be old enough and mature enough as a people to accept our history with dignity, without resort to comparisons which are generally odious.   (Ibid., 230).

For Reconstructionist leaders an individual must be foremost an American and only secondarily a Jew. Such a conviction led Kaplan to set aside the traditional objection to intermarriage. Jews, he maintained, should not regard intermarriage as illegitimate since America:

> is certain to look with disfavour upon any culture which seeks to maintain itself by decrying the intermarriage of its adherents with those of another culture. By accepting a policy which does not decry marriages of Jews with Gentiles, provided the homes they establish are Jewish and their children are given a Jewish upbringing the charge of exclusiveness and tribalism falls to the ground.   (Ibid.)

According to Kaplan and his followers, the *sancta* of American life must be celebrated: to further this aim Kaplan, Eugene Kohn and a Christian J. Paul Williams published *Faith in America*, a collection of non-denominational prayers, poems, songs, literary selections, and historical documents to be used by churches, synagogues, public assemblies, and patriotic societies on national holidays.

Yet it is obvious that such an endorsement of American culture runs counter to the aim of reconstructing Judaism as a civilization. As we have seen, Reconstructionist Jews seek to perpetuate the folk religion of the Jewish people. This pattern of belief and practice is an elitist system including rituals and ceremonies, doctrines and dogma, and a religious organization headed by religious authorities. It is different from – and often conflicts with – the secular orientation of American life. Thus there is an inevitable tension between the religion of Israel and the social norms of modern life; regrettably Reconstructionist Judaism has failed to acknowledge that a clash between these two ideological systems is inevitable and irresolvable.

Another serious inconsistency relates to the Reconstructionist view of the supernatural. As we have seen, Kaplan rejected the traditional understanding of divine reality. In his view the Deity is a cosmic process that makes for human salvation. Adopting a pragmatic approach, he envisaged God as the power in humanity and nature which directs human beings to seek value and meaning. For

Kaplan, the word 'salvation' denotes a striving in one's culture for the fulfilment of human destiny – a naturalistic interpretation without other-worldly implications. Such a view implies that revelation should be understood as a natural process of discovery as the Reconstructionist Prayer Book states; it was not God who revealed the *Torah* to Israel, but the *Torah* which revealed God to Israel. This implies that the *Torah* is the source of the Jewish conception of God rather than God being the source of *Torah*.

This naturalistic interpretation of the central doctrines of Judaism is counterbalanced within Reconstructionism by an insistence that the *sancta* of Jewish life be maintained. For Kaplan and his followers, the Jewish tradition is grounded in the folkways of the people. Judaism is not simply a religion: it constitutes a way of life. The *sancta* of the Jewish heritage, Reconstructionism asserts, commemorates what the community believes to be most valuable, provides historical continuity, and strengthens the collective consciousness of the nation. For this reason, the practices of the past must be retained. The difficulty with such an approach, however, is that Jewish observance is traditionally grounded in God's will. According to the faith, God revealed the 613 commandments to Moses on Mount Sinai, and guided the development of the Oral law. For millennia, Jews believed that by keeping the *Torah* they were obeying God's decree. Without such a conviction, it is unclear why Jews should feel obliged to carry on the tradition. Arguably it would be more consistent for Reconstructionists, as non-supernaturalists, to reformulate the Jewish heritage so that it reflects their fundamental beliefs about the nature of God and the world.

A further difficulty with Reconstructionist ideology concerns its endorsement of a non-theistic approach to Judaism: it is conceptually difficult to envisage Judaism without a supernatural Deity. For nearly 4000 years the Jewish faith was essentially monolithic in character. During the biblical period the ancient Israelites affirmed their belief in one God who created the universe – he brought all things into being, continues to sustain the cosmos, and guides humanity to its ultimate destiny. In the unfolding of this providential scheme, Israel has a central role: as God's chosen people, the nation is to serve as a light to all peoples. Underlying the development of Jewish life and thought through the ages until the modern period there has been a common core of religious belief, variously interpreted by Jewish sages. Yet, it is this religious basis that Reconstructionism seeks to discard in favour of an enlightened understanding of reality. However without this religious foundation, is it possible for Reconstructionist Judaism to be a legitimate heir to the Jewish heritage? It appears instead that as a non-supernatural interpretation of Judaism, Reconstructionism – like Humanistic Judaism – has divorced itself from Jewish civilization despite its avowed claim to preserve the tradition.

In this connection, Reconstructionism as a new development on the Jewish religious spectrum appears unable to meet the spiritual needs of the community as a whole. Despite the attraction of a non-theistic interpretation of the faith for a small segment of Jewry, many Jews are searching for a modern form of spirituality based on the Jewish faith. Though there is considerable uncertainty about traditional Jewish belief, there is an increasing desire to discover a meaningful mode of religiosity. Such a quest for spiritual enlightenment calls for the reformulation of traditional theism rather than a rejection of supernaturalism altogether. Thus, even though Kaplan and his followers believe they are providing an appealing modernized formulation of the Jewish heritage, Reconstructionism as a religious system is incapable of meeting the religious needs of most contemporary Jews.

Finally, in the light of the Reconstructionist rejection of traditional theism, it is inconceivable that under its banner Jewry could unite yearly to reaffirm its faith in the covenant. As we have seen, Kaplan believed that all sectors of world Jewry should assemble in Jerusalem formally to recognize that a new stage in Jewish life has been initiated by the founding of the State of Israel. Yet, it is unclear what such a grouping of representatives would be affirming – certainly it would be impossible for this group to dedicate themselves to any form of religious commitment given the lack of a shared basis of belief. Such a gathering could do nothing more than affirm their allegiance to Israel – a step far removed from Kaplan's desire to reaffirm the covenant which in the past kept Jewry united. Moreover, given the differing criteria within the Jewish community for determining Jewish status, there could not be an agreement about who would be entitled to participate in such a communal initiation ceremony. Jewish Unity Day – rather than drawing all Jews into a Covenant People – would highlight the deep fissures in the modern Jewish community. Reconstructionism, despite its aims to provide world Jewry with a reformulated philosophy of Judaism relevant to contemporary circumstances, is thus riddled with internal contradictions and thereby fails to serve as an overarching religious alternative to the major religious groupings within the community.

7

Humanistic Judaism

Like Reconstructionist Judaism, Jewish Humanism offers a non-theistic interpretation of the Jewish faith. Originating in the 1960s in Detroit, Michigan, under the leadership of Rabbi Sherwin Wine, Humanistic Judaism now numbers about 40 000 members in the United States, Israel, Europe and elsewhere. Distancing itself from all other branches of Judaism, this new movement extols the humanistic dimensions of the faith. On the basis of this ideology, Jewish holidays and life-cycle events have been reinterpreted so as to emphasize their humanistic characteristics; in addition, Humanistic Jews insist that traditional Jewish beliefs must be reformulated in the light of scientific knowledge. Promoting a secular life style, this new conception of Judaism seeks to adjust the Jewish tradition to modernity. However, although Humanistic Judaism has attracted a growing number of followers, its confidence in human potential appears misplaced given the horrific events of the twentieth century. The Holocaust has cast a shadow over any form of Humanism, and it is difficult to envisage such a modernized form of Judaism appealing to world Jewry, particularly those individuals who seek a spiritual solution to the problems of the contemporary age.

THE ORIGINS OF HUMANISTIC JUDAISM

Humanistic Judaism originated in 1965 when the Birmingham Temple in Detroit, Michigan, began to publicize its philosophy of Judaism. In 1966 a special committee for Humanistic Judaism was organized at the Temple to share service and educational material with rabbis and laity throughout the country. The following year a meeting of several leaders of the movement met in Detroit, issuing a statement which affirmed that Judaism should be governed by empirical reason and human needs; in addition, a new magazine, *Humanistic Judaism*, was founded. Two years later, two new

Humanistic congregations were established: Temple Beth Or in Deerfield, Illinois, and a Congregation for Humanistic Judaism in Fairfield County, Connecticut. In 1969 the Society for Humanistic Judaism was established in Detroit to provide a basis for cooperation among Humanistic Jews and in 1970 the first annual conference of the Society met in Detroit. During the next ten years new congregations were established in Boston, Toronto, Los Angeles, Washington, Miami, Long Beach and Huntington, New York. In subsequent years Secular Humanistic Judaism became an international movement with supporters on five continents. The National Federation, consisting of 30 000 members, currently comprises nine national organizations in the United States, Canada, Britain, France, Belgium, Israel, Australia, Argentina and Uruguay.

In 1986 the Federation issued a proclamation stating its ideology and aims:

> We believe in the value of human reason and in the reality of the world which reason discloses. The natural universe stands on its own, requiring no supernatural intervention. We believe in the value of human existence and in the power of human beings to solve their problems both individually and collectively. Life should be directed to the satisfaction of human needs. Every person is entitled to life, dignity and freedom. We believe in the value of Jewish identity and in the survival of the Jewish people. Jewish history is a human story. Judaism, as the civilization of the Jews, is a human creation. Jewish identity is an ethnic reality. The civilization of the Jewish people embraces all manifestations of Jewish life, including Jewish languages, ethical traditions, historic memories, cultural heritage, and especially the emergence of the state of Israel in modern times. Judaism also embraces many belief systems and lifestyles. As the creation of the Jewish people in all ages, it is always changing. We believe in the value of a secular humanistic democracy for Israel and for all the nations of the world. Religion and state must be separate. The individual right to privacy and moral autonomy must be guaranteed. Equal rights must be granted to all, regardless of race, sex, creed or ethnic origin.

In accordance with this philosophy of Judaism, the Federation advocated a new conception of Jewish identity. In answer to the question 'Who is a Jew?', the movement declared:

We, the members of the International Federation of Secular Humanistic Jews, believe that the survival of the Jewish people depends on a broad view of Jewish identity. We welcome into the Jewish people all men and women who sincerely desire to share the Jewish experience regardless of their ancestry. We challenge the assumption that the Jews are primarily or exclusively a religious community and that religious convictions or behaviour are essential to full membership in the Jewish people.

The Jewish people is a world with a pluralistic culture and civilization all its own. Judaism, as the culture of the Jews, is more than theological commitment. It encompasses many languages, a vast body of literature, historical memories and ethical values. In our times the shadow of the Holocaust and the rebirth of the State of Israel are a central part of Jewish consciousness.

We Jews have a moral responsibility to welcome all people who seek to identify with our culture and destiny. The children and spouses of inter-marriage who desire to be part of the Jewish people must not be cast aside because they do not have Jewish mothers and do not wish to undergo religious conversion. The authority to define 'who is a Jew' belongs to all the Jewish people and cannot be usurped by any part of it.

In response to the destructive definition of a Jew now proclaimed by some Orthodox authorities, and in the name of the historic experience of the Jewish people, we therefore, affirm that a Jew is a person of Jewish descent or any person who declares himself or herself to be a Jew and who identifies with the history, ethical values, culture, civilization, community and fate of the Jewish people.

Such an ideology of Judaism is based on a radical reinterpretation of the tradition. According to the major exponent of Humanistic Judaism, Sherwin Wine, the traditional conception of Jewish history is mistaken. In his view, Abraham, Isaac and Jacob never existed. Further, the Exodus account is a myth:

There is no historical evidence to substantiate a massive Hebrew departure from the land of the Pharaohs. As far as we can surmise the Hebrew occupation of the hill country on both sides of the Jordan was continuous. The twelve tribes never left their ancestral land, never endured 400 years of slavery, and never wandered the Sinai desert. (Wine, 1985, 35–6)

Moreover, Moses was not the leader of the Hebrews, nor did he compose the *Torah*. In this light, it is an error to regard the biblical account as authoritative; rather it is a human account of the history of the Israelite nation. Humanistic Judaism, however, rejects this presupposition of traditional Judaism and insists that each Jew should be free to exercise his own personal autonomy concerning questions of religious belief and practice.

Dedicated to Jewish survival, Humanistic Judaism emphasizes the importance of Jewish festivals in fostering Jewish identity. Yet, for Humanistic Jews, they must be detached from their supernatural origins and be reinterpreted in the light of modern circumstances. As Wine explains:

> The Jewish holidays have no intrinsic divine connection. They derive from the evolution of the human species and human culture ... For Humanistic Jews the holidays need to be rescued from rabbinic tyranny and given a secular language and a secular story. (Ibid., 150)

Such an interpretation of traditional Jewish festivals provides a basis for extolling human potential. So, too does Humanistic Judaism's understanding of life-cycle events: the ceremonies connected with these events emphasize the importance of group survival. However, humanistic philosophy – grounded in the conviction that all persons are equal – rejects the practice of male circumcision:

> A Humanistic morality that defends female equality would have a hard time justifying a birth ritual that excludes women ... The *brit* [covenant ceremony] is by its very nature, inconsistent with a Humanistic Jewish value system. (Ibid., 181)

In its place Humanistic Jews have substituted an occasion that provides equal status to boys and girls and dramatizes the connection of the child with the future of the family, the Jewish people and humanity.

Likewise Humanistic Judaism fosters a Humanistic maturity ceremony which reflects the ethical commitments of Humanistic Jews. Ensuring the equality of both sexes, such ceremonies are designed to express the beliefs of the individual celebrants as well as the ideals of the community.

As an important transitional event, the marriage ceremony should also embody Humanistic values. According to Wine, the wedding should embrace the conception of the bride and groom publicly declaring their commitment of support and loyalty to one another. The most important feature of this ritual is the pledge made by both partners in the presence of family and friends. Such a statement should not be simply a ritualistic formula, rather it should be a personal declaration, accompanied with the exchange of rings or other gifts symbolic of their commitment. Humanistic marriage ceremonies also include songs and poetry about love and loyalty, a marriage contract expressive of the couple's personal relationship, and a philosophic statement about the Humanistic meaning of marriage.

Rituals connected with death should similarly be expressive of Humanistic principles. For Humanistic Jews, mortality is an unavoidable and final event. Accepting this truth, it is possible to live courageously and generously in the face of tragedy. 'A Humanistic Jewish memorial service is an opportunity to teach a Humanistic philosophy of life. Both the meditations and the eulogies must serve to remind people that the value of personal life lies in its quality, not in its quantity.' (Ibid., 182)

Humanistic Judaism, then, offers an option for those who wish to identify with the Jewish community despite their rejection of the traditional understanding of God's nature and activity. Unlike Reconstructionist Judaism, with its emphasis on the observances of the past, Humanistic Judaism fosters a radically new approach. The Jewish heritage is relevant only in so far as it advances Humanistic ideals. In addition, traditional definitions and principles are set aside in the quest to create a Judaism consonant with a scientific and pluralistic age. Secular in orientation, Humanistic Jews seek to create a world in which the Jewish people are dedicated to the betterment of all humankind.

THE PHILOSOPHY AND ORGANIZATION OF HUMANISTIC JUDAISM

In *Judaism Beyond God*, Sherwin Wine offered a critique of the different religious movements within the Jewish community. Modern Orthodoxy, Conservatism, Reconstructionism and Reform are, in his view, the 'ambivalents'. Although these groups endorse the secular revolution in their everyday activities, they have one foot in the world of faith and the other in that of reason. However, since these two spheres are incompatible, such a stance is incoherent. Ambivalents, Wine asserted, are experts in avoiding actuality – they seek to avoid any form of painful confrontation. Unable to disown either faith or reason, they attempt to combine the humility of prayer with the dignity of personal freedom.

For Wine modern Orthodoxy avoids facing crucial dilemmas concerning belief in the Messiah, divine reward and punishment, and the world to come. In place of theological commitment, Orthodox Judaism has substituted rigid adherence to traditional observance. Yet without the religious basis of the faith, there is little reason to follow Jewish law. The Conservative movement has similarly failed to confront the challenges of modern secularism and as a result is riddled with theological inconsistency:

> Like modern Orthodoxy, it [Conservative Judaism] chooses to offend no one – or at least, very few, since it deals mainly with appearances, it has difficulty dealing with the substance of belief and integrity. Speaking the ideas of reason and dignity while wearing the costume of faith and humility is precarious theatre. (Ibid., 66)

Reconstructionism differs from Conservative Judaism in its rejection of belief in God; none the less Reconstructionist Jews continue to use the religious vocabulary of the Jewish past. This has resulted in general confusion about the tenets of the faith. Reform Judaism, too, suffers from numerous defects; in particular its emphasis on ethical monotheism is, to Wine, a betrayal of modern secular culture and the Jewish heritage. Humanistic Judaism, however, rejects the authority of the rabbinic tradition; it is also distinct from Conservative, Reform and Reconstructionist Judaism in jettisoning theistic language. Such a shift in perspective is due to the influence of science, capitalism and secular culture which have dramatically transformed Jewish life. As proponents of a secular Jewish lifestyle, Humanistic Jews believe in the power and beauty of human potential, the necessity of reason, the right of each person to satisfy his needs, and the goal of the unity of humankind. In this quest, Humanistic Judaism aspires to create a better future:

> We do not praise what we are. We praise what it is possible for us to become. If human history has featured the base, it has also pre-

sented the noble. If the human saga has revealed the terror of irra-
tional destruction, it has also delivered the marvel of rational survival. If human nature has chosen its movements of petty
selfishness, it has found its seasons of grand compassion. If nations
have killed and slaughtered, they have also made peace. For many
timid spirits cynicism is no more comfortable than hope. It justifies
inaction. But we will not be seduced by this fatal reward. We shall
strive to be what we believe we can become.   (Wine, 1988, 96–7)

Such a modernized vision of Judaism is based on a number of
assumptions concerning the central elements of the faith, as described in detail in the official *Guide to Humanistic Judaism* produced
by the movement.

God

Historically belief in the existence of God served as the foundation of
the Jewish tradition. After the Enlightenment, however, a growing
number of Jews found it increasingly difficult to believe in an
omnipotent, omniscient and benevolent creator and sustainer of the
universe. Instead, a series of alternative theological positions has
emerged within the community:

1. Theism: belief in a Supreme Being, a supernatural creator-God
   who responds to prayer and worship and intervenes actively
   in the lives of people.
2. Deism: belief in a Supreme Being, a supernatural creator who
   does not intervene in the lives of people.
3. Pantheism: belief that God and nature are one and the same,
   or that God and some part of nature, such as life, are one and
   the same.
4. Agnosticism: not knowing whether or not a Supreme Being
   exists.
5. Atheism: belief that a Supreme Being does not exist.
6. Ignosticism: finding the question of God's existence meaningless because it has no verifiable consequences.

Unlike the other branches of Judaism, Humanistic Judaism denies
any form of supernatural belief – instead it is compatible with
agnosticism, atheism and ignosticism. As such, it regards religious
belief as fundamentally psychological in origin:

The deity is the projection of the first and most intimate human experience, the dependence of the child on the parents. Patriarchy, monarchy, and traditional religion go hand in hand. Just as the family requires a father-leader and the nation requires a father-king, so does the universe require a father-God. (*Guide to Humanistic Judaism*, 1993, 27)

Revelation and Authority

Unlike Orthodox Judaism which is based on the doctrine of *Torah MiSinai*, Humanistic Jews rely on reason as the most effective means of arriving at truth. Both Scripture and rabbinic sources are perceived as human in origin: thus they must be submitted to critical evaluation. Viewed in this light, the *Torah* is regarded as an unreliable guide to the history of the Jewish people – Humanistic Jews believe it is full of misunderstanding and confusion. Nor is the *Torah* considered a viable ethical guide:

Much of what [*Torah*] recommends is ethically barbaric; for example, death to homosexuals (Leviticus 20.13) as well as to the person who picks up sticks on the Sabbath (Numbers 15.32–6) or who encourages 'serving other gods' (Deuteronomy 12.7–10). (Ibid., 78)

Yet Humanistic Judaism can derive a number of important moral principles from Scripture. Some of the Bible's ethical teaching (such as the prohibition against murder and theft) are valid from a Humanistic outlook. For Humanistic Jews authority must be individual in nature, a position confirmed by Jewish experience itself:

One of the most prominent characteristics of Jewish history is the vulnerability of Jews. Repeatedly, they learned a painful lesson: Do not trust your fortune to authority. At one moment it might promise safety and prosperity; in the next it might deliver violence and destruction ... the lesson of Jewish history remains valid: Do not trust external authority ... Thus do Humanism and Jewish experience confirm one another. Both demonstrate that (1) there is no authority in the universe, human or divine, that may rightfully impose its power on human beings; and (2) every

person owns himself or herself and possesses the right to determine the purpose and course of his or her life.   (Ibid., 1993, 5–6)

The Jewish People

A central principle of rabbinic Judaism is that the Jewish nation
was elected by God to be his special people, the instrument for the
enlightenment of all humanity. In return for having been divinely
elected, the Jewish community is bound to serve God by obeying
his laws as found in the *Torah* and *Talmud* – the covenant between
the Deity and the people of Israel is fundamental to the faith.
Humanistic Judaism, however, views all human beings as equal.
Their differing worldviews are simply the result of historical, social
and cultural factors; as a consequence, it is a mistake to view one
group as superior to any other.

Adopting a secular perspective, Humanistic Jews reject the traditional interpretation of Jewish history – the account of the Jews in
the Bible and rabbinic literature is seen as a blend of historical fact
and mythic fantasy. The true history of the Jewish nation, however,
is in the process of being discovered through the findings of biblical
criticism, archaeology and scientific investigation. In this light
Humanistic Judaism is able to uncover events of Humanistic import
in the Jewish past. The lesson of history, particularly in the modern
world, is that Jews must look to themselves for deliverance:

Especially in the age of the Holocaust it is very clear that the
events of Jewish history do not point to the existence of a loving
and just God. Rather, they point to the fact that the universe is in-
different to the fate of all men and women, including the Jews. In
the end, Jews like all people, must rely on their own power for
survival, happiness and justice. That message, the message of
Humanism, is the lesson of Jewish history.   (Ibid., 39)

Humanistic Judaism then – unlike Orthodox, Conservative and
Reform Judaism – stresses that Jewish history is ultimately a
human construction. Whereas these other branches of Judaism look
to God's providential concern, Humanistic Jews see only universal
indifference.

Secular Humanistic Judaism, then, offers a non-theistic alternative to Jewish identity and culture, promoting values that have

been largely neglected by the Jewish establishment: rationality, personal autonomy, and the celebration of human values. As a movement, it seeks to create a pluralistic world among all religions and philosophies of life. To carry out these aims, it is organized along the lines shown in Figure 7.1.

JEWISH HOLIDAYS

For Humanistic Jews, the Jewish holidays are of historical and religious significance in so far as they promote Humanistic values. Thus the Sabbath is viewed as a day of peace, restoration and study. Above all it is a time to affirm and celebrate Jewish identity. Following traditional practice, Humanistic Jews are encouraged to observe home and community ceremonies:

> *Shabbat* offers opportunities for both home and community ceremonies: candlelighting, wine and the eating of braided bread (*hallah*), with blessings that express human power and responsibility. *Shabbat* celebrations for Humanistic Jews are tributes to Jewish solidarity, to the shared Jewish past, present and future. They provide opportunities to learn about, articulate, discuss and celebrate Humanistic and Jewish history, philosophy, and values. Humanistic *Shabbat* celebrations recognize the individual's connections to humanity: a family, a community, a nation, the world. (Ibid., 70)

Similarly, the *Havdalah* ceremony at the conclusion of the Sabbath has important Humanistic implications:

> The symbols of *Havdalah* – the twisted candle, the spices, and the wine – may be used Humanistically. The twisted candle represents the many sources of the light of wisdom and beauty. Wine symbolizes joy and fulfilment. The sweet, lingering fragrance of the spice box recalls all that is good and beautiful, and offers hope for happiness and peace in the coming week.   (Ibid.)

Like the adherents of the other branches of contemporary Judaism, Humanistic Jews also view the New Year as spiritually significant – it is a time for reflection, renewal and new beginnings. Humanistic Judaism, however, focuses on the role of self-evaluation

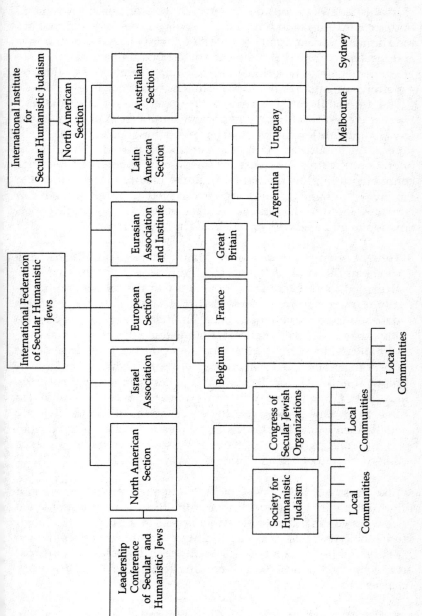

Figure 7.1

rather than divine judgment: *Rosh Hashanah* offers an occasion for Humanistic Jews to consider the possibilities for self-improvement. In this context the sounding of the *shofar* is perceived as summoning the Humanistic community to reflect on their personal shortcomings and resolve to uphold Humanistic values. In a similar vein, the Day of Atonement is seen as signalling the climax of such self-evaluation – it affords an opportunity to make amends and seek forgiveness.

The three Pilgrim Festivals – Passover, *Sukkot* (Booths) and *Shavuot* (Weeks) – also have important significance for Humanistic Jews. Although Jewish Humanism rejects the theological assumptions of the Exodus account, Passover teaches the valuable lesson of liberation: it extols the quest for freedom in a variety of readings commemorating this pivotal event in the history of the nation. On Passover Humanistic Jews are encouraged to recall the ancient Israelites' flight from bondage and resolve to bring about the emancipation of all those who are enslaved in the modern world:

> Tonight is a night of memories. Many years ago our fathers were slaves in the land of Egypt. In bitterness and in hardship they struggled to please their masters and win the precious opportunity of mere survival. Many died from the heat of work; others perished from the cold of despair. Through the agonies of oppression, they searched their hearts for one thing that would make life bearable. They searched for hope and found it. They dreamed of freedom and believed that one day it would be theirs. Tonight is a night of hope. Ancient legend has it that, in a moment of surprise, a prophet called Elijah will return to earth and make all people free. In his time he protected the weak and the poor and fearlessly challenged wicked authority. In all ages his name was a word of comfort and pleasant expectations. Passover invokes his presence and, with it, the vision he brings.   (Wine, 1988, 269)

Like Passover, *Sukkot* was celebrated in ancient times as a major Pilgrim festival; it was a reminder of the Exodus from Egypt when Jews were commanded to construct booths and dwell in them. For Humanistic Jews *Sukkot* is significant in that it symbolizes human mastery of the environment – it is a tribute to agricultural, industrial and technological advance. According to the *Guide to Humanistic Judaism*:

> *Sukkot* offers an opportunity for communities to come together, to experience the out-of-doors, to recognise the interconnected-

ness of humanity, and to acknowledge responsibility for the environment. In ancient times, Jews gathered in booths for the harvest to increase efficiency. For Humanistic Jews, *Sukkot* offers an opportunity to work together to build the *sukkah*, which then can become a centre of an outdoor celebration: a picnic under a roof open to the sun or stars, or a community bonfire that evokes memories of family cookouts or camp overnights. (*Guide to Humanistic Judaism*, 1988, 74)

Traditionally *Shavuot*, the third Pilgrim Festival, was celebrated as a symbol of the giving of the law on Mount Sinai. For Humanistic Jews the *Torah* marks the beginning of Jewish literature; *Shavuot* thus is understood as a time to celebrate the study of Jewish sources. Through the ceremony of confirmation, boys and girls are charged to renew a commitment to Humanistic values. Here, too, Wine provided various readings for this important holiday such as the following:

Poets and sages wandered through the centuries of our history and wove the strands of our heritage with the flair of their talents. In the special joy of *Shavuot* we remember their gifts and reach out with gratitude to use their creation. To be Jewish is to bask in the sun of their fame. To be human is to sense the urgency of their words. People of the past who plant the seeds of wisdom in the minds of others bequeath to the present the harvest of a better world. Others have sowed and we have reaped; we shall sow and others will reap. (Wine, 1988, 280)

As far as *Hannukah* is concerned, Humanistic Jews seek to reinterpret this celebration of the Maccabean victory over the Syrians. Rather than envisaging this holiday as a triumph for Orthodoxy, Jewish Humanists focus on the courage of the Maccabees. Just as these champions of traditional Judaism seized control over the Temple, Humanistic Jews are encouraged to take the future into their own hands. *Hannukah* is thus seen as an endorsement of human dignity, ingenuity and hope. Humanistic Jews celebrate *Hannukah* as a reminder that human beings can use their abilities to enhance the quality of life. To reinforce this message the symbol of light is a dominant motif:

The symbol of *Hannukah* is the eight-branched candelabrum, or *hannukah*, commonly called a *menorah*. Community celebrations and family parties feature candlelighting ceremonies, *latkes*, songs and *dreidel* games. The flickering *Hannukah* lights are a reminder of the Jewish people's struggles, courage and fragile triumphs. The flames are a link to the past and a tribute to the dignity of Jews everywhere. (*Guide to Humanistic Judaism*, 1993, 31)

Purim, too, is interpreted by Humanistic Jews as a celebration of Jewish heroism. The Book of Esther which is read during this holiday relates how Haman – the enemy of the Jews – was defeated by Esther, the king's wife, and her uncle Mordecai. These heroes of the Jewish people serve as a source of courage in facing modern challenges: this is the central theme of the Humanistic Purim Youth Service:

> Many people, many Jews, think of themselves as weak and help-less. They run away from problems and refuse to face their enemies. But others stand their ground and challenge their foes. They value their courage. Brave people become leaders. They become human examples to follow. They become heroes ... *Gibbor* is a Hebrew word. It means 'hero'. Purim is the holiday of *gibbor*, the festival to honour heroes ... Esther and Mordecai stand for all the heroes of Jewish history. They are symbols of strength, power, courage and loyalty. (Wine, 1988, 265–6)

For Humanistic Jews *Tu Bi-Shevat* (The New Year of Trees) also has symbolic significance. Originally this festival was a spring holiday, but with the rise of Zionism it was transformed into a cele-bration of the Jewish homeland. This link to Israel has special meaning for Humanistic Judaism; by planting trees in the State of Israel Humanistic Jews are able to affirm their commitment to Jewish survival. In addition, this holiday functions as a reminder of the im-portance of the natural environment. Thus the *Guide to Humanistic Judaism* recommends the creation of ecological Humanistic pro-grammes on *Tu Bi-Shevat*:

> A holiday honouring trees and their fruit is a natural time for Humanistic Jews to examine their relationship to this planet and how best it can be preserved for future generations. Earth Day ceremonies and fairs are fitting Humanistic celebrations of *Tu Bi-Shevat*. Community tree plantings might symbolize tree planting in Israel or preservation of the world's rain forest. Programmes

that emphasize humanity's unique relationship to nature and the need to preserve, conserve and recycle resources stimulate an awareness of the majesty of nature that lies at the heart of a Humanistic celebration of *Tu Bi-Shevat*. (*Guide to Humanistic Judaism*, 1988, 80)

LIFE-CYCLE EVENTS

Like the other branches of contemporary Judaism, Jewish Humanism has embraced a variety of ceremonies dealing with birth, puberty, marriage and death. Yet unlike the Jewish holidays, these events are perceived as having universal significance – in each case commemorations associated with each stage point beyond the Jewish community to all humankind:

Birth

Throughout history Jews have celebrated the birth of a child. In the biblical and priestly period parents named their babies after their birth: often these names were associated with hope aroused by the birth, current events, dedication to God, and the names of animals and plants. By the first century CE important changes to this pattern occurred: girls continued to be named at birth whereas the naming of male child was connected with the act of circumcision on the eighth day after birth. At this time the family normally named the child after a deceased relative. By the Middle Ages, baby-naming took place in the synagogue. Boys received their names during the *brit* (circumcision) ceremony; girls were named on the fourth Sabbath after they were born. Associated with these ceremonies, the *pidyon ha-ben* (redemption of the first-born son) was practised from biblical times. Because a first-born male child was regarded as belonging to God, it was necessary to buy the baby back from the priest. When the infant was about a month old, the father redeemed him for five shekels of silver.

Distancing themselves from these traditional practices, Humanistic Jews are committed to a number of principles regarding childbirth: (1) male and female children are to be treated equally; (2) children of intermarried couples should have equal status regardless whether their mother or father is Jewish; (3) the birth celebration should affirm the baby's connection to the Jewish people and to the rest of humanity. Within this context Humanistic birth celebrations are viewed as having two basic functions: naming the child and welcoming it into the community. Normally a birth celebration is held about a month after the baby is born: it can take place either at home, in the Temple, or at another public place. Regarding circumcision and *pidyon ha-ben*, Humanistic Judaism generally views both ceremonies as sexist and theistic; as a result the child-welcoming and baby-naming ceremonies are perceived as preferable.

In *Celebrations*, Sherwin Wine provided several examples of prayers to be recited when conferring a name such as the following:

> Life needs hope. It needs anticipation. It needs striving. It needs the future. So often our days are filled with the past, with regret for things not done, with the thought of events we cannot change. But when a new child is born, the direction of life turns forward. We become aware of our power to mould the shape of the world to come. We become aware of our power to create, to share, to teach, to train. A child is the gift of the future in the present. It is a potential waiting to be fulfilled. If we extend to him/her the gift of our love, s/he will share with us, in return, the gift of hope.
>
> May your new son/daughter fill your life with new excitement and new anticipation. May s/he give you a new sense of positive power. May s/he bring forth from you all your capacity to love and to nurture. May the name s/he bears, _____, be a sign of the strength of your commitment to him/her and of his/her commitment to life.   (Wine, 1988, 318)

Puberty

The entrance into adulthood has traditionally been marked by the *bar mitzvah* ceremony. The practice of calling a 13-year-old boy to read from the *Torah* symbolized this transition. In modern times the *bat mitzvah* ceremony was introduced for girls; Humanistic Jews, however, have altered this *rite de passage*. In contemporary society age 13 no longer represents the commencement of adulthood; rather this stage of development marks the advent of adolescence. As a result 13-year-old children are capable of responding to religion in a relatively more mature fashion. A Humanistic *bar* or *bat mitzvah* is therefore designed to encourage the development of spiritual capacities – the ceremony itself signifies a young person's desire to become increasingly responsible for his or her own decisions. This transition can be indicated in a variety of ways: by reading a *Torah* portion along with an interpretive address; alternatively the boy or girl can undertake a study of the life of a Humanist, Jewish hero or suitable subject under the supervision of a tutor. According to the *Guide to Humanistic Judaism*:

> Preparation for a Humanistic *bar* or *bat mitzvah* gives a young person the opportunity to grow intellectually, emotionally, and spiritually; to develop skills and self-confidence; and to experience a meaningful connection to the Jewish people and to humankind. The event provides an opportunity for family and community to join in celebrating and applauding those achievements and to reaffirm their own commitments. (Wine, 1988, 7–8).

Associated with *bar* and *bat mitzvah*, Humanistic Judaism endorses the Confirmation ceremony as an opportunity to explore the philosophical, ethical and spiritual dimension of Judaism. A Humanistic Confirmation ceremony, which normally takes place on the sixteenth birthday, is designed to provide a young person with the opportunity to demonstrate his/her intellectual and emotional skills as an emerging adult. This is achieved through writing a research paper on a subject of historical or ethical interest. In *Celebration* Sherwin Wine presented a number of prayers to be used for this ceremony:

> This evening we confirm our commitment to Humanism. Humanism is the way we see ourselves and the world we live in. It is the way we see our own power and our place in the order of things. If we are Humanist, we do not dwell on our weakness and our helplessness. We do not linger on our fears and anxieties. We are careful to remember that our limitations can become our excuses. If we think about them too often, we tend to exaggerate them. We become too timid for happiness. If we are Humanists, we start with our limitations, but we do not stop there. (Wine, 1988, 360)

Marriage

Traditionally Jewish marriages were patriarchal in character. Women were the possessions of their husbands; they were purchased from either fathers or brothers, defined in terms of reproduction, and divorced if they failed to produce children. The actual virtues for a wife were obedience, humility, chastity and self-sacrifice. As a result of contact with European culture, however, such attitudes underwent a major transformation – today most modern Jewish women seek to attain a sense of equality with men. Humanistic Judaism welcomes such a revolution in Jewish thinking, endorsing the belief in the value of each person.

Because of this orientation, Humanistic weddings celebrate the equal partnership of husband and wife. Couples are encouraged to participate in the formulation of their own marriage service by determining which symbols they wish to include as well as writing the service. Sherwin Wine's *Celebrations* contains a variety of prayers for such a liturgy including the following:

> [Groom] _____ and [bride] _____ we have all come together, your family and friends, to help you celebrate your love for one another and your decision to be husband and wife.

> At this special time it is very important for you to remember the reasons why you are in love and why you belong together – and especially all the important discoveries you have made about each other. You have certainly discovered how good you are for each other. [Groom] _____ [Bride] _____ has come into your life and transformed it. She has made an enormous difference. And you are a better person because she is there. (Bride) _____ (groom) _____ has come into your life and transformed it. He has made an enormous difference. And you are a better person because he is there.

> Each of you is more complete because you have each other. That is the chemistry of love. True lovers evoke the best from those they love and make them aware of feelings and possibilities.   (Ibid.)

Death

Unlike traditional Judaism, Jewish Humanism does not promise eternal life. Rather it accepts the finality of death. According to the *Guide to Humanistic Judaism*, a Humanistic philosophy of death:

1. Recognizes that, although death may be painful and tragic for those who survive and may be profoundly regretted, there is nothing in death to fear, any more than one fears sleeping.

One may well be afraid of the pain that may precede death, as one may be afraid of, and would try to avoid, pain generally. But, in the absence of consciousness or feelings after death, there is no reason to fear death itself.

2. Respects the intelligence and feelings of mourners and does not pretend that an incomprehensible, but wonderful, benefit has befallen the deceased.

3. Respects the life of the deceased by honouring it rather than alleged mystical forces that have taken it away.

4. Provides memorial ceremonies for the purpose of helping the living accept their loss by strengthening them with the presence, encouragement, and love of friends and family. (*Guide to Humanistic Judaism*, 1993, 17)

In this spirit, the Humanistic memorial service emphasizes the importance of facing the reality of death:

Death is something individual. Against the collective stream of life, it seems powerless. Particular flowers fade and die, but every spring repeats them in the cycle of nature. Individual man is a brief episode, but humanity bears the mark of immortality, renewed in every generation by the undying spark of life. We are, each of us, greater than ourselves. We survive in the children we create. We endure in the humanity we serve.

As an individual, separate and distinct, each of us is temporary, an ephemeral chapter in the saga of the universe. As a moment in the never-ending process of life, each of us is immortal, an expression of the persistent thrust of vital energy. The leaves of last year's summer have died and have vanished into the treasury of mother earth, but each one lives on in the renewal of every spring. Every person dies, but humanity survives. Every living thing perishes, but life persists. (Wine, 1988, 377)

CRITIQUE

Humanistic Judaism constitutes a decisive departure from the Jewish past, designed for those unable to subscribe to a belief in a supernatural deity but who nonetheless desire to identify as Jews. No doubt it will appeal to individuals for whom secular

Humanism provides an ideological framework for the improvement of modern life. Yet Humanistic Judaism suffers from a number of important deficiencies. First, in the light of the horrific events of the twentieth century, it is difficult to sustain confidence in human progress; if anything, the suffering brought about by two World Wars, the dropping of the atomic bomb, and the subsequent series of conflicts over the last five decades illustrates man's basic inhumanity.

The optimism generated by the advance of science and technology in the nineteenth century has therefore been superseded in this century by deep-seated pessimism about human potential. The philosophical assumptions of Jewish Humanism are thus at odds with a contemporary perception of human irrationality and evil. In the face of the horrors of the Holocaust, for example, such statements as the following from the *Guide to Humanistic Judaism* appear naive, unrealistic and dangerous:

> The chief power available for dealing with human problems is human power.   (35)

> What unites all Humanistic ethical viewpoints is a reliance upon reason rather than faith or intuition in arriving at standards to guide human behaviour.   (20–1)

> Humanistic Judaism embraces rationality as the best way not only of approaching truth but of managing life.   (61)

A second difficulty with Humanistic Judaism concerns its rejection of theism. Throughout his writings Sherwin Wine emphasizes that Humanistic Jews have freed themselves from traditional theology: Thus he wrote in *Celebrations*:

> As a way of life Humanism initially seems less satisfying than the 'glitz' of supernatural religion. It provides no loving God, no happy ending for the good and the righteous, no perfect order for the universe, no immortality for the soul. But, in the end, it rewards its 'believers' with the special pleasure of dignity. Despite the harshness of reality, Humanists know that they have the right and the power to be masters of their own lives, that they have the strength to confront the world as it is and not as fantasy makes it appear, that they have the opportunity to serve the future and not the past.   (Wine, 1988, 16)

In Wine's view the secular revolution has profoundly challenged the traditional understanding of God as a transcendent creator and sustainer of the universe who is intimately involved in human affairs. In *Judaism Beyond God*, he argued that theological language is now devoid of meaningful significance:

> The age of reason did not kill God through angry disbelief. It disposed of him in a much more deadly fashion. It made him too vague to be interesting. Theology passed from the excitement of hell, fire and brimstone to the boredom of abstraction with capital letters. The 'All', the 'One', the 'Ground of Being' are like the emperor's clothing. You are not even sure they are there, And if they are, who cares? Ultimately, the masters of contemporary religion refused to admit to any God that was meaningful. He lingered on as a word of reverence. Most people believed – but there was nothing to believe in.   (Wine, 1985, 34–5)

With the eclipse of theological belief, the natural world has taken precedence: the modern age has witnessed scientific advance on the one hand and religious retreat on the other.

For Wine and other Humanists such a revolution is to be welcomed, but it is difficult to see how the formulation of a Judaism without God could serve as a viable alternative for contemporary Jewry. As we have seen, committed Jews still subscribe to many of the central principles of the faith even if they have undergone modifications. There is no doubt that the events of the twentieth century have deeply affected Jewish consciousness, yet Jewry as a whole has not embraced either agnosticism or atheism. On the contrary, there are signs of an emergent spirituality within all branches of contemporary Judaism. Given this development, most Jews would not be drawn to the arid rationalism of Jewish Humanism – it is simply unimaginable that its liturgy extolling human potential with no reference to God could offer the spiritual sustenance religious Jews seek in a post-Holocaust world.

A further difficulty with Humanistic Judaism relates to its understanding of the Jewish holidays. Repeatedly in his writings Sherwin Wine stressed that Jewish festivals needed to be reinterpreted in the light of Humanistic values. Initially, he argued, they were connected with mythical and historical events; later under the influence of the rabbis Jewish festivals became means for expressing rabbinic ideals. For Humanistic Jews, he wrote:

Jewish holidays – as they are generally presented – are less than satisfactory. While they were not invented by the leaders of rabbinic Judaism, they were appropriated by them and put to rabbinic use. Religious authority made them convenient vehicles for rabbinic propaganda and for the rabbinic view of history.   (Ibid., 144)

While stressing the need for the continuation as such ceremonies, Wine insisted that they needed to be reclaimed for Humanistic use: within a Humanistic perspective the prayers and stories alluding to supernatural intervention should be eliminated – in their place the holidays should become occasions for celebrating human integrity, courage and steadfastness. Further, Wine stressed that it was necessary to discard a number of holidays which were not worth reinterpretation, such as the Fast of Esther, the 17th of Tammuz, and the 9th of Av.

For most Jews such a radical departure from tradition would have little appeal. As we have seen, those Jews affiliated to Hasidism and Orthodox Judaism are adamantly committed to the retention of all traditional features of the Jewish heritage, and even Conservative, Reform and Reconstructionist Jews are eager to preserve the major Jewish festivals. Therefore there is little scope for Humanistic Judaism's proposal to reinterpret some ancient Jewish festivals and discard others. Moreover, the non-theistic festival liturgy of Jewish Humanism would strike most Jews as odd. Readings for *Yom Kippur* for example, such as the following – devoid of any reference to divine forgiveness – would inevitably fail to evoke an appropriate penitential response from most worshippers:

The Day of Atonement is a time when we feel at one with all our vital connections, we do not really choose to be Jewish. We discover that we are. For some of us Jewishness is a minor enterprise, subordinate to what we deem more important concerns. For many of us Jewish identity is a major commitment, absorbing important energy and time. The style of a healthy religion allows for many degrees of commitment and for many expressions of identity. If we all dance to the same Jewish tune, we will bore ourselves with uniformity. Some Jews see the Jewish future by looking at the Jewish past. They view identity through the eyes of an authoritarian state and believe that loyalty is obedience to the old way. But others view the Jewish future as a richness of options. We take what we receive and we mould it to our needs. (Wine, 1988, 220)

The Humanistic liturgy for life-cycle events – similarly lacking any reference to God – would also be unacceptable to the vast majority of Jews. Traditionally these sacred occasions were infused with a sense of the holy; Humanistic Judaism's insistence on emptying them of such spiritual meaning would inevitably be rejected by Jews across the religious spectrum.

Religious Jews would also no doubt be disturbed by Humanistic Judaism's interpretation of the Jewish past. As we have seen, Sherwin Wine categorically denied the traditional understanding of Jewish history as providentially determined; instead he insisted that events are the result of human intention and action. A Humanistic approach to Jewish history, he emphasized, needs a naturalistic orientation:

The supernaturalist approach of the priestly and rabbinic theologians who edited the Bible and the *Talmud* is unacceptable. And the semi-supernaturalist approach of contemporary historians who describe Jewish survival as a unique 'mystery' is equally unacceptable. The course of Jewish behaviour and Jewish endurance are open to public investigation. If they are presently known, they are not permanently unknowable. 'Mystery' and 'enigma' are contemporary cover-ups for supernatural direction. (Wine, 1985, 118)

Again, such an attempt to view events as simply the result of natural causes would be unacceptable to most committed Jews. In all the major branches of contemporary Judaism there is a general acknowledgement that human history is in some way shaped by divine providence however understood. Humanistic Judaism thus fails as a solution for Jewish existence in the future: its proposals for a reinterpretation of Judaism are far too extreme for the Jewish community as a whole.

8

Zionism

In addition to the various branches of modern Judaism, Zionism as a religious and political ideology has had a profound effect on Jewish consciousness. Initially a number of pious Jews in the nineteenth century believed in the coming of the Messiah and linked this yearning to an advocacy of a return to the Holy Land. Pre-eminent among such individuals, Yehuda hai Alkalai argued that Jewish settlers should establish colonies in Palestine in anticipation of the Messianic age; a similar view was adopted by Zwi Hirsch Kalischer who maintained that the Messianic Age will take place following the creation of a Jewish homeland. Paralleling these religious aspirations, modern secular Zionists such as Moses Hess, Leon Pinsker, and Theodor Herzl stressed that the problem of anti-Semitism could only be solved through the creation of a Jewish state. Through the efforts of early pioneers the state of Israel was eventually established, and in the ensuing years it has been defended from repeated Arab attack. Yet despite the centrality of Israel in Jewish life, it is difficult to see how Zionism as a solution to Jewish survival can serve as the underpinning of Jewish life in the twenty-first century.

RELIGIOUS ZIONISM

Throughout history Jews have longed to return to the Holy Land they inhabited in ancient times – for thousands of years this quest animated messianic aspirations. At the beginning of the nineteenth century there emerged a new trend within religious Orthodoxy, the advocacy of an active approach to Jewish messianism. Rather than adopt a passive attitude towards the problem of redemption, these writers maintained that the Jewish nation must engage in the creation of a homeland in anticipation of the advent of the Messiah. Pre-eminent among such religious Zionists was Yehuda hai Alkalai, born in 1798 in Sarajevo to Rabbi Sholomo Alkalai, the spiritual leader of the local Jewish community. During his youth he lived in Palestine where he was influenced by kabbalistic thought. In 1825 he served as a rabbi in Semlin in Serbia; in 1834 he published a booklet entitled *Shema Yisrael* in which he advocated the establishment of Jewish colonies in Palestine, a view at variance with the traditional Jewish belief that the Messiah would come through an act of divine deliverance. When in 1840 the Jews of Damascus were charged with blood libel, Alkalai became convinced that the Jewish people could be secure only in their own land. Henceforth he published a series of books and pamphlets explaining his plans of self-redemption.

In his *Minhat Yehuda* he argued on the basis of Scripture that the Messiah would not miraculously materialize; rather, he would be preceded by various preparatory events. In this light the Holy Land needed to be populated by Jewry in preparation for messianic deliverance: This new redemption would, he wrote,

> be different; our land is waste and desolate, and we shall have to build houses, dig wells, and plant vines and olive trees. We are, therefore, commanded not to attempt to go at once and all together to the Holy Land ... the Lord desires that we be redeemed in dignity; we cannot, therefore, migrate in a mass, for we should then have to live like Bedouins, scattered in tents all over the fields of the Holy Land. Redemption must come slowly. The land must by degrees, be built up and prepared. ('The Third Redemption', in Hertzberg, 1959, 105)

For Alkalai, redemption was not simply a divine affair – it was also a human concern requiring labour and persistence.

This demystification of traditional messianic eschatology extended to Alkalai's advocacy of Hebrew as a language of communication. Traditionally Hebrew was viewed as a sacred language; it was not to be profaned by daily use. Alkalai, however, recognized the practical importance of having a single language for ordinary life in Palestine. He wrote:

> I wish to attest to the pain I have always felt at the error of our ancestors, that they allowed our Holy Tongue to be so forgotten. Because of this our people was divided into seventy peoples; our one language was replaced by the seventy languages of the lands of exile. If the Almighty should indeed show us his miraculous

favour and gather us into our land, we would not be able to
speak to each other and such a divided community could not
succeed.　(Ibid., 106)

It would be a mistake, he continued, to think that God would send
an angel to teach his people all seventy languages. Instead the
Jewish people must ensure that Hebrew was studied so that it
could be used for ordinary life: 'We must redouble our efforts to
maintain Hebrew and to strengthen its position. It must be the basis
of our educational work'. (Ibid.)

How can this process of redemption be accomplished? Alkalai
stressed the importance of convening an assembly of those dedicated to the realization of this goal. Thus he asserted that the redemption must begin with efforts by Jews themselves. They must
'organize and unite, choose leaders, and leave the lands of exile.
Since no community can exist without a governing body, the very
first new ordinance must be the appointment of the elders of each
district, men of piety and wisdom, to oversee all the affairs of the
community'. (Ibid.)

Reinterpreting the concept of the Messiah ben Joseph, he argued
that this assembly of elders was in fact what was meant by the
promise of the Messiah, the son of Joseph. For Alkalai, the process
of deliverance followed a different sequence from what is depicted
in traditional sources. The organization of an international Jewish
body was, he believed, the first step to the redemption because out
of this organization would emerge a fully authorized assembly of
elders, and from the elders, the Messiah, son of Joseph, would
appear. The vision of this first messianic figure should thus be understood as a process involving the emergence of a political leadership among the Jewish nation that would prepare the way for
divine deliverance.

According to Alkalai, it was not impossible for Jews to carry out
this project. The sultan, he maintained, would not object to such an
aim since he knew his Jewish subjects were loyal. What was required was that the Jewish people create a company along the lines
of fire insurance or railroad companies. This body should then
appeal to the sultan to give back the ancestral home to the Jewish
people for an annual rent. 'Once the name of Israel is again applied
to our land,' he declared, 'all Jews will be inspired to help this
company with all the means at their disposal. Though this venture
will begin modestly, its future will be very great.' (Ibid., 107)

Another early pioneer of religious Zionism was Zwi Hirsch Kalischer, the rabbi of Toun in the province of Posen. An early defender of Orthodoxy against the advances made by Reform Judaism, he championed the commandments prescribing faith in the Messiah and devotion to the Holy Land. In 1836 he expressed his commitment to Jewish settlement in Palestine in a letter to the head of the Berlin branch of the Rothschild family. 'The beginning of the redemption', he wrote, 'will come through natural causes by human effort and by the will of the governments to gather the scattered of Israel into the Holy Land.' (Ibid., 109–10)

Such a conviction did not actively engage Kalischer until 1860 when a society was organized in Frankfurt-on-Oder to encourage Jewish settlement in Palestine. After joining this group, he published a Zionist work, *Derishat Zion*, which appeared in 1862. In this treatise he advocated the return of Jews to their native soil. The redemption of Israel, he argued, would not take place miraculously:

> The Almighty, blessed be his Name, will not suddenly descend from on high and command his people to go forth. Neither will he send the Messiah from heaven in a twinkling of an eye, to sound the great trumpet for the scattered of Israel and gather them into Jerusalem. He will not surround the holy city with a wall of fire or cause the holy Temple to descend from heaven. (Avineri, 1981, 53)

Instead the redemption of Israel would take place slowly, through awakening support from philanthropists and gaining the consent of other nations to the gathering of the Jewish people into the Holy Land.

This view, Kalischer maintained, was inherent in Scripture. Thus the prophet Isaiah declared:

> In days to come Jacob shall take root, Israel shall blossom and put forth shoots, and fill the whole world with fruit ... In that day from the river Euphrates to the Brook of Egypt the Lord will thresh out the grain, and you will be gathered one by one, O people of Israel. And in that day a great trumpet will be blown, and those who were lost in the land of Assyria and those who were driven out to the land of Egypt will come and worship the Lord on the holy mountain at Jerusalem. (Isaiah 27.6, 12–13)

According to Kalischer, this passage implies that not all of Israel will return from exile at once, but instead will be gathered by degrees. This concept of redemption, he continued, is also contained in Isaiah 11.10: 'In that day the root of Jesse shall stand as an ensign to the peoples; him shall the nations seek, and his dwellings shall be glorious.' Here, he asserted, both a first and second gathering are intended. The first ingathering will be to work the land, after which the nation will blossom forth to a glorious extent.

The coming of the Messiah must therefore be preceded by the creation of a Jewish homeland. It was not enough to wait for miracles; instead Jews must act to bring about this event. Quoting from a medieval devotional book, he asserted:

> When many Jews, pious and learned in the *Torah*, will volunteer to go to the Land of Israel and settle in Jerusalem, motivated by a desire to serve, by purity of spirit, and by love of holiness; when they will come, by ones and twos, from all four corners of the world; and when many will settle there and their prayers will increase at the holy mountain in Jerusalem, the Creator will then heed them and hasten the day of redemption. ('Seeking Zion', in Hertzberg, 1959, 112–13)

Kalischer was aware that there were many Jews who would refuse to support those who were poor in the Holy Land. Such an attitude, he believed, was an argument put forward by Satan, since the people of Palestine had risked their lives to become pioneers. 'In this country', he wrote, 'which is strange to them, how could they go about finding a business or occupation, when they had never in their lives done anything of this kind? Their eyes can only turn to their philanthropic brethren, of whom they ask only enough to keep body and soul together, so that they can dwell in that land which is God's portion on earth'. (Ibid., 113)

For Kalischer, practical steps must be taken to fulfil this dream of resettlement. What was required was that an organization be created to encourage emigration, and farms and vineyards be purchased and cultivated. Such a programme would be a ray of deliverance to those then languishing in Palestine due to poverty and famine; this situation would be utterly changed if those able to contribute to this effort were inspired by the vision of a Jewish homeland. An advantage of this scheme would be to bring to fruition those religious commandments that attach to working the soil of the Holy Land. Even those Jews who supervised the labourers would be aiding in the working of the land and would therefore have the same status as if they had personally fulfilled these commandments. But beyond all this, Kalischer was convinced that Jewish farming would be a spur to messianic redemption. The policy of active participation in the cultivation of the soil would not divert the people from the task of divine service; rather such labour would add dignity to God's *Torah*. By working the land, Jews would be dedicating themselves to bringing about the advent of the messianic age.

In addition, such a policy would raise the dignity of the Jewish people among the nations, for then the foreign peoples would say of the children of Israel that they had the will to redeem the land of their ancestors. In conclusion, Kalischer declared:

> Let us take to heart the examples of the Italians, Poles, and Hungarians, who laid down their lives and possessions in the struggle for national independence, while we, the children of Israel, who have the most glorious and the holiest of lands as our inheritance, are spiritless and silent. We should be ashamed of ourselves! All the other peoples have striven only for the sake of their own national honour; how much more should we exert ourselves, for our duty is to labour not only for the glory of our ancestors but for the glory of God who chose Zion. (Ibid., 114)

Because Kalischer was financially independent, he was able to engage in a variety of activities to bring about the fulfilment of this vision. In 1866 he was instrumental in persuading a group to purchase land for colonization on the outskirts of Jaffa. Eventually he influenced the Alliance Israélite Universelle – the organization founded in France in 1860 to protect Jewish rights throughout the world – to establish an agricultural school in Jaffa in 1870. Nonetheless Orthodox critics of his views denounced what they believed was a departure from tradition.

SECULAR ZIONISM

Modern secular Zionism began with the writings of Moses Hess. Born in Bonn, Germany, he published his first philosophical work, *The Holy History of Mankind, by a young Spinozist*, in 1837. By 1840 he had settled in Paris where he was active in socialist circles; from 1842 to 1843 he served as the Paris correspondent of the *Rheinische Zeitung*, edited by Karl Marx. In 1862 he published *Rome and Jerusalem*, a systematic defence of Jewish nationalism.

Anti-Jewish sentiment, he believed, was unavoidable. Progressive Jews thought they could escape from Judeophobia by recoiling from any Jewish national expression, yet the hatred of Jews was inescapable. No reform of the religion was radical enough to avoid such sentiments, and even conversion to Christianity could not relieve the Jews of this disability. 'Jewish noses', he wrote, 'cannot be reformed, and the black, wavy hair of the Jews will not be changed into blond by conversion or straightened out by constant combing' (Hertzberg, 121). For Hess, Jews would always remain strangers among the nations: nothing could alter this state of affairs. The only solution to the problem of Jew-hatred was for the Jewish people to come to terms with their national identity.

According to Hess, the restoration of Jewish nationalism would not deprive the world of the benefits promoted by Jewish reformers who wished to dissociate themselves from the particularistic dimensions of the Jewish heritage. On the contrary, the values of universalism would be championed by various aspects of the Jewish national character. Judaism, he contended, was the root of the modern universalist view of life. Until the French Revolution, the Jewish people were the only nation whose religion was both national and universalist. It was through Judaism that the history of humanity could become sacred, namely a unified development which had its origin in the love of the family. This process could be completed only when members of the human race were united by the holy spirit.

Such a conception of history was grounded in the Jewish messianic vision of God's kingdom on earth. From the beginning of their history, Hess noted, the Jews had been bearers of the faith in a future messianic epoch. This conviction was symbolically expressed through Sabbath observance. 'The biblical story of the creation is told only for the sake of the Sabbath ideal', he wrote. 'It tells us, in symbolic language, that when the creation of the world of nature was completed, with the calling into life of the highest organic being of the earth – man – the Creator celebrated his natural Sabbath, after the completion of the task of world history, by ushering in the messianic epoch' (Hertzberg, 131). Biblical Sabbath precepts thus inspired Jews with a feeling of certainty that a divine law governed both the world of nature and the world of history. This belief, rooted in the spiritual life of the Jewish nation, pointed to a universal salvation of the world.

What was required today, Hess asserted, was for Jewry to regenerate the Jewish nation and to keep alive the hope for the political rebirth of the Jewish people. For Hess a Jewish renaissance was possible once national life reasserted itself in the Holy Land. In the past the creative energies of the people deserted Israel when Jews became ashamed of their nationality. But the holy spirit, he wrote, would again animate Jewry once the nation awakened to a new life. The only question remaining was how it might be possible to stimulate the patriotic sentiments of modern Jewry as well as liberate the Jewish masses by means of this revived national loyalty. This was a formidable challenge, yet Hess contended that it must be overcome. Although he recognized that there could not be a total emigration of world Jewry to Palestine, the existence of a Jewish state would act as a spiritual centre for the Jewish people and for all of humanity. It was, he stated, the duty of all Jews to carry 'the yoke of the Kingdom of heaven' until the very end.

The Russian pogroms of 1881 had a profound impact on another early Zionist, Leon Pinsker, driving him from an espousal of the ideas of the Enlightenment to the determination to create a Jewish homeland. Born in Tomaszów in Russian Poland in 1821, Pinsker attended a Russian high school, studied law in Odessa, and later received a medical degree from the University of Moscow. Upon returning to Odessa, he was appointed to the staff of the local city hospital. After 1860, Pinsker contributed to Jewish weeklies in the Russian language and was active in the Society for the Spread of Culture among the Jews of Russia. However, when Jews were massacred in the pogroms of 1881 he left the Society, convinced that a more radical remedy was required to solve the plight of Russian Jewry. In 1882 he published *Autoemancipation*, a tract containing similar themes to those found in Hess's writings. He subsequently became the leader of the new Hibbat Zion movement, and in 1884 convened its founding conference.

In *Autoemancipation*, Pinsker asserted that the Jewish problem was as unresolved in the modern world as in former times. In essence, this dilemma concerned the unassimilable character of Jewish identity in countries where Jews were in the minority. In such cases there was no basis for mutual respect between Jews and non-Jews. 'The Jewish people', he wrote, 'has no fatherland of its own, though many motherlands; it has no rallying point, no centre of gravity, no government of its own, no accredited representatives. It is everywhere a guest, and nowhere at home' (Pinsker, 1932, 6). This situation was aggravated by the fact that the Jewish people did not feel a need for an independent national existence; yet without such a longing, there was no hope for a solution to Jewish misery.

Among the nations of the world, Pinsker asserted, the Jews were like a nation long since dead: the dead walking among the living. Such an eerie, ghostly existence was unique in history. The fear of the Jewish ghost had been a typical reaction throughout the centuries, and had paved the way for current Judeophobia. This prejudice had through the years become rooted and naturalized among all peoples of the world. 'As a psychic aberration', he wrote, 'it is hereditary; as a disease transmitted for two thousand years, it is incurable' (ibid. 8). Such Jew-hatred had generated various charges against the Jewish people: throughout history Jews had been accused of crucifying Jesus, drinking the blood of Christians, poisoning wells, exacting usury, and exploiting peasants. Such accusations were invariably groundless – they were trumped up to quiet the conscience of Jew-baiters. Thus Judaism and anti-Semitism had been inseparable companions through the centuries, and any struggle against this aberration of the human mind was fruitless.

Unlike other peoples, the Jew was inevitably a stranger. Having no home, he could never be anything other than an alien. He was not simply a guest in a foreign country; rather he was more like a beggar and a refugee. The Jews were aliens, Pinsker stated, who could have no representatives because they had no fatherland. Because they had none, because their home had no boundaries behind which they could entrench themselves, their misery also had no bounds. It was a mistake, Pinsker continued, to think that the legal emancipation of Jewry would result in social emancipation. This, he believed, was impossible. The isolation of the Jew could not be removed by any form of official emancipation since the Jew was eternally an alien. In summary, he asserted, 'For the living, the Jew is a dead man; for the natives, an alien and a vagrant; for property holders, a beggar; for the poor, an exploiter and a millionaire; for patriots, a man without a country; for all classes, a hated rival' (Hertzberg, 1959, 188).

Such natural antagonism between Jew and non-Jew had resulted in a variety of reproaches levelled by both parties at one another.

From the Jewish side, appeals to justice were frequently made to improve the condition of the Jewish community. In response, non-Jews attempted to justify their negative attitudes by groundless accusations. A more realistic approach, however, would involve the recognition that the Jewish people had no choice but to reconstitute themselves as a separate people. In recent times, Pinsker pointed out, there had been a growing awareness of the need for a Jewish homeland.

The Jewish struggle to attain this goal had an inherent justification that belonged to the quest of every oppressed people. Although this endeavour might be opposed by various quarters, the battle must continue – the Jewish people had no other way out of their desperate position. There was a moral duty to ensure that persecuted Jews wherever they lived had a secure home. In this respect, it was a danger, Pinsker stated, for Jews to attach themselves only to the 'Holy Land'. What was required was simply a secure land for the Jewish nation.

For Pinsker, the present moment was a decisive time for the revival of national aspirations. History appeared to be on the side of world Jewry in its longing for a national homeland. Even in the absence of a leader like Moses, the recognition of what Jewish people needed most should arouse a number of energetic individuals to take on positions of responsibility. Already, he noted, there were societies who were pressing for the creation of a Jewish nation. They must now invoke a national congress, and establish a national directorate to bring to fruition these plans: 'Our greatest and best forces – men of finance, of science, and of affairs, statesmen and publicists – must join hands with one accord in steering toward the common destination' (Hertzberg, 1959, 196). Of course not all Jews would be able to settle in this Jewish homeland. Yet, it would serve as a refuge for those who sought to flee from oppression and persecution.

In conclusion, Pinsker contended that the Jews were despised because they were not a living nation. It was an error to believe that civil and political emancipation would raise Jewry in the estimation of other peoples. Instead the only proper remedy for the Jewish problem was the creation of a Jewish nationality, of a people living on its own soil. Jews must reassert their national self-respect, and cease to wander from one exile to another. At present there were forces helping to bring about this vision, and the international Jewish community must work towards this end. No sacrifice, he declared, would be too great, to reach the goal which would assure that the Jewish nation's future was secure.

More than any other figure Theodor Herzl has become identified with modern secular Zionism. Born on 2 May 1860 in Budapest, Hungary, he was the only son of a rich merchant. After studying at a technical school and high school in Budapest, he went with this family to Vienna where he enrolled in the law faculty of the university. In 1884 he received a doctorate and worked for a year as a civil servant; subsequently he wrote plays, and in 1892 was appointed to the staff of the *Neue Freie Presse*. As its Paris correspondent, he witnessed the Dreyfus Affair and became convinced that the Jewish problem could only be solved by the creation of a homeland for the Jewish people. In May 1895 Herzl requested an interview with Baron Maurice de Hirsch to interest him in the establishment of a Jewish state. When the Baron expressed little sympathy for the project, Herzl hoped the Rothschilds would be more receptive and wrote a 65-page proposal outlining his views. This work was an outline of his *The Jewish State* which appeared in February 1896; this was followed by a utopian study, *Alteneuland* (Old-New Land), published in 1902.

Herzl's analysis of modern Jewish existence was not original – many of his ideas were preceded in the writings of Moses Hess and Leon Pinsker. Yet what was novel about Herzl's espousal of Zionism was his success in stimulating interest and debate about a Jewish state in the highest diplomatic and political circles. This was due both to the force of his personality and the passionate expression of his proposals. Convinced of the importance of his views, Herzl insisted that the building of a Jewish homeland would transform Jewish life.

In the preface to *The Jewish State* Herzl contended that his advocacy of a Jewish homeland was not simply a utopian scheme; on the contrary, his plan was a realistic proposal arising out of the appalling conditions facing Jews living under oppression and persecution. The plan, he argued, would be impracticable if only a single individual were to undertake it. But if many Jews were to agree on its importance its implementation would be entirely reasonable. Like Pinsker, Herzl believed that the Jewish question could only be solved if the Jews constituted themselves as one people.

Old prejudices against Jewry are ingrained in Western society – assimilation would not act as a cure for the ills that beset the Jewish people. There was only one remedy for the malady of anti-

Semitism: the creation of a Jewish commonwealth. In *The Jewish State* Herzl outlined the nature of such a social and political entity. The plan, he argued, should be carried out by two agencies: the Society of Jews and the Jewish Company. The scientific programme and political policies which the Society of Jews would establish should be carried out by the Jewish Company. This body would be the liquidating agent for the business interests of departing Jews, and would organize trade and commerce in the new country. Given such a framework, immigration of Jews would be gradual. Initially the poorest would settle in this new land. Their tasks would be to construct roads, bridges, railways and telegraph installations. In addition they would regulate rivers and provide themselves with homesteads. Through their labour trade would be created, and in its wake markets. Such economic activity would attract new settlers, and thus the land would be populated.

Those Jews who agreed with the concept of a Jewish state should rally round the Society of Jews and encourage its endeavours. This was the way to give it authority in the eyes of governments, and in time ensure that the state was recognized through international law. If other nations were willing to grant Jews sovereignty over a neutral land, then the Society would be able to enter into negotiations for its possession. Where should this new state be located? Herzl proposed two alternatives: Palestine or Argentina. Argentina, Herzl noted, was one of the most fertile countries in the world, extending over a vast area with a sparse population. Palestine on the other hand was the Jews' historic homeland. If the sultan were persuaded to allow the Jews to repossess this land, the Jewish community could in return undertake the complete management of the finances of Turkey. In this way the Jews could form a part of a wall of defence for Europe and Asia, and the holy places of Christendom could be placed under some form of international extraterritoriality. There were therefore advantages for both these options, and Herzl asserted that the Society should take whatever it was given and whatever Jewish opinion favoured.

In the conclusion of this tract Herzl eloquently expressed the longing of the entire nation for the creation of such a refuge from centuries of suffering:

What glory awaits the selfless fighters for the cause! Therefore I believe that a wondrous breed of Jews will spring up from the earth. The Maccabees will rise again. Let me repeat once more

my opening words: The Jews who will it shall achieve their state.
We shall live at last as free men on our own soil, and in our own
homes peacefully die. The world will be liberated by our
freedom, enriched by our wealth, magnified by our greatness.
And whatever we attempt there for our own benefit will rebound
mightily and beneficially to the good of all mankind. ('The
Jewish State', in ibid., 1959, 225–6)

SPIRITUAL ZIONISM

Like Alkalai and Kalischer, Asher Zvi Ginsberg (later known as
Ahad Ha-Am) was concerned with the spiritual redemption of the
Jewish people, although his thought is devoid of traditional
Jewish ideas of messianic deliverance. Born in Skvira in the
Russian Ukraine on 18 August 1856, he initially received a traditional Jewish education. In 1868 his family moved to an estate
which his wealthy father leased; there he studied the works of
medieval Jewish philosophers and writers of the Enlightenment.
At the age of twenty he pursued French and German literature
and philosophy, and later unsuccessfully attempted to continue
his study in various European capitals. In 1886 he moved to
Odessa where he began to publish articles dealing with contemporary Jewish life.

His first essay, 'Wrong Way', which appeared in 1889, set the
stage for his role within the Hovevei Zion movement. In this work
he advocated the return to Zion, but remained critical of a number
of aspects of the movement's platform. In a later essay, 'The Jewish
State and the Jewish Problem', written after his return from the
First Zionist Congress, he discussed Max Nordeau's opening statement to the Congress. According to Nordeau, the major problem
facing East European Jewry was economic misery, whereas
Western Jewry was confronted by the failure of the Emancipation
to provide a firm base for Jewish identity in modern society.
According to Nordeau, these dilemmas point to the need for the
creation of a Jewish state in Palestine.

For Ahad Ha-Am, however, the matter is more complicated.
Assuming that the Zionist movement attained this goal, what
would occur when the Jewish state absorbed the first wave of immigrants? Would the Jewish problem be solved? Clearly not all
Jews throughout the world (numbering ten million) would be able

to settle in Palestine. What would be the result if only a small section of the world Jewish population emigrated? Ahad Ha-Am argued that the economic problems facing East European Jewry would not be solved for those who remained behind. The Jewish state could only contribute to cultural and spiritual regeneration. Thus the central dilemma faced by Zionism was how the spiritual perplexities of Jews in the diaspora could be resolved by the creation of a Jewish homeland.

According to Ahad Ha-Am, Zionism was able to solve the problems of Western Jewry more readily than to ameliorate the condition of Jews in Eastern Europe. The Jew in the West was separated from Jewish culture and simultaneously alienated from the society in which he resided. The existence of a Jewish state would enable him to solve the problems of national identity, compensating him for his lack of integration into the culture of the country in which he lived:

> If a Jewish state were re-established (in Palestine), a state arranged and organized exactly after the pattern of other states, then he [the Western Jew] could live a full, complete life among his own people, and find at home all that he now sees outside, dangled before his eyes, but out of reach. Of course, not all the Jews will be able to take wing and go to their state; but the very existence of the Jewish state will raise the prestige of those who remain in exile, and their fellow citizens will no more despise them and keep them at arm's length as though they were ignoble slaves, dependent entirely on the hospitality of others. (Ha-Am, 1962, 74–5)

It was this ideal which was able to cure the Jew in the West of his social unease, the consciousness of his inferiority in lands where he was an alien.

In Eastern Europe, however, such a solution was inadequate. With the disappearance of ghetto life, Judaism lost its hold on the Jewish population. In the past, Jews were able to sustain their traditions through common experience. The passing of this closed society led to the disintegration of the Jewish heritage. For Ahad Ha-Am, it was impossible for Eastern European Jews to return to the traditional religious symbolism of the ghetto. What was required was the establishment of a new Jewish social identity in Israel:

Judaism needs at present but little. It needs not an independent state, but only the creation in its native land of conditions favourable to its development: a good-sized settlement of Jews working without hindrance in every branch of culture, from agriculture and handicrafts to science and literature. This Jewish settlement, which will be a gradual growth, will become in course of time the centre of the nation, wherein its spirit will find pure expression and develop in all its aspects up to the highest degree of perfection of which it is capable. Then from the centre the spirit of Judaism will go forth to the great circumference, to all the communities of the diaspora, and will breathe new life into them and preserve their unity; and when our national culture in Palestine has attained that level, we may be confident that it will produce men in the country who will be able, on a favourable opportunity, to establish a state which will be truly a Jewish state, and not merely a state of Jews.   (Ibid., 78–9)

Israel was thus to be a state infused with Jewish values, and not simply a homeland for the Jewish people; it must embody the religious and cultural ideas of the Jewish past. According to Ahad Ha-Am, the strength of Judaism resided in the prophetic emphasis on spiritual values; a Jewish state devoid of such an orientation would lose the support of diaspora Jewry. A secular state was not viable, he argued, because 'a political ideal which does not rest on the national culture is apt to seduce us from our loyalty to spiritual greatness, and to beget in us a tendency to find the path of glory in the attainment of material power and political dominion, thus breaking the thread that unites us with the past, and undermining our historical basis' (Ha-Am, 1962, 80).

Without spiritual ideals, political power may become an end in itself. To clarify this point, Ha-Am used the example of Judaea under Herod the Great:

History teaches us that in the days of the Herodian house Palestine was indeed a Jewish state, but the national culture was despised and persecuted, and the ruling house did everything in its power to implant Roman culture in the country, and frittered away the national resources in the building of heathen temples and amphitheatres, and so forth. Such a Jewish state would spell death and utter degradation for our people. Such a Jewish state ... would not be able to give us a feeling of national glory; and the national culture, in which we might have sought and found our glory, would not be implanted in our state and would not be the principle of its life.   (Ibid., 80–1)

After visiting Jewish settlements in Palestine, Ahad Ha-Am wrote an essay, 'Truth from the Land of Israel', filled with his impression of the country. Deploring land speculation, he called on the Hovevei Zion to intervene in this odious practice. In addition, he focused on the dilemmas faced by Zionism because of the existence of the sizeable Arab population. This people, he maintained, must be confronted by those wishing to settle in the land. As early as 1891 he recognized that the Arab Palestinians might press for the creation of a national movement. It was a mistake to believe that Palestine was devoid of a native population: 'We tend to believe abroad that Palestine is nowadays almost completely deserted, a non-cultivated wilderness, and anyone can come there and buy as much land as his heart desires. But in reality this is not the case. It is difficult to find anywhere in the country Arab land which lies fallow' (Avineri, 1981, 122).

What was required was a sense of realism. Jews should not regard themselves as superior to their Arab neighbours. Instead they should perceive that the Arabs are fiercely proud and determined:

We tend to believe abroad that all Arabs are desert barbarians, an asinine people who do not see or understand what is going on around them. This is a cardinal mistake ... The Arabs, and especially the city dwellers, understand very well what we want and what we do in the country; but they behave as if they do not notice it because at present they do not see any danger for themselves or their future in what we are doing and are therefore trying to turn to their benefit these new guests ... But when the day will come in which the life of our people in the land of Israel will develop to such a degree that they will push aside the local population by little or much, then it will not easily give up its place.   (Ibid., 123)

In order to flourish in the land of their ancestors Ahad Ha-Am insisted that the Jewish people act with love and respect to those Arabs in their midst.

Although Ahad Ha-Am's vision of the return to the Holy Land was not filled with messianic longing, his idealization of the spiritual, religious and cultural dimensions of Judaism and their embodiment in a Jewish state was rooted in Jewish messianism. For Ahad Ha-Am, it would not be a divinely appointed Messiah who would bring about the realization of God's Kingdom on earth. Rather this would be the task of the Jewish people themselves. Through the creation of a Jewish state, the spiritual values of the faith were to materialize in the Holy Land.

Like other modern religious and spiritual writers, Aharon David Gordon was anxious to confront the problem of Jewish regeneration in the Holy Land. In formulating his conception of Jewish life in Palestine, he grounded his outlook in a mystical conception of the interaction of human beings and nature. Born in a village in the province of Podolia, Gordon spent his youth in a farming village on an estate which his father managed for the family of Baron Horace Günzburg. After his marriage, he served as an official from 1880 to 1923 on a large tract of land the Günzburgs leased for farming. At the age of forty-seven, he emigrated to Palestine where he worked as a labourer in the vineyards and wineries of Petah Tikva. Later he worked in Galilee; his final days were spent in Degania, one of the earliest *kibbutzim*.

According to Gordon, manual labour was central to both personal and national salvation. In an essay, 'Some Observations', published in 1910, he outlined two alternatives facing the Jewish community in Palestine. The first was 'the practical way of the world wise ... the continuation of exile life, with all its shortsighted practical wisdom'. For Gordon exile was not simply geographical dislocation: it involved psychological and existential alienation, combining dependence on others and estrangement from creative life. The second alternative called for a renaissance of Jewish life: the way of manual labour. This latter option, he believed, would renew the national energies of the Jewish people:

> We have as yet no national assets because our people have not paid the price for them. A people can acquire a land only by its own effort, by realizing the potentialities of its body and soul, by unfolding and revealing its inner self. This is a two-sided transaction, but the people come first – the people comes before the land. But a parasitical people is not a living people. Our people can be brought to life only if each one of us recreates himself through labour and a life close to nature. (Hertzberg, 1959, 376)

Gordon's understanding of Jewish life in the diaspora was related to his theories of anthropology and psychology. To Gordon a person could become fully human only through contact with nature. Physical labour was thus essential for personal growth and fulfilment. In this light Jewish existence in the diaspora was a distorted mode of living, not only because the Jewish nation had lost its homeland, but also because it lacked the land in which Jews could realize their full human potential through physical work. In Gordon's view, a Jewish national renaissance would not take place simply through migration: it must involve a return to the self through the cultivation of the land. A fundamental distinction must hence be drawn between a transference of exiles to the Holy Land, and a radical reconstruction of Jewish life through agricultural employment.

Such a radical analysis calls for the total transformation of Jewish life. The way of national rebirth, he wrote,

> embraces every detail of our individual lives. Every one of us is required to refashion himself so that the *Galut* [diaspora] Jew within him becomes a truly emancipated Jew; so that the unnatural, defective, splintered person within him may be changed into a natural, wholesome human being who is true to himself; so that his *Galut* life, which has been fashioned by alien and extraneous influences, hampering his natural growth and self-realization, may give way to one that allows him to develop freely, to his fullest stature in all dimensions. ('Some Questions', in ibid., 376)

Such a process of rehabilitation must take place if Jewish exile is to cease, even if Palestine becomes populated with Jewish emigrants.

According to Gordon, traditional Jewish life in the diaspora was richer than modern existence in the post-Emancipation world. Prior to the Emancipation Jews sought to ameliorate their position without abandoning *Torah* Judaism. Yet now material prosperity had overshadowed all other values. To counteract this corrosive attitude, the 'religion of nature' must become the dominant ideology in Palestine. In an essay entitled 'Labour' Gordon insisted that the Jewish people is linked to its homeland; if it is divorced from agricultural labour, it becomes disfigured and emasculated. In their advocacy of a Jewish state, modern Zionist writers have overlooked the fundamental requirements for a vibrant national life:

A people that was completely divorced from nature, that during two thousand years was imprisoned within walls, that became inured to all forms of life except to a life of labour, cannot become once again a living, natural, working people without bending all its willpower toward that end. We lack the fundamental element: we lack labour (not labour done because of necessity, but labour to which man is organically and naturally linked), labour by which a people becomes rooted in its soil and its culture. ('Labour', in Avineri, 1981, 155)

What is lacking in contemporary Zionism, he argued, is a recognition of the essential link between man and nature. This is the cosmic element of national identity. Jews who have been uprooted must learn to know the soil and prepare it for the transplantation of the Jewish nation. It is necessary to study climatic conditions and everything required to grow agricultural produce: 'We who have been torn away from nature, who have lost the savour of natural living – if we desire life, we must establish a new relationship with nature, we must open a new account with it' (ibid., 157).

This quest to bring about a radical transformation in Jewish consciousness was motivated by a utopian vision of Jewish life in Palestine. Although Gordon's thinking lacked the religious framework of Orthodox Jewish Zionists, it had quasi-religious connotations reminiscent of previous writers who longed for the redemption of the Jewish nation.

THE EARLY STRUGGLE

The quest for a Jewish state was set in motion by the events of the nineteenth century. Following the inspiration of early Zionist leaders, the First Zionist Congress met on 29 August 1897 in the Great Hall of the Basle Municipal Casino under the leadership of Theodor Herzl. Subsequently Herzl cultivated important figures in Turkey, Austria, Germany and Russia to further his plans. In 1902 a British Royal Commission on Alien Immigration was appointed, with Lord Rothschild as one of its members. On 7 July 1902 Herzl appeared before the Commission, declaring that further Jewish immigration to Britain should be accepted but that the ultimate solution to the refugee problem was the recognition of the Jews as a people and the finding by them of a legally recognized home.

This appearance brought Herzl into contact with the Colonial
Secretary, Joseph Chamberlain, who subsequently suggested to
Herzl that a Jewish homeland could be established in Uganda.
Fearful of the plight of Russian Jewry, Herzl was prepared to
accept the proposal. As a result Lord Lansdowne, the Foreign
Secretary, wrote in a letter:

> If a site can be found which the [Jewish Colonial] Trust and His
> Majesty's Commission consider suitable and which commends
> itself to HM Government, Lord Lansdowne will be prepared to
> entertain favourable proposals for the establishment of a Jewish
> colony of settlement, on conditions which will enable the members
> to observe their national customs.   (Sanders, 1984, 37–8)

When Herzl read Lansdowne's letter to the Zionist Congress, a
number of Russian delegates who viewed the Uganda Plan as a betrayal of Zionism walked out. At the next Congress, Uganda was
formally rejected as a place for a national homeland.

At the time of Herzl's death, Zionism had become an established
movement, yet it expressed a minority view in the Jewish world.
Until the First World War all branches of Judaism were generally
opposed to secular Zionism, and assimilationists saw no attraction
in a Jewish state in the Middle East. After Herzl's death, David
Wolffsohn became the leader of the Zionists and continued to
agitate for the creation of a Jewish national home. In Britain Chaim
Weizmann pressed for the acceptance of this plan with the support
of the liberal MP Herbert Samuel. In a meeting on 9 November 1914
with the Foreign Secretary, Sir Edward Grey, Samuel asked about a
homeland for the Jewish people. In reply Grey said that the idea had
always had a strong sentimental attachment for him, and he would
be prepared to work for it if the opportunity arose. Later in the day
Samuel attempted to enlist the support of Lloyd George, Chancellor
of the Exchequer. When Samuel later put his plan to the Cabinet, it
was resisted by his cousin Edwin Montagu. In a letter to Venetia
Stanley written on 28 January 1915 the Prime Minister referred to
Samuel's plea for a Jewish homeland in Palestine: 'We might plant
in this not very promising territory about 3 or 4 million Jews and
this would have a good effect on those (including I suppose himself)
who were left behind' (Brock, 1952, 406–7). During this period
Weizmann pressed on with his proposals. On 18 August 1916 Lord
Robert Cecil recorded his meeting with Weizmann:

He (Weizmann) said with great truth that even in this country a
Jew always had to give an explanation of his existence and he
was neither quite an Englishman nor quite a Jew, and that the
same thing was equally true with much more serious results in
other countries ... Perhaps a phrase he used may convey something of the impression which he made. He said: 'I am not romantic except that Jews must always be romantic, for to them
reality is too terrible.'   (Ibid., 313–14)

Later in the year when Lloyd George became Prime Minister and
Arthur Balfour was appointed Foreign Secretary, the Zionist cause
was given a more sympathetic hearing. In January 1917 British
troops began the assault on Palestine; at the same time the Tsar was
overthrown and the provisional Prime Minister Kerensky ended
Russia's anti-Semitic code. At the end of the month Germany
engaged in U-boat warfare, thereby drawing America on to the
Allied side. In the light of these events, the US government became
a supporter of a Jewish home in Palestine. In the same year Balfour
as Foreign Secretary wrote to Lord Rothschild, the head of the
English Jewish community, promising British commitment to a
Jewish homeland in Palestine. The original draft of this letter (the
text of which was agreed on by both sides beforehand) stated that
Palestine should be reconstituted as a whole as a Jewish national
home with internal autonomy, and that there should be an unrestricted right of Jewish immigration. This document was not approved by the Cabinet until 31 October 1917, and substantial
changes had been made. Palestine was not equated with the national home, nor was there any reference to unrestricted Jewish immigration. Further, the rights of the Arabs were safeguarded. The
central passage of the letter, subsequently known as the Balfour
Declaration, read:

His Majesty's Government view with favour the establishment in
Palestine of a national home for the Jewish people, and will use
their best endeavours to facilitate the achievement of this object,
it being clearly understood that nothing shall be done which may
prejudice the civil and religious rights and political status
enjoyed by Jews in any other country.

A month after the Balfour Declaration was published, General
Allenby captured Jerusalem. When Weizmann went to meet him in

1918, Allenby was overwhelmed by military and administrative difficulties. Weizmann was told the time was not propitious to implement the British plan: 'Nothing can be done at present', he stated. 'We have to be extremely careful not to hurt the susceptibilities of the population' (Johnson, 1987, 431). Yet despite such obstacles as well as opposition from various quarters Britain secured the Palestine mandate at the peace negotiations and steps were taken to create a national Jewish homeland.

At the end of the nineteenth century a number of agricultural settlements, funded by such philanthropists as Moses Montefiore and Edmund de Rothschild, were established in Palestine by Jewish settlers (the first *Aliyah*). At the beginning of the twentieth century in the wake of Russian pogroms, a second wave of Jewish immigrants (the second *Aliyah*) emigrated to the Holy Land. These pioneers set up the new garden suburb of Jaffa (later Tel Aviv) and founded *kibbutzim* as well as agricultural settlements. In 1909 the young men of the second *Aliyah*, who had previously participated in Jewish defence groups in Russia, established the Society of Shomerim (Watchmen) to protect these new settlements. Under the leadership of the Russian-born writer Vladimir Jabotinsky and the Russian war hero Joseph Trumpeldor, a Jewish regiment (Zion Mule Corps) was founded, and participated in the First World War. After the war neither the Zionist authorities nor the British showed any desire to keep the Jewish Legion in existence. Jabotinsky, however, believed its continuation was necessary for Jewish survival and formed a self-defence organization (which later became the Haganah).

With the rise of Arab nationalism, the Jewish settlements in Palestine came increasingly under threat. In March 1920 the Arabs attacked Jewish settlements in Galilee and Trumpeldor was killed; this was followed by Arab riots in Jerusalem. In response, Jabotinsky's self-defence force went into action and Jabotinsky and others were arrested, tried by a military court, and given 15 years' hard labour. Arab rioters were also convicted and imprisoned. Following these events, Lloyd George sent out Herbert Samuel as High Commissioner, to the fury of the Arab population. Intent on implementing the Balfour Declaration – which aimed to safeguard the civil and religious rights of non-Jewish communities – Samuel criticized the Zionists for failing to recognize the importance of Arab nationalist aspirations. On 10 August 1921 he wrote to Weizmann: 'It is upon the Arab rock that the Zionist ship may be wrecked.' To the Palestinian Jewish leaders, he cautioned:

You yourselves are inviting a massacre which will come as long as you disregard the Arabs. You pass over them in silence ... You have done nothing to come to an understanding. You know only how to protest against the government ... Zionism has not yet done a thing to obtain the consent of the inhabitants and without this consent immigration will not be possible. (Johnson, 1987, 437)

Despite such cautionary advice, the Zionists had little resources for appeasing the Arab population in the early 1920s and were therefore not anxious to heed Samuel's words. Nonetheless Samuel pursued a policy of even-handedness, pardoning the Arab extremists who had started the riots of 1921. Following this act, he confirmed Sheikh Hisam, who was elected Grand Mufti of Jerusalem by the electoral college of pious Arab Muslims, in preference to the extremist Haj Amin Al-Husseini. Subsequently the Al-Husseini family and the nationalist extreme wing who had led the 1920 riots embarked on a campaign against the electoral college. Throughout Jerusalem they put up posters which proclaimed: 'The accursed traitors, whom you all know, have combined with the Jews to have one of their party appointed Mufti.'

Within the British staff an anti-Zionist, Ernst T. Richmond (who acted as an adviser to the High Commissioner on Muslim affairs), persuaded Sheikh Hisam to step down and urged Samuel to allow Haj Amin to take his place. On 11 July 1921 Samuel saw Haj Amin, who gave assurances that he and his family would be dedicated to peace. Three weeks later riots occurred in Jaffa and elsewhere in which forty-five Jews were killed. This error of judgement was compounded when Samuel fostered the creation of a supreme Muslim Council which was transformed by the Mufti and his followers into a means of terrorizing the Jewish population. Further, Samuel encouraged Palestinian Arabs to contact their neighbours to promote Pan-Arabism. As a result the Mufti was able to generate anti-Zionist feeling within the Pan-Arab movement.

Despite these setbacks the British were insistent on implementing the intention of the Balfour Declaration to create a homeland for the Jewish people in Palestine. In this quest egalitarian principles were paramount. Thus in a meeting of the Imperial Council on 22 June 1921 the Canadian Prime Minister Arthur Meighen asked: 'How do you define our responsibilities in relation to Palestine under Mr Balfour's pledge?' In response, Winston Churchill,

Colonial Secretary, stated: 'To do our best to make an honest effort to give the Jews a chance to make a national home for themselves.' Meighen then asked if this meant they would take control of the government. Churchill replied that they could do so if they became a majority in the country. Meighen then asked if this meant pro rata with the Arab population. To this Churchill said: 'Pro rata with the Arab. We made an equal pledge that we would not turn the Arab off his land or invade his political and social rights' (ibid., 440).

Although the British government initially agreed that all Jews should be free to emigrate to Palestine, immigration eventually became a pressing issue. After the Arab riots, Samuel suspended Jewish immigration, and three boatloads of Jews fleeing from Poland and the Ukraine were sent back from Israel. According to Samuel, mass migration could not be allowed; not surprisingly this policy led to vehement Jewish protests. Under Samuel's successor Lord Plumer the country prospered, yet Jewish resentment continued. Although Weizmann adopted a moderate stance towards Palestinian development, other leaders such as Jabotinsky were more impatient. In 1922 Churchill ended the ban on immigration, but his White Paper none the less insisted that immigration must reflect the economic capacity of the country. Unwilling to accept British policy Jabotinsky believed that immigration should be the sole concern of Jewish authorities. On this basis, he left the Zionist executive in 1923, and in 1925 founded the Union of Zionist Revisionists which sought to attract the largest number of Jews in the shortest possible time. This movement was hailed in Eastern Europe where its young wing Betar wore uniforms and received military training.

Despite such efforts to encourage Jewish immigration the Jewish population in Palestine grew gradually. By 1927 only 2713 immigrated whereas 5000 left the country. Three years later the number of arrivals and departures were about the same. But from 1929, as the economic and political situation grew worse throughout Europe, a large number of Jews sought to enter the country. In 1929 a massacre took place in Palestine in which 150 Jews were killed; this led to a further limit on immigration despite the fact that hundreds of thousands of Jews sought entry into Palestine. As more and more Jews were allowed to settle, Arab resentment intensified. Each year there were more than 30 000 arrivals, and in 1935 the number grew to 62 000. In response, in April 1936 a major Arab uprising took place. On 7 July 1937 a commission headed by Lord Peel recommended that Jewish immigration be reduced to 12 000 a year, and restrictions were placed on land purchases. In addition a three-way partition was suggested: the coastal strip, Galilee and the Jezreel valley should be formed into a Jewish state, whereas the Judaean hills, the Negev and Ephraim should be the Arab state. This plan was rejected by the Arabs and another revolt took place in 1937. In the following year, the Pan-Arab conference in Cairo adopted a policy whereby all Arab communities pledged they would take action to prevent further Zionist expansion.

After the failure of the tripartite plan in London in 1939 the British abandoned the policy of partition. In May 1939 a new White Paper was published stating that only 75 000 more Jews could be admitted over five years, and thereafter none except with Arab agreement. At the same time Palestine should proceed with plans to become independent. Although there were then about 500 000 Jews in Palestine, the Arabs still constituted the majority in the country. As a result the Arabs would be in a position to seize control of Palestine and expel the Jewish people.

THE ESTABLISHMENT OF A JEWISH STATE

The 1930s witnessed various divisions within the Zionist ranks. In 1931 Weizmann was forced to give up the presidency of the World Zionist Congress due to pressure from the Mizrahi. In the same year elections to the Zionist Assembly resulted in a split between Mapai (with 31 seats), the Revisionists (16 seats), and Mizrahi (five seats). In the military sphere the Revisionists, Mizrahi and other Zionists split from the Haganah to form the Irgun. At this time the Revisionists accused Mapai of collusion with the British; the Revisionists were condemned by Mapai as fascists. On 16 June 1933 the head of the Political Department, Chaim Arlosoroff, was murdered; two extreme Revisionists were arrested and charged, but later acquitted. Yet despite such internal divisions, after the outbreak of war in 1939 the establishment of a Jewish state became the central concern of all Zionists.

Although the Jews supported the Allies, Jewry was committed to overturning British policy as enshrined in the 1939 White Paper. During this period the British attempted to prevent illegal immigrants from landing in Palestine: if their ships got through they were captured and deported. In November 1940 the *Patria* which was about to set sail for Mauritius carrying 1700 deportees was sabotaged by the Haganah. It sank in Haifa Bay with the loss of 250 refugees. Two years later the *Struma*, a refugee ship from Romania, was refused landing permission, turned back by the Turks, and sunk in the Black Sea with the death of 770 passengers. Such events, however, did not alter Britain's determination to prevent the entry of illegal immigrants.

In 1943 Menachem Begin, formerly chairman of Betar, took over control of the Revisionist military arm, the Irgun. With 600 agents under his control, he blew up various British buildings. On 6 November 1944 the ultra-extreme group, the Stern Gang (which had broke away from the Irgun), murdered Lord Moyne, the British Minister for Middle Eastern Affairs. Outraged by this act, the Haganah launched a campaign against both the Sternists and the Irgun. While he was fighting the British and other Jews, Begin organized a powerful underground force in the belief that the Haganah would eventually join him in attacking the British. In 1945 a united Jewish Resistance movement was created which embraced the various Jewish military forces, and on 31 October it began sabotaging railways. In retaliation the British made a raid on the Jewish Agency on 29 June 1946, arresting 2718 Jews. Begin, however, persuaded the Haganah to blow up the King David Hotel where a segment of the British administration was located. When Weizmann heard of this plan he was incensed, and the Haganah was ordered to desist. Begin refused, and on 22 July 1946 the explosion took place, killing 27 British, 41 Arabs, 17 Jews and five others. In consequence the Haganah commander Moshe Sneh resigned, and the resistance movement divided. The British then proposed a tripartite plan of partition which was rejected by both Jews and Arabs. Exasperated by this conflict, the British Foreign Secretary, Ernest Bevin, declared he was handing over this dispute to the United Nations.

Despite this decision, Begin continued with his campaign of terror, insisting on the right of the Irgun to retaliate against the British. In April 1947 after three members of the Irgun were convicted and hanged for destroying the Acre prison fortress, Begin ordered that two British sergeants be hanged. Such an act of revenge provoked worldwide condemnation, and anti-Jewish riots took place throughout Britain. These incidents encouraged the British to leave Palestine as soon as possible.

They also coincided with the succession of Harry S Truman as President of the United States. Sympathetic to the Jewish cause and anxious for the support of American Jewry in the 1948 election,

Truman pressed for the creation of a Jewish state. In May 1947 the Palestinian question came before the United Nations, and a special committee was authorized to formulate a plan for the future of the country. The minority recommended a binational state, but the majority suggested that there be both an Arab and a Jewish state as well as an international zone in Jerusalem. On 29 November this recommendation was endorsed by the General Assembly.

After this decision was taken, the Arabs began to attack Jewish settlements. Although the Jewish commanders were determined to repel this assault, their resources were inconsiderable compared with the Arab side. The Haganah had 17 600 rifles, 2700 sten-guns, about 1000 machine guns, and approximately 20 000–43 000 men in various stages of training. The Arabs on the other hand had a sizeable liberation army as well as the regular forces of the Arab states including 10 000 Egyptians, 7000 Syrians, 3000 Iraqis, and 3000 Lebanese as well as 4500 soldiers from the Arab Legion of Transjordan. By March 1948 over 1200 Jews had been killed; in April Prime Minister Ben Gurion ordered the Haganah to link the Jewish enclaves and consolidate as much territory as possible under the United Nations plan. Jewish forces then occupied Haifa, opened up the route to Tiberias and eastern Galilee, and captured Safed, Jaffa and Acre. On 14 May Ben Gurion read out the Scroll of Independence in the Tel Aviv Museum:

> By virtue of our national and intrinsic right and on the strength of the resolution of the United Nations General Assembly, we hereby declare the establishment of a Jewish state in Palestine, which shall be known as the State of Israel.

On 11 June a truce was concluded, but in the next month conflict broke out and the Israelis seized Lydda, Ramleh and Nazareth as well as large areas beyond the partition frontiers. Within ten days the Arabs agreed to another truce, but outbreaks of hostility continued. In mid-October the Israelis attempted to open the road to the Negev settlements and took Beersheba. On 12 January 1949 armistice talks took place in Rhodes and an armistice was later signed by Egypt, Lebanon, Transjordan and Syria. These events created the ongoing Arab-Palestinian problem: 656 000 Arab inhabitants fled from Israeli-held territories: 280 000 to the West Bank; 70 000 to Transjordan; 100 000 to Lebanon; 4000 to Iraq; 75 000 to Syria; 7000 to Egypt; and 190 000 to the Gaza Strip.

On the basis of the 1949 armistice, the Israelis sought agreement on the boundaries of the Jewish state. The Arabs, however, refused to consider this proposal – instead they insisted that Israel return to the 1947 partition lines without giving any formal recognition of the new state. Further, despite the armistice, *fedayeen* bands continued to attack Israeli citizens, and boycotts and blockades sought to injure Israel's economy. After King Abdullah was assassinated on 20 June 1951, a military junta ousted the Egyptian monarch; on 25 February 1954 President Gemal Abdul Nasser gained control of the country. From September 1955 the Soviet bloc supplied weapons to the Arabs, and this encouraged Nasser to take steps against the Jewish State. From 1956 he denied Israeli ships access to the Gulf of Aqaba (they had already been prevented from using the Suez Canal). In April 1956 he signed a pact with Saudi Arabia and Yemen, and in July he seized the Suez Canal. Fearing Arab intentions, Israel launched a pre-emptive strike on 29 October, and in the war that followed Israel captured all of Sinai as well as Gaza, and opened a sea route to Aqaba.

At the end of the Sinai War Israel undertook to withdraw from Sinai as long as Egypt did not remilitarize it and UN forces formed a protective cordon sanitaire. This arrangement endured for ten years, but attacks still continued during this period. In 1967 Nasser launched another offensive, and on 15 May he moved 100 000 men and armour into Sinai and expelled the UN army. On 22 May he blockaded Aqaba; several days later King Hussein of Jordan signed a military agreement in Cairo. On the same day Iraqi forces took up positions in Jordan. In the face of this Arab threat, Israel launched a strike on 5 June, destroying the Egyptian air force on the ground. On 7 June the Israeli army took the Old City, thereby making Jerusalem its capital. On the next day the Israeli forces occupied the entire Left Bank, and during the next few days captured the Golan Heights and reoccupied Sinai.

Despite such a crushing defeat, the Six Day War did not bring security to the Jewish state. Nasser's successor President Anwar Sadat expelled Egypt's Soviet military advisers in July 1972, cancelled the country's political and military alliance with other Arab states, and together with Syria attacked Israel on Yom Kippur, 6 October 1973. At the outbreak of war the Egyptians and the Syrians broke through Israeli defences, but by 9 October the Syrian advance had been repelled. On 10 October the American President Richard Nixon began an airlift of advanced weapons to Israel; two days later the Israelis engaged in a counter-attack on Egypt and moved towards victory. On 24 October a cease-fire came into operation.

Later, when the Labour coalition lost the May 1977 election and handed over power to the Likud headed by Menahem Begin, Sadat offered to negotiate peace terms with Israel. On 5 September 1978 at the American presidential home Camp David, the process of reaching such an agreement began and was completed thirteen days later (although another six months were required before a detailed treaty was formulated). The treaty specified that Egypt would recognize Israel's right to exist and provide secure guarantees for her southern border. In return Israel would hand over Sinai. In addition she would undertake to negotiate away much of the West Bank and make concessions over Jerusalem as long as a complementary treaty was agreed with the Palestinians and other Arab countries. This latter step, however, was never taken – the proposal was rejected by the Palestinian Arabs. This meant that Israel was left with the responsibility for overseeing Arab occupied territories.

In the years that followed, Arab influence grew immeasurably, due to the Arabs' control of oil in the Middle East. As the price of oil increased, Arab revenue provided huge sums for the purchase of armaments. At the UN the Arab world exerted its power, and in 1975 the General Assembly passed a resolution equating Zionism with racism. Further, Yasser Arafat, leader of the Palestine Liberation Organization, was accorded head of government status by the UN. Fearing the growing threat of Palestinian influence and terrorism, Israel launched an advance into southern Lebanon in June 1982, destroying PLO bases. This Israeli onslaught and subsequent occupation served as the background to the killing of Muslim refugees by Christian Falangist Arabs in the Sabra and Shatilla camps on 16 September 1982. Throughout the world this atrocity was portrayed as Israel's fault. In response to this criticism, the Israeli government ordered an independent judicial inquiry which placed some blame on the Israeli Minister of Defence, Ariel Sharon, for not having prevented the massacre.

After the Israeli conquest during the Yom Kippur War, the State of Israel took control of the Occupied Territories. In the following years the Palestinians staged demonstrations, strikes and riots against Israeli rule. By 1987 the Palestinians in the West Bank and Gaza were largely young educated people who had benefited from formal education. Yet despite such educational advances, they suffered from limited job expectations and this situation led to political radicalism. Such frustration came to a head on 9 December 1987 in Jabaliya, the most militant of the Gaza refugee camps. An Israeli patrol was trapped there during a protest about the death of four Jabaliya residents who were killed in a road accident the previous day. The soldiers shot their way out, killing one youth and wounding ten others. This event provoked riots throughout the Occupied Territories. By January 1989, the Israeli Defence Forces declared that 352 Palestinians had died, more than 4300 were wounded, and 25 600 arrested. In addition, 200 Arab homes had been sealed or demolished. As hostilities increased, the *intifada* (resistance) demonstrated that occupying the West Bank and the Gaza Strip would be a perpetual problem.

CRITIQUE

As we have observed, the early proponents of secular Zionism were convinced that Judeophobia is unavoidable in Western society. Thus Moses Hess in *Rome and Jerusalem* decreed that it is impossible for Jews to escape from Jew-hatred no matter what steps are taken towards emancipation and liberation: neither Jewish reform nor conversion to Christianity can provide a means of overcoming such sentiments. For Hess, only the restoration of Jewish nationalism could enable Jewry to gain social, political and economic equality. Similarly, Leon Pinsker in *Autoemancipation* argued for the creation of a national homeland in the wake of the Russian pogroms of 1881. Although initially a fervent supporter of the Enlightenment, Pinsker asserted that the Jewish problem could only be solved through Jewish statehood. In the diaspora the Jews were like the dead among the living, but with the creation of a Jewish society they would be able to regain their self-respect and communal integrity. Again, in *The Jewish State*, Theodor Herzl espoused Zionism as a remedy for anti-Semitism. Convinced of the necessity of a home for those who were oppressed, Herzl maintained that the building of a Jewish state would transform Jewish life; no longer would Jews be vulnerable to attack.

These predictions about the elimination of Jew-hatred have not been realized in this century. On the contrary, anti-Semitism has been intensified by the establishment of a Jewish state. In the Muslim world Arab writing is penetrated with anti-Semitic motifs, images and stereotypes drawn from the past. The Arab press frequently castigates Jews for their crimes against humanity: in political cartoons Israel is personified by hooked-nosed and hunchbacked figures with wispy beards, skull caps and black hats. Headlines call for the destruction of the Jewish state. In addition books and articles reiterate the traditional account of Muhammad's betrayal by the Jewish people. Similar anti-Jewish agitation has also been a constant theme of European history since the Second World War. Such contemporary hostility to the Jewish people illustrates that the flames of anti-Semitism have not been quenched by the creation of a Jewish state. Rather the founding of a Jewish homeland in Israel appears to have had precisely the opposite effect. Diaspora existence did not disappear once Israel was established: there was simply not enough space in Palestine to accommodate world Jewry, and in any case the majority of Jews did not wish to emigrate. Thus Jews still live as aliens in foreign lands where they continue to be the target of persecution, and the existence of a Jewish homeland in the Middle East has simply exacerbated hostility towards the Jewish people who are characterized, particularly in Arab lands, as usurpers and exploiters.

A second dilemma arising from the creation of a homeland relates to Jewish empowerment. With the establishment of the state of Israel, the Jewish people have become a major political force after 2000 years of exile. Having endured the horrors of the Holocaust, world Jewry today is unified in its dedication to Jewish survival: the rallying call of the Jewish nation has become: 'Never Again!' Yet how is the Jewish community to respond to the social responsibilities of political empowerment? In discussing this issue, a number of conservative Jewish writers from across the religious and political spectrum have stressed that pragmatic considerations must be paramount as the State of Israel struggles to endure against formidable odds. Such a policy of *realpolitik*, they maintain, will inevitably countenance the occasional use of immoral strategies to achieve desired ends – this is the price of nationhood. According to these pragmatists, if Judaism and the Jewish people are to survive, there must be constant vigilance against those forces which seek to undermine the existence of Jewry: anti-Semitism must be countered wherever it exists, no matter what the political, economic, social, spiritual or moral cost may be.

Such a philosophy, however, is inherently flawed. From its inception, the idea of Israel as a homeland for the Jewish people was animated by an idealistic vision of the Jewish future. It was not enough simply to ensure a Jewish presence in the Holy Land: what is required instead is an attempt to create a utopian Jewish exist- ence in the land that was promised to Abraham, Isaac and Jacob. Such utopianism was at the heart of the quest to return to Zion. Hence, arguably, contemporary Israeli society is under an obliga- tion to live up to the moral prescriptions of the *Torah* – Jewish life in Israel must be infused with the ethical values of the faith. In partic- ular, as an empowered people the Israelis have the duty to consider the plight of all those who are currently undergoing hardship and deprivation in the Jewish state. In this context the State of Israel should give heed to the Palestinian quest for human dignity. A number of early Zionists were acutely aware of the needs of the Arab population in Palestine. Nonetheless, for 5000 years Jews and Arabs have sought to conquer one another. This terrible chapter in the history of modern Judaism must now come to an end.

A third difficulty with Zionism concerns the status of Israel in modern Jewish life. For nearly 4000 years the Jewish people longed for a homeland of their own. From the time of Abraham to the present this yearning has been at the centre of the Jewish faith. As God's chosen people, the promise of a return to Zion sustained Jewry through persecution and suffering. Yet in the light of the events of the twentieth century, a fundamental shift has occurred in Jewish consciousness. For many Jews it has become extremely difficult to believe that God will stand by his people in times of dis- aster. Increasingly for Jewry a void exists where once the Jewish people experienced God's presence, and as a result modern Israel has been invested with many of the attributes previously reserved for the Deity. Hence in the post-Holocaust world the traditional conception of a divine redeemer and deliverer has been eclipsed by a policy of Jewish self-protection. It is the Holy Land which is viewed as ultimately capable of providing a safe haven for those in need: Israel – not the God of history – is perceived as the protector of the Jewish people.

A shift away from theological commitment poses profound difficulties for the future. Even if a Palestinian homeland were created in the Middle East, this would be no guarantee for the sur- vival of modern Israel. The threat of a nuclear holocaust would in all likelihood continue as an ever-present reality. What if Israel were destroyed, and the Jewish State wiped off the map? How could the Jewish community endure yet another tragedy of this order without belief in God and redemption? For those Jews who have substituted the Holy Land for God himself, the destruction of Israel would be the ultimate tragedy.

In substituting the political Israel for traditional religious belief, modern Zionism has turned on its head the story of Jacob wrestling with the angel. According to the Book of Genesis, the patriarch Jacob wrestled with the messenger of God until dawn at the ford of Jabbok. When this messenger saw that he could not prevail against Jacob, he touched the hollow of Jacob's thigh which was thereby put out of joint. As dawn appeared, the messenger said: 'Let me go, for the day is breaking.' But Jacob replied: 'I will not let you go, unless you bless me.' And he said: 'What is your name?' He said: 'Jacob'. Then the angel said: 'Your name shall no more be called Jacob, but Israel, for you have striven with God and with men, and have prevailed' (Genesis 32. 26–9). This incident was the origin of the name Israel (meaning 'he who struggles with God') which subsequently became the designation of Jacob's twelve sons, and eventually of the entire nation.

Here Jacob struggled and through God, he became Israel. Yet in the contemporary world it appears that political Israel has prevailed and has become a substitute for God. In the quest to provide a refuge for all who are oppressed and persecuted, the State of Israel has eclipsed religious faith. Such an altered perspective is profoundly disturbing because it provides no religious sustenance for the nation. From earliest times Jews have viewed God as an all-powerful creator, the omnipotent Lord of the universe, capable of doing everything. In his omniscience he is aware of all things that take place in the universe including the human heart. In addition God is active in world affairs. Not only is he the source of all, he chose the Jews, guides their destiny and directs all history to its final consummation. As holy righteous and merciful Lord, he is the loving father to all who call upon him. It is this conception of the Deity, enshrined in the Jewish tradition, that has always animated the faithful.

Israel may not survive, and if the Jewish people forget the religious foundations of the tradition in their passion for the land, then they also may disappear from history. The State of Israel is not an ultimate insurance policy – it is simply a human attempt to bring about the realization of Jewish yearning for a homeland. Through centuries of hardship, the nation remained faithful to their hope of restoration in the land of their ancestors – through their religious faith, the sense of destiny and nationhood was preserved. Since 1948 when Israel became a Jewish state, the hope of a return to the Promised Land became a reality. Yet if Israel is a state like any other, it is subject to the political vicissitudes of all other earthly institutions. If the Jewish people are to survive into the third millennium, it is not enough for them to assert their identity merely through supporting the State of Israel. Thus despite world Jewry's general acceptance of the State of Israel, Zionism does not provide a comprehensive ideological basis for Jewish living in the twenty-first century.

9

A New Philosophy of Judaism

Given the deficiencies of Orthodox, Hasidic, Reform, Conservative, Reconstructionist and Humanistic Judaism, as well as Zionism, what is now required is a new philosophy of Judaism which could serve as a unifying basis for modern Jewish life. Arguably such a reinterpretation of the Jewish heritage should be based on a revised vision of Judaism in which the traditional view of God's nature and activity is not seen as definitive and final. Rather the Jewish faith should be perceived simply as one way among many of making sense of Divine Reality. Aware of the inevitable subjectivity of all religious belief, Jews should feel free to draw from the past those elements of the Jewish faith which they regard as spiritually meaningful. Unlike the main branches of Judaism, this new interpretation is based on the concept of personal autonomy, allowing each individual independence of thought and action. Such a liberal approach would more accurately reflect the realities of everyday Jewish life in which each Jew is in fact at liberty to select for himself which features of the tradition he wishes to observe. This new philosophy of Judaism would thus acknowledge the true character of modern Jewish life and extol the principle of personal freedom which has become the hallmark of the modern age.

THE INADEQUACIES OF CONTEMPORARY JUDAISM

In the post-Enlightenment world Jewry is no longer united by a cohesive religious system; rather the Jewish people has fragmented into a wide range of subgroups espousing competing interpretations of the tradition. All of these movements seek to provide a basis for Jewish existence in contemporary society yet in different ways their solutions are inadequate and none is able to provide a universally acceptable philosophy for the community as a whole.

212

Orthodox Judaism, for example, has generally not faced up to the serious challenges posed to religion by science. Modern scientific discoveries have illustrated that the biblical account of creation is no longer credible, nor is the traditional belief in the resurrection of the dead plausible; further, the scientific explanation of history has replaced the more primitive interpretation of biblical events. In addition, the critical findings of biblical scholars have illustrated that the doctrine of *Torah MiSinai* is fundamentally flawed: in the light of the findings of biblical archaeology and textual analysis it is inconceivable that Moses could have been the author of the Pentateuch. Orthodox thinkers have also failed to recognize the serious theological implications of the Holocaust – for many Jews the belief in an all-powerful and benevolent Deity who lovingly watches over his chosen people is no longer credible. Rather than provide a persuasive defence of theism, Orthodox leaders have simply affirmed the central tenets of the faith without seeking to demonstrate their validity.

Like Orthodox Judaism, Hasidism also has not come to terms with the findings of biblical scholarship. Unwilling to confront the overwhelming evidence that the *Torah* was composed at different times in the history of ancient Israel, Hasidic Jews proclaim – without providing a justification for their view – that God revealed the *Torah* in its entirety to Moses on Mount Sinai and that therefore the prescriptions contained in Scripture are authoritative. Moreover, Hasidic writers piously accept kabbalistic cosmological doctrines without acknowledging that these theories conflict with scientific investigations into the origin of the universe. The concept of the *zaddik* (righteous person) as a spiritually elevated individual able to act as an intermediary on behalf of his people is also unquestioningly accepted even though most Jews have rejected such a notion of authoritarianism. A final difficulty with Hasidic theology concerns the concept of divine providence; to the modern Jewish mind it is inconceivable that human suffering, particularly during the Nazi period, could be a result of divine providence. For most Jews the religious ideas and life-style of Hasidism, as well as its perception of the role of women in society, are outmoded relics from a bygone age.

Moving across the religious spectrum, Reform Judaism is also beset with various difficulties even though its supporters maintain that it provides a relevant form of Judaism for contemporary Jewry. The main difficulty with Reform is that it has failed to provide a coherent framework for belief and practice. With respect to religious convictions, sociological studies reveal that religious opinion within the movement ranges from traditional belief to atheism. And as in the sphere of religious doctrine, there is a comparable disagreement with regard to Jewish law. Even though Reform Judaism has attempted to provide a common basis for Jewish practice, reformers have been unable to reach a consensus about which traditional laws should be retained: in attempting to formulate a modern Code of Jewish Law, subjective judgement prevails. As a consequence modern Reform Judaism lacks a coherent ideology for its adherents. This is not a temporary deficiency, but an inevitable outcome resulting from the abandonment of the fundamentals of the faith.

In a similar vein, Conservative Judaism suffers from a lack of coherence. Within the movement there is considerable uncertainty about the status of Jewish belief and practice. Some traditionalists, for example, assert that Scriptural and rabbinic law is authoritative for the Jewish people; others demand halakhic change. Regarding theological beliefs, some thinkers view God as a personal, supernatural being active in history; others contend that God should be conceived in non-personal terms since his nature transcends human understanding. At the other end of the spectrum, there are some Conservative writers who reject the notion of supernaturalism altogether: in their view God should be understood as a creative power in the cosmos. Similar disagreement also exists about the doctrine of revelation. Some more traditionally minded Conservative Jews believe that God revealed the *Torah* even though not every word in the Pentateuch was communicated to Moses; other writers, however, interpret revelation as a process of divine encounter.

Another area of dispute concerns the belief that the Jews are God's chosen people: even thought the Conservative prayer book has retained the traditional formula 'You have chosen us from all the nations', for many Conservative Jews the notion of chosenness must be modified to account for God's active involvement in the life of all human beings. Hence, like Reform Judaism, Conservatism is bedevilled with disagreement over the most central aspects of the tradition even though it has sought to conserve the central features of the faith.

Reconstructionist Judaism differs from these other forms of Judaism in that it has explicitly rejected a belief in an external Deity. Under the influence of Mordecai Kaplan, Reconstructionist Jews have sought to reinterpret Judaism to meet the demands of modern life. In his writings Kaplan argued that it is no longer possible to believe in a supernatural Deity; instead he maintained that the idea of God must be redefined. Promoting a naturalistic explanation of transcendence Kaplan called for the re-establishment of a network of organic Jewish communities that would ensure the self-perpetuation of the Jewish heritage. The central difficulty with such a view is that, on the one hand, Reconstructionism has deliberately eliminated any form of theism from its philosophy while, on the other, it has retained the central features of the Jewish faith. Thus, although Reconstructionist Jews do not believe in a God who responds to prayer, in practice their worship is essentially no different from what takes place in traditional synagogues. Similarly, the religious observances of Reconstructionist Judaism parallel what is found in Conservative Judaism but they are in no way connected with God's decree. Reconstructionism therefore is riddled with internal inconsistency: as a movement it seeks to perpetuate a traditional Jewish life-style while simultaneously rejecting the religious foundations on which such an adherence to the Jewish heritage has previously been based.

Like Reconstructionist Judaism, Jewish Humanism has also rejected a belief in a supernatural God. Yet – distancing itself from Reconstructionism – it has sought to provide an alternative lifestyle consonant with the principles of the movement. Extolling humane values, it strives to offer a mode of Jewish existence attuned to the modern age. Even though such an ideology may appeal to some Jews drawn to secular ideology, it is difficult to see how it could serve as a basis for Jewish living in contemporary society. In the light of the horrific events of the Holocaust, it has become increasingly difficult for most Jews to be confident about human progress. The basic assumptions of Humanistic Judaism are thus at odds with a growing sense of pessimism about the human potential for evil. Further, Humanist Judaism's reformulation of Jewish life-cycle events and holidays would in all likelihood hold little attraction for the vast majority of Jews who are currently seeking for spiritual sustenance from the tradition.

Turning to modern Zionism, it is clear that the early Zionists were misguided in their conviction that the problem of anti-Semitism could be solved through the creation of a Jewish state. The establishment of a Jewish homeland in the Middle East has if anything increased anti-Jewish attitudes in the Arab world and elsewhere – in recent years there has been an explosion of hostility toward the Jewish community in both first and third-world countries. Another difficulty facing Zionist ideology is the espousal of pragmatic policies on the part of the Israeli government; such attitudes are far removed from the utopianism that fuelled early Zionist thinkers and pioneers. Increasingly Israel has adopted policies devoid of any Jewish content, at times profoundly opposed to the humane values of the tradition. Yet, paradoxically, the state of Israel has nonetheless been invested with a sense of holiness – for many Jews it is perceived as the stronghold of the Jewish people in a post-Holocaust age. Such a conception is a dangerous inversion of spiritual values given Israel's vulnerability in a nuclear age.

It is clear then that none of these Jewish ideologies – Orthodoxy, Hasidism, Reform Judaism, Conservative Judaism, Reconstructionist Judaism, Jewish Humanism and Zionism – is adequate for the modern age. What is required instead is a new interpretation of Judaism which acknowledges the depth of Jewish diversity in contemporary society. The central feature of this new conception – which I will refer to as Open Judaism – is the principle of personal autonomy. Open Judaism would allow all individuals the right to select those features from the tradition which they find spiritually meaningful.

Unlike the various branches of modern Judaism, this new conception of the tradition would espouse a truly liberal doctrine of individual freedom, seeking to grant persons full religious independence. Adherents of Open Judaism would be actively encouraged to make up their own minds about religious belief and practice. It might be objected that such extreme liberalism would simply result in chaos – such criticism, however, fails to acknowledge the state of religious diversity within contemporary Jewish society. As we have seen, in all branches of Judaism, there has been a gradual erosion of centralized authority; although many rabbis have attempted to establish standards for the members of their communities, there is a universal recognition that in the end each Jew will define for himself which aspects of the heritage are personally relevant. In short, in the modern Jewish world there is a conscious acceptance of the principle of personal autonomy, even if in some quarters it is only grudgingly accepted. Open Judaism would hence be in accord with the spirit of the age; its endorsement of personal decision-making would be consonant with the nature of Jewish existence. Grounded in an acceptance of the nature of the contemporary Jewish community, its philosophy reflects the realities of everyday life, in Israel and the diaspora.

A THEOLOGY OF OPEN JUDAISM

For two millennia Jews have maintained that the *Torah* was given by God to Moses on Mount Sinai. Such a belief served as the basis for the conviction that the Five Books of Moses – including history, theology and legal precepts – have absolute authority. As a result Orthodox Judaism and Hasidism refuse to accept any modernist interpretations of the Pentateuch. As the Israeli scholar Zvi Werblowsky explained:

> Jewish Orthodoxy has ... staunchly upheld the theory of verbal inspiration in its extremist form – at least so far as the Pentateuch is concerned. Higher criticism of the Pentateuch is flatly rejected and is considered a major heresy. The underlying assumption is that the whole fabric of traditional Judaism would crumble if its foundations, the notion of Divine legislation to Moses, were to be exchanged for modernist ideas about historical growth and the composite nature of sacred texts.   (Jacobs, 1964, 218)

Arguably, however, what is now required is a new theological understanding which will provide a framework for Jewish existence for the next millennium. What is needed is a theological structure consonant with a contemporary understanding of Divine Reality. In recent years an increasing number of theologians have called for a Copernican revolution in our understanding of religion. Following the Kantian distinction between the World-as-it-is (the Noumenal World), and the World-as-perceived (the Phenomenal World), these writers argue that Divine Reality-as-it-is-in-itself should be distinguished from Divine Reality-as-conceived in human thought and experience. Such a contrast, they point out, is in fact a major feature of many of the world's faiths. As far as Judaism is concerned, throughout the history of the faith there has been a conscious awareness of such a distinction between God-as-he-is-in-himself and human conceptions of the Divine. Scripture, for example, frequently cautions against describing God anthropomorphically. Thus Deuteronomy states: 'Therefore take good heed to yourselves. Since you saw no form on the day that the Lord spoke to you at Horeb out of the midst of the fire' (Deut.4.5). Again Exodus 33:20 declares:

> And he said, 'You cannot see my face; for man shall not see me, and live.' And the Lord said, 'Behold there is a place by me

where you shalt stand upon the rock; and while my glory passes
I will put you in a cleft of the rock, and I will cover you with my
hand until I have passed by; then I will take away my hand, and
you shall see my back; but my face shall not be seen.'

In rabbinic literature there are comparable passages which suggest
that human beings should refrain from attempting to describe God.
Thus the Palestinian teacher Abin said: 'When Jacob of the village
of Neboria was in Tyre, he interpreted the verse "For thee, silence is
praise, O God" to mean that silence is the ultimate praise of God. It
can be compared to a jewel without price: however high you ap-
praise it, you will undervalue it.' In another talmudic passage a
story is told of the prayer reader who was rebuked by the scholar
Hanina. This individual praised God by listing as many of his attributes as he could. When he finished, Hanina asked if he had ex-
hausted the praises of God. Hanina then said that even the three
attributes 'The Great', 'The Valiant' and 'The Tremendous' could
not legitimately be used to describe God were it not for the fact that
Moses used them and they subsequently became part of the Jewish
liturgy. This text concludes with a parable: if a king who possesses
millions of gold pieces is praised for having millions of silver pieces
such praise disparages his wealth rather than glorifies it.

The latter development of such a view was continued by both
Jewish philosophers and mystics. In his treatise, *Duties of the Heart*,
for example, the eleventh-century philosopher Bahya Ibn Pakudah
argued that the concept of God's unity involves the negation from
God of all human and infinite limitations. According to Bahya, if
we wish to ascertain the nature of anything, we must ask two fundamental questions: (1) if it is; and (2) what it is. Of God, however,
it is possible to ask only if he is. And once having established his
existence, it is not possible to go on to enquire about his nature,
since it is beyond human understanding. Given this standpoint,
how is one to make sense of the descriptions of God in Scripture
and the Jewish liturgy? For Bahya there are three main attributes
which should be understood in a negative sense: God's existence,
unity and eternity. Even when these three attributes are expressed
positively, they are in fact understood negatively. Hence, to say
that God exists, implies that he is not non-existent. When one
asserts that he is one, this means that there is no multiplicity in him.
And, finally, when he is depicted as eternal, this signifies that he is
not bound by time. God's nature is thus inscrutable; none the less,

we do have knowledge about him. Concerning other positive attributes (such as his goodness), these can be understood in a positive sense because unlike the other three attributes, they deal with God's acts rather than his essence.

In the *Guide for the Perplexed*, the twelfth-century Jewish philosopher Moses Maimonides also focused on the concept of negative attributes. For Maimonides the ascription to God of positive attributes is a form of idolatry because it suggests that his attributes are coexistent with him. To say that God is one, Maimonides contended, is simply a way of negating all plurality from his being. Even when one asserts that God exists, one is simply affirming that his non-existence is impossible. Positive attributes are only admissible if they are understood as referring to God's acts. Attributes which refer to his nature, however, are only permissible if they are applied negatively. Moreover, the attributes which refer to God's actions imply only the acts themselves – they do not refer to the emotions from which these actions are generated when performed by human beings.

Following Maimonides, the fifteenth-century philosopher Joseph Albo in *Ikkarim* maintained that God's attributes, referring to God's nature can only be employed in a negative sense. On the other hand, attributes which refer to God's acts can be used positively as long as they do not imply change in God:

> But even the attributes in this class, those taken from God's acts, must be taken in the sense involving perfection, not in the sense involving defect. Thus, although these attributes cause emotion in us and make us change from one of the contraries to the other, they do not necessitate any change or emotions in God, for his ways are not our ways, nor are his thoughts our thoughts. (Cohn-Sherbok, 1993, 105)

Like these Jewish philosophers Jewish mystics advocated a theory of negation in describing God. For these kabbalists the Divine is revealed through the powers which emanate from him. Yet God as he is in himself is the *Ayn Sof* (Infinite). As the twelfth-century kabbalist Azriel of Gerona remarked:

> Know that the *Ayn Sof* cannot be thought of, much less spoken of, even though there is a hint of it in all things, for there is nothing else apart from it. Consequently, it can be contained neither by letter nor name nor writing nor anything.   (Cohn-Sherbok, 1995, 171)

Similarly the *Zohar* (Book of Splendour) asserts that the *Ayn Sof* is incomprehensible. It is only through the *sefirot* that the Divine is manifest in the world. Yet Jewish mystics were anxious to stress that the Divine is a unity. Hence a prayer in the *Zohar* ascribed to Elijah stresses the unity of the *Ayn Sof* and the *sefirot* (divine emanations):

> Elijah began to praise God saying: Lord of the universe! You are one but are not numbered. You are higher than the highest. You are above all mysteries. No thought can grasp you at all. It is you who produced the ten perfections which we call the ten *sefirot*. With them you guide the secret worlds which have not been revealed and the worlds which have been revealed, and in them you conceal yourself from human beings. But it is you who binds them together and unites them. Since you are in them, whoever separates any one of these ten from the others it is as if he had made a division in you.   (Ibid., 172)

According to the *Zohar* even the higher realms of the Divine – the stages represented by God's will, wisdom and understanding (*Keter, Hokhmah* and *Binah*) – should be understood negatively. Thus God's will which is represented by the *sefirah Keter* is referred to as *Ayin* (Nothingness) – it is so elevated beyond human understanding that it can only be represented by negation. Concerning divine wisdom, represented by *Hokhmah*, the *Zohar* declares that one can ask what it is but should expect no answer. Likewise the eighteenth-century scholar the Vilna Gaon stated that one can say so little about the *Ayn Sof* that one should not even give it the name *Ayn Sof*.

Here then is a new theological framework – deeply rooted in the Jewish tradition – which can serve as a basis for new vision of Jewish theology in the modern age. Acknowledging the limitation of human comprehension, such a way of unknowing reveals that there is no means by which to ascertain the true nature of Divine Reality as-it-is-in-itself. In the end, the doctrines of Judaism must be regarded as human images constructed from within particular social and cultural contexts. Thus, the absolute claims about God as found in biblical and rabbinic literature should be understood as human conceptions stemming from the religious experience of the Jewish nation: Jewish monotheism – embracing a myriad of formulations from biblical through medieval to modern times – is grounded in the life of the people; in all cases pious believers and thinkers expressed their understanding of God's activity on the basis of their own personal as well as communal encounter. Yet given that Divine Reality as-it-is-in-itself is beyond human comprehension, this Jewish understanding of the Godhead cannot be viewed as definitive and final. Rather, it should be seen as only one among many ways in which human beings have attempted to make sense of the Ultimate. In this light, it makes no sense for Jews to believe that they possess the unique truth about God and his action in the world; on the contrary, universalistic truth-claims about the Divine must give way to a recognition of the inevitable subjectivity of religious convictions.

The implications of this shift from the absolutism of the Jewish past to a new vision of Jewish theology are radical and far-reaching. Judaism – like all other religions – has advanced absolute, universal claims about the nature of the Divine, but given the separation between our finite understanding and Ultimate Reality, there is no way of attaining complete certitude about the veracity of these beliefs. Divine Reality-as-it-is-in-itself transcends human comprehension, and hence it must be admitted that Jewish religious convictions are no different in principle from those found in other religious traditions – all are lenses through which the Ultimate is conceptualized. The Jewish faith, like all other major religions, is built around its distinctive way of thinking and experiencing the Divine, yet in the end Jews must remain agnostic about the correctness of their religious beliefs.

REFORMULATING JEWISH IDENTITY

According to Jewish law, a person born of a Jewish mother is regarded as Jewish. Conversely, however, an individual born of a Jewish father and a non-Jewish mother is not Jewish – such a person is a Gentile. For thousands of years this has been the normative understanding of Jewish identification. This means that someone who is either atheistic, agnostic or non-practising but born of a Jewish mother is nevertheless Jewish. Correct belief or observance is irrelevant. As a result of this legal definition of Jewish status, there are many individuals today who though formally recognized as Jews are in no sense religious – some of these individuals adamantly identify themselves with the community; others refuse such identification. Yet, whatever their response, the Jewish community regards them as belonging to the Jewish fold and accords them various religious rights (such as the right to be married in a synagogue or buried in a Jewish cemetery). Here, then, is a simple concrete criterion of Jewishness.

In modern times, however, such a definition has been obscured for several reasons. First, the Gentile world has not invariably applied this legal criterion of Jewishness to the Jewish populace. Frequently – as took place in Nazi Germany – persons are considered Jews even if they do not qualify by this internal Jewish classification. During the Third Reich, for example, the Citizen Laws defined persons as Jewish if they were simply of Jewish blood. This meant that some of the people murdered by the Nazis would not have been accepted as Jews by the Jewish community.

A second difficulty concerns the decision taken in 1983 by the Central Conference of American Rabbis (the central body of American Reform rabbis) that a child of either a Jewish father or a Jewish mother should be deemed as Jewish assuming that this presumption is confirmed by timely and appropriate acts of identification with the Jewish faith and people. By expanding the criterion of Jewishness to include children of both matrilineal and patrilineal descent the Reform movement thus defined as Jews individuals whom other branches of Judaism regard as Gentiles. This means that neither these persons nor their descendants can be accepted as Jews by the Orthodox religious establishment.

A further difficulty about Jewish status concerns the process of conversion. According to tradition, a non-Jew is permitted to join the Jewish community by undergoing conversion. According to Orthodoxy, conversion is a ritual process involving immersion in a ritual bath (*mikveh*) and circumcision for males. Conversion is to take place in the presence of three rabbis who compose a court of law (*bet din*). This procedure has remained constant through the ages; however, within the non-Orthodox branches of Judaism, there have been various modifications to this process. Conservative Judaism, for example, generally adopts the traditional procedure, but it does not always follow the precise legal requirements. For this reason, most Orthodox rabbis do not recognize Conservative conversions as valid. Similarly, since Reform Judaism has largely abandoned ritual immersion and does not conduct circumcision in the required form, its converts are not accepted by the Orthodox community. Thus Reform and Conservative converts and their offspring as well as converts in the other non-Orthodox branches of

Judaism are deemed to be Gentiles by the Orthodox establishment, and in consequence there is considerable confusion in the Jewish world as to who should be regarded as legitimately Jewish.

Is there any solution to this profound dilemma concerning Jewish status? Given the shift in orientation from the absolutism of the past, Open Judaism would be able to offer a new definition of Jewishness for the modern age. According to this new philosophy of Judaism, Jews should not regard the doctrines of their faith as the true expression of God's will. Rather, contemporary Jewry should adopt a more open stance in which the Divine – instead of the Jewish religion – is placed at the centre of the Universe of faiths. Such a stance would enable Jews to affirm the uniqueness of their own heritage while acknowledging the validity of other approaches to the Ultimate. As we have seen, the theology underpinning this shift of perspective is based on the distinction between Divine Reality as-it-is-in-itself and Divine Reality as-perceived. From this vantage point the truth-claims of all religious systems should be seen as human constructions rather than universally valid doctrines. As a consequence, the various interpretations of the Jewish faith should no longer be perceived as embodying God's final and decisive revelation for humanity.

Such a new vision of the Jewish heritage calls for a revaluation of the traditional commitment to belief and practice. In the past Jewish doctrines were regarded as binding upon all Jews. No longer, however, is it possible to regard Judaism in this way – this new philosophy in which the Jewish faith is regarded simply as one faith among many calls for an attitude of openness. If the Jewish faith is ultimately a human construct growing out of the experiences of the nation over four millennia, it must be susceptible to reinterpretation and change. Aware of the inevitable subjectivity of religious belief, each Jew should feel free to draw from the tradition those features which he finds religiously significant. In other words, the authoritarianism of the past should give way to personal autonomy in which all persons are at liberty to construct for themselves a personal system of religious observance relevant to their own needs.

Such theological liberalism offers a new orientation to the current perplexities regarding Jewish identity. A solution to this problem is to redefine Jewishness – with Open Judaism's non-dogmatic reinterpretation of religious doctrine, there is no reason to regard the traditional legal understanding of Jewishness as binding.

Instead, Jewish identity could be redefined along the lines suggested by Humanistic Judaism. As we have seen, Humanistic Jews are anxious to avoid any form of racism in their definition of Jewishness; nor do they seek to impose a religious test on converts. Rather, they desire to accept within the Jewish fold all those who wish to identify themselves with the Jewish people. Similarly, Open Judaism – with its emphasis on religious openness and personal autonomy – could offer a similar definition of Jewishness. Distancing itself from either biological descent or correct belief and practice, Open Judaism would welcome as Jews all those, regardless of ancestry, who desire to be identified in this fashion. On this basis, Jewish identity would be solely a matter of personal choice. In other words, Jewishness would be construed as an optional identification rather than the result of matrilineal or patrilineal descent or religious conviction formally accepted by a rabbinic body. Being a Jew would then be an option open to all. Although such reinterpretation of Jewish status would not be acceptable to the major branches of Judaism, it would eliminate the uncertainty surrounding the question: Who is a Jew? Open Judaism's simple answer would be: all those who wish to adopt such an identification. Following the formulation of Jewishness as propounded by Humanistic Judaism, Open Judaism's definition of Jewishness would be expressed along the following lines:

> Open Judaism welcomes into the body of the Jewish people all those who sincerely wish to identify as Jews regardless of their ancestry. Rejecting the traditional definition of Jewishness, Open Judaism affirms that a Jew is any person irrespective of birth who declares himself to be Jewish and identifies with the Jewish heritage.

A related complication about Jewish status which could be resolved by the principles of this new philosophy of Judaism concerns the remarriage of female Jews who, though divorced in civil law, have failed to obtain a Jewish bill of divorce (*get*). Orthodox Judaism does not recognize their divorces as valid, and any subsequent liaison, even when accompanied by a non-Orthodox Jewish marriage ceremony or civil marriage, is regarded as adulterous. Further, the children of such unions are stigmatized as illegitimate (*mamzerim*) and barred from marrying other Jews unless they are also *mamzerim* or proselytes. Reform Judaism – as well as other

non-Orthodox movements – has abandoned this religious procedure in favour of civil divorce; such a rejection of Jewish law has
widespread implications given the high incidence of divorce in contemporary society. In recent years the Jewish divorce rate in
Western countries has increased enormously: in the 25–29 year-old
age group, 15 per cent of all households were separated or divorced. Such a statistic combined with the fact that non-Orthodox
groups constitute the majority of American Jews has led the
Orthodox scholar Irving Greenberg to conclude that there will be
100 000–200 000 *mamzerim* in America by the year 2000 (Sacks, 1993,
184). There is thus no doubt that the growing number of *mamzerim*
will be acute in the future, thereby deepening the schism between
Orthodox and non-Orthodox Jewry.

Alarmed by the implications of this problem for Jewish unity a
number of Orthodox scholars have proposed various solutions. The
Orthodox legal authority, Moses Feinstein, for example, issued a
ruling which was aimed at removing the difficulty concerning the
status of children of Reform second marriages. According to
Feinstein, a marriage ceremony itself is invalid if it is not observed
by two witnesses. Since those present at Reform marriages are most
likely to be Reform Jews, it is probable that they violate Jewish law
in such a fashion that they would be disqualified as witnesses.
Hence Reform marriages are not legally valid. Therefore, there is no
need for a Jewish divorce – in this light children from remarriages
should not be considered *mamzerim*. By annulling such marriages,
Feinstein's aim was to eliminate the status of illegitimacy from the
children of remarriages where the first marriage had been conducted under Reform auspices.

Such a complex strategy for dealing with this issue, however,
would be unnecessary within the context of Open Judaism. As we
have seen, this new philosophy of Judaism would promote individual decision-making, unfettered by the religious restraints of the
past. Extolling the principle of self-determination, Open Judaism
would encourage each person to exercise his personal autonomy in
determining which aspects of the tradition he wishes to retain or
discard. Departing from the legalism of Orthodoxy as well as the
prescriptive nature of the various branches of non-Orthodoxy,
Open Judaism would therefore provide a basis for the wholesale
rejection of this category: this would mean that the children of all
remarriages undertaken without first obtaining a *get* would be regarded as untainted by the stigma of illegitimacy. Such a solution

has of course already been advocated by the Reform community itself – the status of *mamzer* is deemed null and void. Nonetheless the ideology of Open Judaism provides an ideological basis for such a rejection: given Open Judaism's reinterpretation of religious doctrine, there is no reason to regard any traditional categories of Jewish status as binding upon contemporary Jewry as a whole.

JEWISH BELIEF IN A NEW AGE

In the past traditional Jews regarded the tenets of Judaism as absolute and final. For this reason the twelfth-century Jewish philosopher Moses Maimonides asserted that anyone who denies the cardinal principles of Judaism is a heretic: 'When a man breaks away from any of these fundamental principles of belief,' he wrote, 'then of him it is said, "he has gone out of the body of Israel", and he denies the root truth of Judaism.' In consequence, such individuals will be doomed to everlasting punishment: 'Each one ... even if he is an Israelite, has no share in the world to come.' (Jacobs, 1988, 14–16). While less extreme than Orthodoxy, the various branches of non-Orthodox Judaism similarly have uncompromising views of religious belief – Reform, Conservative, Reconstructionist and Humanistic Jews contend that their respective world-views are correct. Thus across the Jewish religious spectrum, the varied theistic interpretations of the nature and activity of God as well as the perspectives of non-theistic Judaism are viewed as objectively valid.

Open Judaism, however, challenges such dogmatism. On the basis of the distinction between Divine Reality as-it-is-in-itself and Divine Reality as-perceived, it is no longer credible to assert that one's religious views are categorically true. Within the framework of Open Judaism, various philosophies of the Jewish tradition found in contemporary branches of Judaism should be viewed as lenses through which the Ultimate has been differently conceptualized. The implications of this new outlook are of profound importance in the shaping of Judaism for the future. A philosophy of Judaism in which religious doctrines are seen as ultimately human in origin calls for an attitude of openness. Aware of the inevitable subjectivity of religious belief, absolute claims about Ultimate Reality should be construed as human conceptions stemming from the experience of the Jewish people through their long history.

On the basis of this revised understanding of Jewish doctrine, Jewish monotheism – embracing myriad formulations from biblical through medieval to modern times – should be perceived as grounded in the life of the nation. In all cases, devout believers, thinkers and mystics have expressed their understanding of God's nature and activity on the basis of their own spiritual apprehension. Yet given that Divine Reality as-it-is-in-itself is beyond human comprehension, such a formulation should be viewed as only one mode among many different ways of apprehending the Real. In this light, it makes no sense for Jews of whatever persuasion to believe that they possess unique truth about Ultimate Reality; on the contrary, universalistic truth-claims should give way to a recognition of the inevitable subjectivity of all convictions about the Real.

The same conclusion applies to Jewish beliefs about God's revelation. Instead of declaring that God uniquely disclosed his word to the Jewish people in the Hebrew Scriptures as well as through the teachings of rabbinic scholars, Jews should recognize that their Holy Writ is simply one record among many others. Both the Written and the Oral *Torah* have particular significance for Jewry, but this does not imply that these writings contain a uniquely true and superior divine disclosure; instead the *Torah* as well as rabbinic literature should be conceived as a record of the spiritual life of the nation and testimony of its religious quest: as such it should be viewed in much the same light as the New Testament, the *Qur'an*, the *Bagahavad Gita*, and the *Vedas*. For the Jewish people their own sacred literature has special significance, but it should not be regarded as possessing truth for all humankind.

Likewise the doctrine of the chosen people must be revised. In the past Jews believed that God had chosen them from all peoples to be the bearer of his message. Although Jews have derived great strength from the conviction that God has had a special relationship with Israel, such a belief is based on a misapprehension of Judaism in the context of the religious experience of humankind. Given that Divine Reality as-it-is-in-itself transcends human understanding, the belief that God selected a specific people as his agent is nothing more than an expression of the Jewish people's sense of spiritual superiority and impulse to disseminate its religious message. In fact, however, there is simply no way of determining if a single group stands in a unique relationship with God.

Again the ideology of Open Judaism challenges the traditional conviction that God has a providential plan for the Jewish people and for all humanity. The belief that God's guiding hand is manifest in all things is ultimately a human response to the universe: it is not, as Jews have believed through the centuries, certain knowledge. This is well illustrated by the fact that other traditions have proposed a similar view of both general and special providence, yet maintain that God's action in the world has taken an entirely different course. In other cases, non-theistic religions such as Buddhism have formulated conceptions of human destiny divorced from the activity of God or the gods. Such differences in interpretation highlight the subjective nature of all belief systems.

The Jewish conception of the Messiah must also be understood in a similar light. Within the scheme of Open Judaism, the longing for messianic deliverance should be perceived as a pious hope based on both personal and communal expectations. Although this conviction has served as a bedrock of the Jewish faith since biblical times, it is inevitably shaped by human conceptualization. Thus like other doctrines in the Jewish tradition, it is grounded in the experience of the Jewish nation and has undergone a variety of reformulations in the course of the history of the nation. But because Divine Reality as-it-is-in-itself is beyond human comprehension, there is simply no way of ascertaining whether the belief in a personal Messiah accurately mirrors the nature of Ultimate Reality.

Again, this new philosophical understanding of Judaism demands a similar stance concerning the doctrine of the afterlife. Although the belief in the eschatological unfolding of history has been a central feature of the Jewish heritage from rabbinic times to the modern period, it is simply impossible to determine whether these events will in fact occur in the future. In our finite world – limited by space and time – certain knowledge about such issues is unobtainable. Belief in an afterlife in which the righteous of Israel will receive their just reward has sustained the Jewish people through suffering, persecution and tragedy, yet from a pluralistic outlook these doctrines can be no more certain than any other elements of the Jewish religious tradition.

The implications of this shift from the absolutism of the past to a new vision of Jewish theology are radical and far reaching. The various branches of modern Judaism including non-theistic movements have advanced absolute, universal truth claims about the nature of the world – but given the separation between our finite understanding and the Real as-it-is-in-itself, there can be no way of attaining complete certainty about the veracity of these beliefs. The

Real transcends human comprehension, and hence it must be admitted that Jewish religious beliefs are in principle no different from those found in other religious faiths – all are lenses through which the Ultimate is conceptualized. Judaism, in its various forms, like all other world religions, is built around its distinctive way of thinking and experiencing the Divine.

Given such an agnostic interpretation of the Jewish faith, what belief system is appropriate for the adherents of Open Judaism? For those who subscribe to this new philosophy of Judaism, there is a broad range of options. For those of a traditional disposition, it would be possible to adopt a mode of Judaism embracing the central features of the Jewish heritage. Here an advocate of Open Judaism would accept the conventional picture of God as a supernatural deity who created and sustains the universe. In essence, such a view would be the same as that found in Orthodox Judaism and Hasidism, as well as right-wing Conservative and Reform Judaism. Yet there is one fundamental difference between conventional theism and theism as understood within this new philosophy of Judaism. For the traditionalist, this view of the Godhead is accepted unquestioningly – there is no debate about its validity. For a follower of Open Judaism, on the other hand, religious belief would be conceived as a tentative hypothesis. Aware of the conjectural nature of all religious convictions, he would acknowledge that his conceptualization of Ultimate Reality is a humanly constructed concept by which the Divine is conceptualized.

Other adherents of Open Judaism might, however, desire to espouse a modified form of theism in which various elements of the traditional understanding of God are revised. Within Open Judaism such theological adjustments would be in harmony with its emphasis on personal decision-making. A cardinal aspect of this new Jewish ideology is the appropriateness of religious modification to the time-honoured doctrines of the faith. This signifies that all divine attributes as well as theological concepts could be subjected to change. Hence the various modifications to traditional Orthodox teaching proposed by Reform, Conservative, Reconstructionist and Humanistic Jewish thinkers would be admissible. Moreover, there would be no compulsion for such altered notions to be accepted by all members of the community; on the contrary, it would be impossible for adherents of Open Judaism to formulate a statement of belief akin to the Platforms produced by the Reform movement. Instead, each person would be encouraged to formulate his own personal interpretation of Judaism in accord with his religious leanings.

Such openness would also permit an even more radical reconsideration of Jewish belief. Open Judaism would, for example, regard Mordecai Kaplan's or Sherwin Wine's non-supernaturalistic interpretation of Judaism as acceptable. In both cases there is an explicit rejection of theism and the substitution of a naturalistic understanding of the Divine. As we have noted, Kaplan defined God as 'the source of all the authority, organizing forces and relationships which are forever making a cosmos out of chaos'; Wine goes even further in rejecting any form of supernaturalistic language. Such ideas are far removed from traditional theism or even a modified form of traditional belief, yet Open Judaism – with its emphasis on individual freedom – would permit such naturalistic conceptualizations. Religious options within this new philosophy of Judaism thus range across the theological spectrum from traditional belief to atheistic naturalism.

REINTERPRETING JEWISH PRACTICE

As we have seen, until the time of the Enlightenment the Jewish people were united by a common religious inheritance. In the post-Enlightenment world, however, the Jewish community has broken up into a variety of subgroups espousing differing and competing ideologies. Thus across the religious spectrum, there is a wide variety of interpretations of the tradition: Orthodox and Hasidic Judaism are dedicated to the perpetuation of biblical law as interpreted through the centuries by rabbinic sages; Conservative and Reconstructionist Judaism seek to preserve many of the central features of traditional Judaism while allowing for modification; Reform and Humanistic Judaism actively encourage the reformulation of the Jewish tradition to meet contemporary circumstances. As far as non-affiliated Jews are concerned, there is widespread variation in practice: some individuals, even though they are not formally attached to synagogues, still follow certain practices such as circumcision; others have totally detached themselves from any form of Jewish activity.

In addition to these differing approaches to the Jewish heritage, there is a broad range of observance among the adherents of each branch of Judaism. In each movement there has been a gradual erosion of centralized authority. Although many rabbis have attempted to establish standards for the members of their communities, there is a universal recognition that in the end each Jew – regardless of formal affiliation – will define for himself which aspects of the Jewish heritage are personally relevant. Modern Jews are ultimately guided by their own consciences. Moreover, the rabbinic establishment is no longer able to impose sanctions on those who have ignored its rulings. In short, in the modern Jewish world there is a conscious acceptance of the principle of personal autonomy even if in some quarters it is only reluctantly accepted.

As a radical alternative to the more structured models of the Jewish faith represented by the major branches of Judaism, Open Judaism would provide a new foundation for dealing with the realities of modern Jewish life. By advocating the principle of personal autonomy, its philosophy would be in accord with the spirit of the age; its endorsement of personal decision-making would be consonant with the nature of modern Jewish life. Open Judaism is grounded in an acceptance of the nature of contemporary Jewish existence: its advocacy of individual liberty and freedom of choice reflects the actual conditions of Jewish living in the twentieth century.

The central feature of modern Jewish existence is the principle of personal autonomy despite a general lack of conscious recognition in the Jewish community of its pervasiveness. Open Judaism, however, not only acknowledges this characteristic of Jewish life, it celebrates freedom of choice as a positive virtue. In all spheres of activity, modern democratic societies foster individual decision-making; so too in the religious domain personal liberty – unrestrained by centralized coercion – should be regarded as a cardinal axiom of any theological system. Unique among the various interpretations of Judaism, Open Judaism would endorse such a canon of action as its guiding rule.

There is an intersection between this new philosophy of Judaism and the religious ideology propounded by Alvin Reines, Professor of Philosophy at the Hebrew Union College. Reines' approach to religious life – Polydoxy – is similarly based on the principle of autonomous choice. According to Reines, in the modern world each individual should be allowed to exercise personal autonomy since no religion is able to prove that a divine revelation has taken place which would set limits on personal decision-making:

The principle has been laid down that every person is religiously free, possessing an ultimate right to religious self-authority. Now, if this principle is to be rebutted by any members of a religious community, they must demonstrate that they possess absolute authority, namely a right to authority over the other members superior to the latter's own right to authority over themselves. The only way in which the members who wish to exercise authority in a religious community can demonstrate possession of this superior right is to show that they have received the right from a theistic God.   (Reines, 1987, 22–3)

Underlying such a stance is what Reines refers to as the Freedom Covenant: It states that:

every member of a religious community possesses an ultimate right to religious self-authority, and that every member of the religious community pledges to affirm the ultimate religious self-authority of all other members in return for their pledge to affirm her or his own. The corollary of the Freedom Covenant is that the freedom of each member of the community ends where the other member's freedom begins.   (Ibid., 25)

This new interpretation of religion is called 'Polydoxy' because those who subscribe to such a system would in all likelihood hold differing beliefs regarding such subjects as revelation, immortality and the meaning of the word 'God'. Hence Polydoxy contrasts with all forms of Orthodoxy in that its adherents are under no compulsion to accept a particular theological doctrine. Within Polydoxy, practices cannot be determined by any small group or through a majority vote. Instead, individuals are free to embrace those observances which they find religiously significant. As far as authority is concerned, each member of a Polydox community is free to exercise his own judgement. Paralleling this ideological position, Open Judaism would encourage Jews to determine for themselves which Jewish practices are religiously meaningful; as in the sphere of Jewish belief, personal autonomy is of paramount importance.

As we have seen, the major branches of non-Orthodox Judaism do not accept biblical and rabbinic law as binding; in their different ways these movements have redefined the scope of Jewish law. Yet despite such liberalism, Conservative, Reform, Reconstructionist and Humanistic Judaism are prescriptive in their interpretation of the legal tradition. Open Judaism however, like Polydoxy, would stimulate each individual Jew to determine for himself which Jewish practices should be followed. Thus, more traditionally minded supporters of Open Judaism might desire to follow the Orthodox pattern of Jewish observance, including daily worship, attendance at Sabbath and Festival services, and a strict adherence to ritual law. In terms of outward appearances, their Jewish lifestyle would resemble that of pious Orthodox, Conservative or Reconstructionist Jews. Indeed, such individuals might feel most comfortable as members of Orthodox, Conservative or Reconstructionist synagogues. Yet as followers of this new philosophy of Judaism, they would acknowledge that their personal religious choices are no more valid than those of the less observant.

Jews less conservative in approach, on the other hand, might wish to abandon or modify various features of Jewish law. Such individuals, for example, might wish to distance themselves from the vast number of prescriptions surrounding Jewish worship, home observance and personal piety – instead they would seek to formulate a Jewish lifestyle more in keeping with the demands of modern life. As we have seen, this has been the policy of Reform Judaism from its inception; for these less observant Jews, Reform Judaism would in all likelihood offer the most acceptable religious attitude. None the less, even if they were members of a Reform congregation, as followers of Open Judaism they would acknowledge that their individual decisions should in no way set a standard for others. Rather, as exponents of this new liberated philosophy of Judaism, they would be under an obligation to respect the choices of all Jews, no matter how observant or lax.

Open Judaism would also accept as valid the resolve of Jews who desire to express only minimal recognition of their Jewishness. Such persons, for example, might choose to ignore Jewish law altogether in their everyday lives and only attend synagogue on the High Holy Days or for the *yartzeit* of a parent. Alternatively, they might simply wish to be married or buried under Jewish auspices without belonging to a synagogue. Open Judaism – as an all-embracing fluid system extolling personal autonomy as a fundamental tenet – would accept the legitimacy of even such a nominal form of Jewish identification.

Open Judaism, therefore, as a philosophy of Judaism, does not set out to establish itself as an organized movement within the ranks of modern Jewry. Different from the various branches of religious Jewish life with their own seminaries, rabbis, congregational structures and educational facilities, Open Judaism should be seen as a new ideology, a vision of Judaism based on a revised conception of Divine Reality. Liberal in orientation, it offers all Jews – no matter what their particular religious affiliation – a remodelled conceptualization of Jewish life more in accord with the realities of Jewish existence. As an overarching framework for Jewish observance, it respects the manifold religious choices made by contemporary Jews: within Open Judaism, Jewish practice, whatever its form, is accepted as valid.

JUDAISM AND GLOBAL THEOLOGY

Given the shift away from the absolutism of the past, Open Judaism provides a radically new basis for interfaith encounter as well. Previously Jewish thinkers argued that Judaism contains God's fullest revelation to humankind – thus it is the superior religion, surpassing all rivals. Even the most liberal thinkers maintained that all human beings will eventually acknowledge the truth of Jewish monotheism. Such a belief is enshrined in the *Amidah* prayer recited in the Orthodox as well as non-Orthodox worship services:

Therefore do we hope in thee, O Eternal, our God! speedily to behold the effulgence of thy might, removing all idols, and utterly destroying man's vain creations; righting the world by Almighty sovereignty, so that all the children of flesh shall invoke thy name, and toward thee turn all the wicked of the earth. Then shall all the indwellers of the world recognise and clearly see, that unto thee all knees must bend, all tongues swear. In thy presence, O Eternal, our God! shall they kneel and prostrate, ascribing honour to the glory of thy name, and taking upon themselves the yoke of thy supremacy, that thou mayest reign over them fully and for evermore. For sovereignty is thine, and for ever shalt thou reign in glory, as it is written in thy Law: The Eternal shall reign for ever and ever. And it is further said: The Eternal shall be King throughout the earth; on that day the Eternal shall be one, and his name one.

Today, however, in our religiously plural world, it is no longer possible to sustain such an exclusivist position – what is required instead is a redefinition of the theological exploration in view of the recognition that religious doctrines in all the world's faiths are simply human attempts to understand the nature of Ultimate Reality.

The pursuit of religious truth in a global context calls for a dialogical approach along the lines suggested by Wilfred Cantwell Smith:

> The time will soon be with us when a theologian who attempts to work out his position unaware that he does so as a member of a world society in which other theologians equally intelligent, equally devout, equally oral, are Hindus, Buddhists, Muslims and unaware that his readers are likely perhaps to be Buddhists or to have Muslim husbands or Hindu colleagues – such a theologian is as out of date as is one who attempts to construct an intellectual position unaware that Aristotle has thought about the world or that existentialists have raised new orientations, or unaware that the earth is a minor planet in a galaxy that is vast only by terrestrial standards. (Smith, 1962, 123)

The formulation of a Jewish global, interreligious theology rests on two conditions. First, Jewish thinkers must endeavour to learn from traditions other than their own. Global theology undertaken from within the context of Open Judaism requires religious thinkers to investigate what the world's faiths have experienced and affirmed about the nature of Divine Reality, the phenomenon of religious experience, the nature of the self, the problem of the human condition, and the value of the world. Second, Jewish thinkers should endeavour to enter into the thought-world as well as religious experiences of those of other faiths – this can only be achieved by being a participant in their way of life. As noted by Paul Knitter:

> Theologians must 'pass over' to the experience, to the mode of being in the world, that nurtures the creeds and codes and cults of other religions ... [they] must imaginatively participate in the faith of other religions: 'Faith can only be theologized from the inside.' (Knitter, 1985, 226)

Jewish thinkers must therefore strive to enter into the subjectivity of other religions and bring the resulting insights to bear on their own understanding of religion – such reflection demands a multi-faceted approach in which all religions are viewed as independent. With such a global perspective, those who embrace this new philosophy of Judaism should insist that this theological endeavour takes place in a transreligious context. This enterprise requires an encounter in which Jews confront others who hold totally dissimilar truth-claims; such individuals can help Jewish thinkers to discover their own underlying assumptions. In this process Jewish partners should be able to acknowledge the limitations of their own heritage, and as a result make a conscious effort to discover common ground with other faiths. Such interchange is vital to the foundation of a multidimensional religious outlook.

Not only would this new philosophy of Judaism provide a basis for a dialogical engagement with other faiths, it could provide a framework for engagement on a more practical level. No longer should Jews feel constrained to stand apart from the worship services of other religious traditions. Rather a pluralist standpoint in which all faiths are recognized as authentic paths to Divine Reality would encourage the adherents of all faiths – including Jews – to engage in common religious activities. In this regard, a distinction should be made between three different types of interfaith worship:

1. Services of a particular religious community in which members of other faiths are invited as guests. On such occasions, it is usual to ask a representative of the visiting faith community to recite a suitable prayer or preach a sermon, but the liturgy remains the same.
2. Interfaith gatherings of a serial nature. At such meetings representatives of each religion offer prayers or readings on a common theme. Those present constitute an audience listening to a liturgical anthology in which the distinctiveness of each religion is acknowledged, but everyone is free to participate as well.
3. Interfaith gatherings with a shared order of service. In such situations all present are participants, and there is an overarching theme.   (Braybrooke, 1992, 151)

These various kinds of service possess their own particular features. In the first type where adherents of one faith invite others to attend, they are not seeking to make converts – rather there is a conscious recognition of the integrity of other faith traditions. In such an environment, the proponents of Open Judaism should feel

comfortable – ideally Jewish guests at such a service would strive
to enter into the religious experience itself. Advocates of Open
Judaism should not feel hesitant to recite prayers or sing hymns
whose truth-claims do not conform with the truth-claims of
Judaism. Given that Divine Reality as-it-is-in-itself is unknowable,
the different formulations of faith in worship should be perceived
as human constructions which strive to depict the nature of the
Divine. As models of the Real, they guide the believer to the
Ultimate.

Similarly, in the second type of worship service in which there is
a serial reading by representatives of other religions, Open Judaism
would welcome the opportunity to share the Jewish liturgical tradition. Those who espouse this new philosophy of Judaism should
not hesitate to join in the liturgy from other traditions when appropriate. In accord with a pluralist stance, such serial services are
based on mutual respect and allow each community an equal part
in worship.

Turning to the third form of worship service in which there is a
joint liturgy, Open Judaism would encourage Jews to pray with
members of other faiths. In such contexts, participants are often
invited to worship the One Eternal One – the ground of being to
which all religious dogma and ritual point as the Divine Mystery.
This form of service is particularly amenable to this new philosophy of Judaism in which final Reality is viewed as beyond human
comprehension. In services of this type the distinctiveness of each
religion is acknowledged – there is no attempt to replace the
regular liturgy of the individual faith communities. Yet there is the
implicit assumption that in worship, the followers of all the world's
religions stand before the Ultimate which they have described in
different ways. The third form of worship hence is consonant with
the principles of Open Judaism – it affirms other faiths while simultaneously recognizing the limitations of all human concepts of the
Real.

Open Judaism – as a new ideology of Judaism for the twenty-first
century – thus not only provides a basis for reformulating the
Jewish faith in the light of contemporary theological reflection, it
also serves as a framework for interfaith encounter on the deepest
level. If Judaism is to survive, what is now required is the formulation of modern conception of Judaism based on the recognition that
the Jewish view of Divine Reality is ultimately grounded in human
reflection. As such, Jews should no longer proclaim that their reli-

gious beliefs are absolute; instead these should be understood as no different in principle from those found in other religions. Such a theology of religious pluralism in which the Jewish faith is perceived simply as one religion among others demands an attitude of openness and receptivity. Unlike all the other branches of modern Judaism, this interpretation of Judaism paves the way to a sympathetic appreciation of the riches of other religions, and calls for fruitful dialogue with the adherents of other faith-communities in a global context.

10

Conclusion: Judaism in the Twenty-First Century

The Enlightenment brought about major changes in Jewish life. No longer were Jews insulated from non-Jewish currents of culture and thought, and this transformation of Jewish existence led many Jews to seek a modernization of Jewish worship. The earliest reformers engaged in liturgical revision, but quickly the spirit of reform spread to other areas of Jewish life; eventually modernists convened a succession of rabbinical conferences in order to formulate a common policy. Such a radical approach to the Jewish tradition provoked a hostile response from a number of leading Orthodox scholars, a reaction which led to the establishment of the neo-Orthodox movement. Simultaneously the Hasidic movement, grounded in *kabbalah*, similarly sought to revitalize Jewish life. The founder of this new development, the Baal Shem Tov, attracted a wide circle of followers and eventually under the influence of his successor Dov Baer, Hasidism spread throughout Eastern Europe. Like Reform Judaism, this departure from tradition engendered considerable hostility on the part of rabbinic authorities, yet in time it became a major defender of the traditional Jewish way of life in the face of increasing secularism.

The modern period has also witnessed the creation of other non-orthodox subgroups. In the middle of the nineteenth century Zacharias Frankel pursued a less radical interpretation of the tradition than that advanced by Reform Judaism: this new development, subsequently known as Conservative Judaism, took root in the United States under the influence of Solomon Schechter. Today Conservative Judaism ranks as one of the major Jewish movements on the American scene. As an offshoot of Conservative Judaism, Reconstructionism was established in this century by the Jewish thinker Mordecai Kaplan. Adopting a non-supernatural understanding of Jewish civilization, it too gained a strong foothold on the American continent. In the 1960s another non-supernatural form of Judaism was advanced by Rabbi Sherwin Wine: Humanistic Judaism, like Reconstructionism, has rejected Jewish theism in favour of a Humanistic approach to the Jewish past. For Wine and his followers, Judaism must be divested of its supernatural elements if it is to function as a vibrant force in contemporary society. What is important, Humanists argue, is the Humanistic value system implicit within the Jewish heritage. In addition to these religious movements, Zionism as an ideology has also generated widespread acceptance among all sections of Jewry. Initially Zionists believed that all Jews should reside in the Holy Land; however today there is a general recognition that Israel greatly benefits from the presence of Jews in the diaspora.

As we have seen, all these ideologies suffer from various defects, and it is therefore difficult to see how any form of modern Judaism could serve as a basis for Jewish life in the twenty-first century. Due to its unwillingness to acknowledge the findings of biblical scholarship, Orthodox Judaism promotes an anachronistic understanding of the origins and nature of Scripture; further, it is unable to provide a coherent account of divine providential care in the face of the overwhelming tragedies of the current era. In addition, by uncritically accepting the traditional doctrine of *Torah MiSinai*, Orthodoxy has failed to recognize the evolutionary character of the Jewish legal system. Like Orthodox Judaism, Hasidism has also adopted an unenlightened approach to scientific discovery – instead it champions an archaic conception of cosmology based on kabbalistic lore as well as an unsupported conception of the composition of the Bible. Moreover, its endorsement of the role of the *zaddik* as an intermediary between human beings and God is an antiquated survival of the authoritarian Jewish past, totally unsuited to the modern world.

Turning to the varied branches of non-Orthodox Judaism, Reform Judaism is untenable as a religious system due to its lack of internal consistency. Not only are Reform Jews divided over the fundamental principles of the Jewish heritage, there is no common agreement as to the central features of a Reform Jewish life-style despite Reform's proclamations of common policy. Instead Reform Judaism embodies a wide variety of followers who differ dramatically over the interpretation of the faith.

Conservative Judaism also lacks a coherent religious framework for modern Jewish living: within the movement there are divergent groups espousing radically different philosophies of Judaism. The major weakness of Conservatism is its internal disharmony over the fundamental features of the faith. Although Conservative Jews seek to preserve traditional Judaism, there is no consensus over which features of the Jewish heritage should be preserved. Indeed the inability of the movement to produce agreed statements of policy (like the Platforms issued by the Reform movement) illustrates Conservative Judaism's chaotic character.

As far as the non-supernatural interpretations of Judaism are concerned, Reconstructionist Judaism is beset by numerous difficulties. The advocacy of loyalty to Judaism on the one hand and the endorsement of secular values on the other is internally inconsistent: a Jewish life-style and secular values are incompatible, regardless of Kaplan's assurances. Another serious defect relates to Kaplan's view of the supernatural. Jewish observance is traditionally grounded in an acceptance of divine revelation, yet it is precisely this theological foundation that Reconstructionism rejects. But what sense can be made of the notion of Jewish civilization if it is not based on God's will? Humanistic Judaism's naturalistic interpretation of Jewish life is similarly inadequate. Jewish Humanists seek to preserve the Humanistic features of Judaism while abandoning theism. However without such a basis it is difficult to see how such a conception of Judaism would be able to sustain the Jewish people. Further, Humanistic Judaism's endorsement of human potential is at odds with the horrific events of this century which have eclipsed the optimistic assumptions of the post-Enlightenment age. Zionism – as a non-religious option for modern Jewry – also fails to provide an ideological basis for Jewish living in the next century. The creation of the state of Israel has not eliminated the problem of anti-Semitism nor has it provided a guarantee for Jewish survival.

Thus none of the options we have surveyed appears to provide a solid foundation for Jewish existence in the future. Arguably what is required therefore is a new philosophy of Judaism which acknowledges the plurality of approaches to the Jewish heritage which currently exist within the Jewish world. As we have seen, all the modern branches of Judaism espouse different conceptions of the tradition. Yet the adherents of each movement are at liberty to decide for themselves which beliefs and practices are personally relevant. Despite the pronouncements of leaders of each subgroup, all Jews in fact select those features of the tradition which they find meaningful – this is true for Orthodox Jews as much as for members of Reform, Conservative, Reconstructionist and Humanistic congregations. In past centuries such freedom was not allowed; instead the Jewish establishment was able to coerce members of the community to conform to its dictates. But today this is no longer the case; rather there is a conscious recognition that Jews are free to make up their own minds. Coercion in the community has virtually disappeared except in the narrow sphere of personal status where the different movements are empowered to enforce various standards. Hence, the hallmark of the modern age is the guarantee of personal autonomy. This is the basic under-pinning of Jewish life in Western democratic societies. Just as Jews are free to make personal choices about all aspects of their every-day existence – from place of residence to holiday travel – they are at liberty to decide for themselves how to conduct their religious lives.

A vibrant philosophy of Judaism for the twenty-first century must acknowledge the universality of this central feature of the modern world. Open Judaism – as depicted in Chapter 9 – seeks to grant all Jews full religious independence. Drawing on the insights of Polydox Judaism, this new ideology would allow each member of the Jewish community an inalienable right to religious autonomy. In other words, the freedom of each person would end only where another person's freedom began. The central feature of this new concept of Judaism is therefore the principle of personal liberty: Open Judaism would grant all Jews the right to select those aspects of the tradition which they find religiously significant. Adherents of this interpretation of the faith would be encouraged to make up their own minds about both belief and practice. No one – no rabbi or rabbinical body – would be permitted to decide which observances are acceptable. In other words, Open Judaism would foster the same conception of personal liberty that is essential to a democratic society. This vision of a truly liberal form of Judaism would thus be consonant with the realities of everyday Jewish life – in democratic societies Jews in fact do decide for themselves which features of the Jewish tradition they wish to adopt or reject.

This notion of Judaism as an amorphous religious system can perhaps best be illustrated by the analogy of the supermarket. If we imagine Jewish civilization as a vast emporium with articles from the past arranged in long aisles and individual Jews with shopping trolleys, Open Judaism would encourage each person to select from the shelves those items he wishes to possess. Orthodox Jews would leave with overflowing trolleys; Conservative and Reconstructionist Jews would depart with less; Reform and Humanistic Jews with even fewer commodities; and non-affiliated Jews with hardly any. This image of the supermarket emphasizes the non-judgemental character of Open Judaism. Just as when shopping each person is able to make selections without the fear of coercion or criticism, so within this open model of Judaism individuals would be allowed to decide for themselves which features of the Jewish past they desired to incorporate into their own lives. Shoppers in such a Jewish market-place would be free agents, charting their own personal path through the tradition. Further, as in a supermarket where there is no critical assessment made by other shoppers or by the supermarket staff of the choices made, so within Open Judaism censorious evaluations of the decisions of others would have no place.

As previously indicated, this philosophy of Judaism, as a new orientation to Judaism more in accord with the realities of every-day Jewish life, would welcome into this Jewish market-place all those who seek such identification regardless of their background. Open Judaism would regard all individuals as members of the Jewish community if they wished to be included. In the past Orthodoxy defined as Jews all those who are of maternal Jewish descent; in addition, traditional Judaism provided a formalized means of conversion, and recently Reform Judaism has modified this definition of Jewishness to include all those born of a Jewish mother or Jewish father. As a result there is widespread uncertainty within the Jewish community as to who qualifies as a Jew. Like Humanistic Judaism, Open Judaism provides a simple solution to this dilemma: all those who desire to be known as Jews would be granted this status without the necessity of demonstrating Jewish descent or undergoing an official ceremony of recognition. The only criterion of Jewishness would be a sincere desire to identify in this way. A radical shift would thus be required away from formal recognition to self-identification, a change which can be represented diagramatically. For Orthodox Jews only those born of matrilineal descent or properly converted through specified legal procedures can be deemed Jewish – all others are non-Jews even if they have been converted by non-orthodox Jewish subgroups (Figure 10.1).

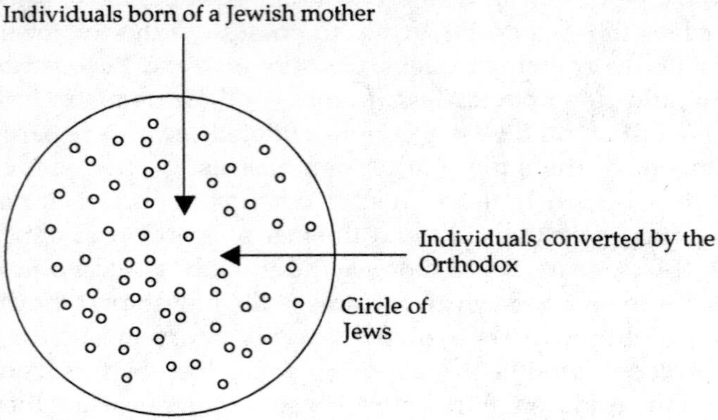

Individuals born of a Jewish mother

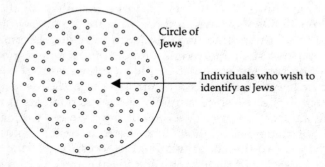

Individuals converted by the Orthodox

Circle of Jews

Figure 10.1   The Jewish world according to Orthodox Judaism

Within Open Judaism, on the other hand, members of the Jewish community would not have to meet such stringent criteria; instead all those who, for whatever reason, wish to identify as Jews would be accepted into the fold:

Circle of Jews

Individuals who wish to identify as Jews

Figure 10.2   The Jewish world according to Open Judaism

As noted previously, Open Judaism as a solution to Jewish living in the next century is not conceived of as an alternative denomination alongside Orthodox, Hasidic, Reform, Conservative, Reconstructionist and Humanist Judaism. It is rather an ideology which can be embraced by the members of all religious groupings as well as the unaffiliated. Traditionally-minded Jews, for example, who are supporters of Orthodox or Hasidic Judaism could be advocates of Open Judaism as long as they were willing to grant legitimacy to all modes of Jewish living, including the most lax. For such individuals, traditional Judaism would provide the most satisfactory and religiously compelling form of Judaism, but as followers of Open Judaism they would accept that alternative forms of Judaism could be equally satisfying for others. Hence, there would be a conscious recognition of the validity of all Jewish options.

Turning to non-Orthodox alternatives, those who accept the ideology of Open Judaism would similarly acknowledge the validity of patterns of belief and practice other than their own. Thus Reform Jews, while not concurring with Orthodox, Conservative, Reconstructionist or Humanistic interpretations of the faith would respect the choices of those who subscribed to these systems. Conversely the same would apply to Conservative, Reconstructionist and Humanistic Jews when confronted with the views of others. And as far as non-affiliated Jews are concerned, the members of the various non-Orthodox movements who accept the principles of Open Judaism would be committed to a policy of tolerance of those who had deliberately sought to distance themselves from organized religion.

What is needed then is a revolution in Jewish thinking. From post-Enlightenment times to the present the various religious subgroups in the community have been anxious to stress that they are the legitimate heirs of biblical and rabbinic Judaism. As far as Orthodoxy is concerned, traditionalists have generally subscribed to the belief that Orthodox Judaism (including Hasidism) constitutes the only true form of Judaism. Such a stance is represented as follows:

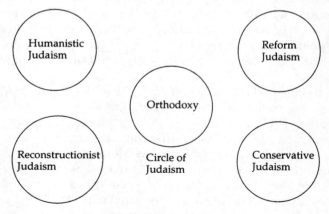

Figure 10.3   Orthodox Judaism

Here Orthodoxy is perceived as the only legitimate expression of the Jewish faith – it constitutes the true centre of Jewish religiosity whereas the various non-Orthodox movements are viewed as heretical.

Non-Orthodox movements, however, are less exclusivist in orientation – they generally do not exclude other interpretations of Judaism; rather they propose an inclusivist conception of the different forms of post-Enlightenment Judaism in which other Jewish religious systems are included but as less suitable for the modern age than their own (Figure 10.4).

Open Judaism, however, calls for a reversal of this conceptualization of modern Judaism. Instead of placing any particular movement at the centre of the various Jewish subgroups, they are all arranged inside the circle of Judaism without any differentiation made about their respective claims: all are perceived as valid for contemporary Jews (Figure 10.5).

As indicated previously, such an altered vision of the various religious groupings is based on a new understanding of Divine reality. In the past, Jewish theologians and philosophers stressed that God is unknowable: he is the Infinite who lies beyond human conceptualization. Such philosophers as Maimonides formulated the doctrine of negative attributes to explain such a theory – in his view, God as-he-is-in-himself cannot be known. Scripture reveals God's actions rather than his essence. For the kabbalists, God is the *Ayn Sof* who lies beyond human comprehension; the unknowable source of all, he manifests himself in the cosmos through a series of divine emanations. Drawing on these insights, Open Judaism emphasizes the total unknowability of the Divine. Yet, unlike previous Jewish theories, this new philosophy of Judaism is theologically non-dogmatic in character: the theology of Open Judaism draws a radical distinction between Reality as-it-is-in-itself and Reality-as-perceived.

Open Judaism acknowledges the fact that each religious tradition affirms its own superiority – all rival claims are viewed as misapprehensions of Ultimate Reality. From a pluralistic perspective, however, Open Judaism asserts that there is simply no means by which it is possible to ascertain which, if any, of these spiritual paths accurately reflects the nature of the Real as-it-is-in-itself. In the end, the varied truth-claims of the world's faiths must be regarded as human icons which are constructed from within specific social and cultural contexts. Hence from this standpoint, it is im-

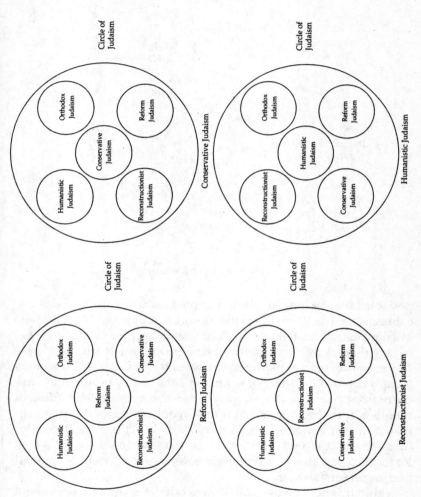

Figure 10.4 Non-Orthodox Judaism

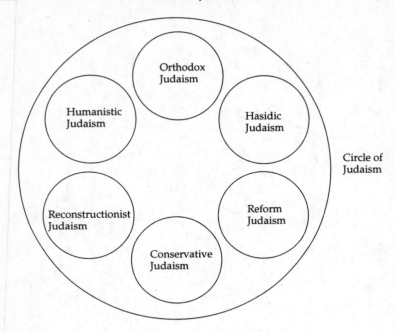

Figure 10.5   Open Judaism

possible to make judgements about the validity of the various conceptions of the Divine in the world's religions. Neither Jew,
Muslim, Christian, Hindu nor Buddhist has any justification for believing that his own tradition embodies the uniquely true and superior religious path – instead the adherents of all the world's faiths
must recognize the inevitable human subjectivity of religious conceptualization. Such a theology calls for a complete reorientation of
religious apprehension. What is now required is for Jews to accept
that their conceptual system, form of worship, life-style and scriptures are in the end nothing more than lenses through which
Reality is perceived, but the Divine as-it-is-in-itself is beyond
human understanding.

   Within this new theological framework the absolute claims about
God contained in the Bible and the rabbinic tradition should be
viewed as human conceptions stemming from the religious experience of the ancient Israelites as well as later generations of Jewish
sages. Jewish monotheism – embracing a myriad of formulations
from biblical through medieval to modern times – is rooted in the

life of the people. In all cases pious believers and thinkers have expressed their understanding of God's activity on the basis of their personal as well as communal encounter with the Divine. Yet given that the Real as-it-is-in-itself is beyond human comprehension, this Jewish understanding of the Godhead cannot be viewed as definitive and final. Rather, it must be seen as only one among many ways in which human beings have attempted to make sense of the Ultimate. In this light, it makes no sense for Jews to believe that they possess the unique truth about God and his action in the world; on the contrary, universalistic truth-claims about divine Reality must give way to a recognition of the inevitable subjectivity of beliefs about the Ultimate.

As a radical alternative to the more structured models of the Jewish faith, this new philosophy of Judaism provides a non-dogmatic foundation for integrating Jewish belief and practice into modern life. Within this framework, all those who wish to be identified as Jews would be encouraged to find their own path through the Jewish heritage. Such a fluid system, attuned to the realities of everyday Jewish life, provides a comprehensive vision of Jewish existence in the next century. Unlike the current subgroups within the Jewish world, Open Judaism celebrates the plurality of Jewish belief and practice in the modern age. Respectful of the differences in the community, this new conception of Judaism – based on a recognition of the inevitable subjectivity of religious belief – furnishes an overarching ideological basis for Jewish living in a pluralistic age. As a remedy for the bitter divisions that beset the Jewish community, this new approach to the Jewish heritage offers the hope of unity beyond diversity for the next millennium.

Bibliography

Adler, Morris, 1964. 'The Philosophy of the Conservative Movement', *Review* (USA), 16, no. 4 (Winter).

Agus, J., 1959. *The Evolution of Jewish Thought* (Abelard Schuman).

Arzt, M., 1955. 'Conservative Judaism', in Theodore Friedman, *What is Conservative Judaism?* (Horizon).

Avineri, S. 1981. *The Making of Modern Zionism* (Basic Books).

Baeck, L., 1948. *The Essence of Judaism* (Schocken).

Bamberger, B., 1964. *The Story of Judaism* (Schocken).

Baron, S.W., 1952–76. *A Social and Religious History of the Jews* (Columbia University Press).

Ben-Sasson, H.H., 1976. *A History of the Jewish People* (Harvard University Press).

Bergman, S.H.,1963. *Faith and Reason: An Introduction to Modern Jewish Thought* (Schocken).

Berkovitz, E., 1973. *Faith after the Holocaust* (KTAV).

Berkovitz, E., 1974. *Major Themes in Modern Philosophies of Judaism* (KTAV).

Berkovitz, E., 1983. *Not in Heaven* (KTAV).

Bokser, B.Z., June 1941. 'Doctrine of the Chosen People', *Contemporary Jewish Record*.

Bokser, B.Z., 1963. *Judaism, Profile of a Faith* (Burning Bush Press).

Bokser, B.Z., 1964. *Jewish Law: A Conservative Approach* (Burning Bush Press).

Borowitz, E., 1968. *A New Jewish Theology in the Making* (Westminster Press).

Borowitz, E., 1969. *How Can a Jew Speak of Faith Today?* (Westminster Press).

Borowitz, E., 1983. *Choices in Modern Thought* (Behrman House).

Braybrooke, M., 1992. 'Interfaith Prayer', in D. Cohn-Sherbok, ed. *Many Mansions* (Bellew).

Bulka, R., 1984. *The Coming Cataclysm* (Mosaic Press).

Cohen, A. A., 1981. *The Tremendum* (Crossroads).

Cohen, I., 1943. *Vilna*.

Cohn-Sherbok, D., 1988. *The Jewish Heritage* (Basil Blackwell).

Cohn-Sherbok, D., 1989. *Holocaust Theology* (Lamp).

Cohn-Sherbok, D., 1991. *Issues in Contemporary Judaism* (Macmillan).

Cohn-Sherbok, D., 1993. *The Jewish Faith* (SPCK).

Cohn-Sherbok, D., 1993. *Judaism and Other Faiths* (Macmillan).

Cohn-Sherbok, D., 1994. *The Future of Judaism* (T. and T. Clark).

Cohn-Sherbok, D. and L., 1994. *The American Jew* (Harper Collins).

Cohn-Sherbok, D. and L., 1995. *Jewish and Christian Mysticism* (Gracewing).

The Condition of Jewish Belief: 1989 (Jason Aronson).

Dawidowicz, L., 1967. *The Golden Tradition*.

De Lange, N., 1986. *Judaism* (Oxford University Press).

Dorff, G.N., 1979. *Conservative Judaism* (United Synagogue Youth).

Encyclopaedia Judaica (Keter Publishing House, 1972).

Epstein, I., 1975. *Judaism* (Penguin).

Fackenheim, E., 1982. *To Mend the World: Foundations of Future Jewish Thought* (Schocken).

Fackenheim, E., 1987. *What is Judaism?* (Collier).

Feuerlicht, R.S., 1983. *The Fate of the Jews: A People Torn between Israeli Power and Jewish Ethics* (Times Books).

Finkelstein, L., 1948. 'The Things that Unite Us', in Rabbinical Assembly, *Proceedings*, 12.

Freehof, S., 1960. *Reform Responsa* (Hebrew Union College Press).

Freehof, S., 1974. *Contemporary Reform Responsa* (HUC Press).

Freud, S., 1981. *The Future of an Illusion. The Complete Psychological Works of Sigmund Freud* (Hogarth Press).

Friedman, G., 1967. *The End of the Jewish People?* (Hutchinson).

Goldstein, I., 1928. 'Inadequacies in the Status of the Synagogue Today', Rabbinical Assembly, *Proceedings*, 2.

Goodman, S.L. (ed.), 1976. *The Faith of Secular Jews* (KTAV).

Gordis, R., 1970 *Conservative Judaism: A Modern Approach to Jewish Tradition* (Behrman House).

Graetz, H., 1891–98. *A History of the Jews* (Jewish Publication Society).

Grayzel, S., 1968. *A History of the Jews: From the Babylonian Exile to the Present* (New American Library).

Greenberg, I., 1980. *On the Third Era in Jewish History* (National Jewish Resource Centre).

Greenberg, I., 1981. *The Third Great Cycle in Jewish History* (National Jewish Resource Centre.

Greenberg, S., 1955. *The Conservative Movement in Judaism: An Introduction* (United Synagogue of America).

Guide to Humanistic Judaism, 1988, 1993 (Society for Humanistic Judaism).

Guttman, Julius, 1964. *Philosophies of Judaism: The History of Jewish Philosophy from Biblical Times to Franz Rosenzweig* (Holt, Rinehart & Winston).

Ha-Am, A., 1962. *Nationalism and the Jewish Ethic* (Schocken).

Hartman, D., 1985. *A Living Covenant* (New York).

Helmrich, W.B., 1982. *The World of the Yeshiva* (Macmillan).

Hertzberg, A. (ed.), 1959. *The Zionist Idea: A Historical Analysis and Reader* (Athenaeum).

Heschel, A., 1985. *God in Search of Man* (Harper & Row).

Hick, J., 1963, 1973. *Philosophy of Religion* (Prentice Hall).

Hielman, H.M., 1903. *Beit Rabbi*.

Hirsch, S.R., 1960. *The Nineteen Letters on Judaism* (Feldheim).

Husik, I., 1958. *A History of Medieval Jewish Philosophy* (Jewish Publication Society).

Jacob Joseph of Polonnoye, 1954–55. *Told of Yaokou Yosef* (Israel Rev Publisher).

Jacobs, L., 1973. *A Jewish Theology* (Darton, Longman & Todd).

Jacobs, L., 1964. *Principles of the Jewish Faith* (Basic Books).

Jacobs, L., 1988. *Principles of the Jewish Faith*, 2nd edn (Jason Aronson).
Jewish Encyclopaedia (Funk & Wagnalls, 1901–5).
Johnson, P., 1987. *A History of the Jews* (Weidenfeld & Nicolson).
Kaplan, M., 1916. 'The Future of Judaism', *Menorah Journal*, 2, no. 3.
Kaplan, M., 1956. *Questions Jews Ask: Reconstructionist Answers* (Reconstructionist Press).
Kaplan, M., 1962. *The Meaning of God in Modern Jewish Religion* (Reconstructionist Press).
Kaplan, M., 1967. *Judaism as a Civilization* (Schocken Books).
Kaplan, M., 1970. 'The Meaning of God for the Contemporary Jew', in A. Jospe (ed.), *Tradition and Contemporary Experience* (Schocken Books).
Katz, S.T., 1983. *Post-Holocaust Dialogues* (New York University Press).
Kaufman, W., 1976. *Contemporary Jewish Philosophies* (Behrman House).
Knitter, P., 1985. *No Other Name* (Orbis).
Kohler, K., 1968. *Jewish Theology* (KTAV).
Kreitman, B.Z., 1975. 'Conservative Judaism – The Next Step', *Review* (USA), 27, no.3 (Winter).
Kurzweil, Z., 1985. *The Modern Impulse of Traditional Judaism* (KTAV).
Liebman, C., 1975. 'Reconstructionism in American Jewish Life' in J. Neusner (ed.), *Understanding American Judaism* (KTAV).
Lenn, 1972. *Rabbi and Synagogue in Reform Judaism* (CCAR).
Levine, A., 1977. 'Needed – a Definition', *Judaism*, vol. 26, no.3.
Levinthal, I., 1928. Rabbinical Assembly, *Proceedings*, 2.
Maggid Debarav L'Yaakov, 1981.
Mahler, R., (ed.), 1941. *Jewish Emancipation: A Selection of Documents* (American Jewish Committee).
Maimon, S., 1954. *The Autobiography of Solomon Maimon* (East and West Library).
Maimonides, 1981. *The Guide of the Perplexed* (Hebrew Publishing).
Marcus, J., 1938. *The Jew in the Medieval World* (Hebrew Union College).
Margolis, M.L. and Marx, A., 1965. *A History of the Jewish People* (Harper & Row).
Marmur, D. (ed.), 1978. 'British Reform and Jewish Status', *Journal of Reform Judaism*, vol. 25, 2.
Marmur, D., 1982. *Beyond Survival* (Darton, Longman & Todd).
Maybaum, I., 1984. *The Face of God after Auschwitz* (Polak and van Gennep).
Maza, Bernard, 1984. *With Fury Poured Out* (KTAV).
Mendelsohn, M, 1969. *Judaism and Other Jewish Writings* (Schocken).
Meyer, M., 1967. *The Origins of the Modern Jew* (Wayne State University Press).
Meyer, M., 1988. *Response to Modernity: A History of the Reform Movement in Judaism* (Oxford University Press).
Nemoy, L., 1952. *Karaite Anthology* (Yale University Press).
Novak, D., 1989. *Jewish–Christian Dialogue* (Oxford University Press).
Parkes, J., 1964. *A History of the Jewish People* (Penguin).
Philipson, D., 1967. *The Reform Movement in Judaism* (KTAV).
Philo, 1949. *De Opificio Mundi* (Loeb Classical Library).
Pinsker, L., 1932. *Autoemancipation* (London).
Plaut, W.G., 1963. *The Rise of Reform Judaism* (World Union for Progressive Judaism).

Plaut, W.G., 1963. *The Growth of Reform Judaism* (World Union for Progressive Judaism).

Rabinowicz, H., 1970. *The World of Hasidim* (Vallentine Mitchell).

Rabinowicz, H., 1988. *Hasidism: The Movement and its Masters* (Jason Aaronson).

Raphael, M.L., 1984. *Profiles in American Judaism* (Harper & Row).

Reines, A., 1987. *Polydoxy* (Pantheon).

Rosenthal, G., 1973. *Four Paths to One God: Today's Jew and His Religion* (Block).

Rosenthal, G., 1959, 1978. *The Many Faces of Judaism* (Behrman House).

Rosenthal, G., 1980. 'The Foundations of the Conservative Approach to Jewish Law', in Rabbinical Assembly, *Proceedings*.

Rosenthal, S., 1986. *Contemporary Judaism* (Human Sciences).

Rotenstreich, N., 1968. *Jewish Philosophy in Modern Times: From Mendelssohn to Rosenzweig* (Holt, Rinehart & Winston).

Roth, C., 1970. *A History of the Jews* (Schocken).

Rubenstein, R. 1966. *After Auschwitz* (Bobbs-Merrill).

Rudonsky, D., 1967a. *Emancipation and Adjustment: Contemporary Jewish Religious Movements – Their History and Thought* (Behrman House).

Rudonsky, D., 1967b. *Modern Jewish Movements* (Behrman House).

Sachar, A.L., 1967. *A History of the Jews* (Alfred A. Knopf).

Sachar, H.M., 1977. *The Course of Modern Jewish History* (Dell).

Sachs, J., 1993. *One People? Tradition, Modernity and Jewish Unity* (Littman Library).

Sacks, J., 1944. *Will We Have Jewish Grandchildren?* (Vallentine Mitchell).

Sacks, J., 1989. *Traditional Alternatives* (Jews College Publications).

Sanders, R., 1984. *The High Walls of Jerusalem* (Holt, Rinehart & Winston).

Schechter, S., 1959. *Seminary Addresses and Other Papers* (Burning Bush Press).

Seltzer, R., 1980. *Jewish People, Jewish Thought* (Collier Macmillan).

Shibbe Ha-Bescht 1922.

Siegel, S., 1980. 'Approaches to Halachah in the Conservative Movement', in Rabbinical Assembly, *Proceedings*, 42.

Simon, E., 1958. 'Torat Hayyim: Some Thoughts on the Teaching of the Bible', *Conservative Judaism*.

Sklare, M., 1972. *Conservative Judaism* (Schocken).

Smith, W.C., 1962. *The Faith of Other Men* (Canadian Broadcasting Company).

Solomon, N., 1991. *Judaism and World Religion* (Macmillan).

The Condition of Jewish Belief: A Symposium Compiled by the Editors of Commentary Magazine (Macmillan, 1969).

Trepp, L., 1973. *A History of the Jewish Experience* (Behrman House).

Vital, D., 1990. *The Future of the Jews* (Harvard University Press).

Wine, S., 1985. *Judaism Beyond God* (Society for Humanistic Judaism).

Wine, S., 1988. *Celebration* (Prometheus Books).

Wouk, H., 1968. *This is my God* (Doubleday).

Wyschogrod, M., 1983. *The Body of Faith* (Seabury Press).

Index